EXTRA INNINGS
A Memoir

ALSO BY DORIS GRUMBACH

The Spoil of the Flowers
The Short Throat, the Tender Mouth
The Company She Kept
Chamber Music
The Missing Person
The Ladies
The Magician's Girl
Coming into the End Zone: A Memoir

EXTRA INNINGS
A Memoir

DORIS GRUMBACH

W·W·NORTON & COMPANY

New York   London

"To Waken an Old Lady" and excerpt from "January Morning" from *The Collected Poems of William Carlos Williams,* Vol. I. Copyright © 1938 by William Carlos Williams. Reprinted by permission of New Directions Publishing Corporation. Excerpt from "Thirteen Ways of Looking at a Blackbird" from *The Collected Poems* by Wallace Stevens. Copyright © 1923 and renewed 1951 by Wallace Stevens. Reprinted by permission of Alfred A. Knopf, Inc. Excerpt from "One Art" from *The Complete Poems 1927–1979* by Elizabeth Bishop. Copyright © 1979, 1983 by Alice Helen Methfessel. Reprinted by permission of Farrar, Straus and Giroux, Inc. Excerpts from "Sprung Lamb" and "Southern Comfort" by Felicia Lamport from *Political Plumlines* by Felicia Lamport. Copyright © 1984 by Felicia Lamport. Reprinted by permission of Bantam, Doubleday, Dell Publishing Group, Inc.

First Edition

The text of this book is composed in Bembo,
with the display set in Cochin Italic.
Composition and manufacturing by the Haddon Craftsmen, Inc.

Library of Congress Cataloging-in-Publication Data
Grumbach, Doris.
    Extra innings : a memoir / by Doris Grumbach.
        p.   cm.   1. Grumbach, Doris—Diaries.   2. Novelists, American—20th
century—Diaries.   3. Maine—Social life and customs.   I. Title.
    PS3557.R83Z465   1993
    818'.5403—dc20
    [B]   92-42489

ISBN 0-393-03541-7

W. W. Norton & Company, Inc., 500 Fifth Avenue, New York, N.Y. 10110
W. W. Norton & Company Ltd., 10 Coptic Street, London WC1A 1PU

1 2 3 4 5 6 7 8 9 0

As it was, is now, and (let
us hope) ever shall be:
For SHP

September

I am ready to meet my maker. Whether my maker is prepared for the ordeal of meeting me is another matter.

—Winston Churchill, on his seventy-fifth birthday

Proem

*A*t seventy, I wrote a book about how I felt coming into old age, about the unaccountable yet very real despair that accompanied entering my septennial years. Now I am approaching seventy-five. I think it a good time (for my own sake) that I review my life since those intensely despondent days, to see if the customary acceptance has set in, if my view of the world, of my smaller world, and of the world buried within myself, has changed, for better or for worse. Has my gloom lifted? Or has there been some unavoidable intensification of it?

I have chosen to follow the same journal-jotting procedure I used four years ago. Perhaps, in the process of writing, I may come upon some answers to the insistent questions of old age. Or perhaps I will only succeed in recording, month by month, the minor thoughts and activities in the life of an aging woman. It may be that a commonplace record of insignificant exterior doings and interior musings *are* my only possible response to the great philosophical questions. What is it that drives us to examine matters of cosmic significance—birth, faith, suffering, injustice, dying, and death—but the intrusion into our daily lives of niggling irritations and petty trifles.

∽

September 15, 1991: A frightening day, when a book one has
written comes out, when details about my life and reflections,
always before hidden and personal, unexamined by anyone
except for me in all these years, are made public. *Coming into
the End Zone,* a memoir, is published today. There is no
announcement, no conspicuous coming-out party, no
acknowledgment from anyone that this is the day the shrink
wrap of privacy is torn away, the protective cocoon bursts, and
out comes what one hopes is a butterfly, not a worm.

Today my wicked imagination is at work. I have a vision of
hopeful, eager booksellers, before their stores open in
midmorning, rushing to fill their shelf space with my freshly
minted volume, newspaper book editors making last-minute
corrections on reviews to appear next day or, at least, next
Sunday, the publishing-house personnel standing on tiptoe
(editors and publicists alike) anticipating the rush for praise that
can be quoted and books to be sold to ensure the return of their
investment.

But, of course, none of this happens. The fragile butterfly is
'out,' that is about all. It is making its precarious way to God
knows where or to whom or into what unpredictable climate of
faint praise or harsh critical notice. In this same week (to change
the metaphor to a more contemporary one), my small VW Bug
of a book will travel down a six-lane superhighway surrounded,
front and back and on two sides, by huge semi-trailers: a
1,328-page novel by Norman Mailer (*Harlot's Ghost*); a
690-page tome, *Needful Things,* by Stephen King; the sequel to
Gone with the Wind, called, starkly, *Scarlett,* and Anne Tyler's
new novel, not itself of mammoth size but in a gargantuan
150,000-copy printing.

And, bearing down hard on me, as a result of twenty-six

years of writing and rewriting, of fanfare, publicity, praise, and wonderment before the fact of publication, is *The Runaway Soul,* Harold Brodkey's huge novel, 835 pages. Its press release claims that the literate public has been waiting two and a half decades for this book, which, it has also been said by two most reputable critics, Harold Bloom and Denis Donoghue, will establish Brodkey as the greatest writer of this century.

On the other hand, few people besides me are waiting for mine, and I fear it will establish me only as a somewhat cranky elderly person airing her fears, loves, regrets, dislikes, wan hopes, and unaccountable memories.

∽

So there it goes, my all-of-256-page subcompact car, almost a miniature, traveling very cautiously in the slow lane. Its survival out there is perilous. It is outsized, outdistanced, outnumbered, overshadowed in every possible way. Now I require a third simile to explain my feelings: I am like a featherweight fighter sent into the ring to do battle with, let us say (to properly reflect my age and time), Joe Louis, the Brown Bomber, the great pugilist of my youth.

We live in an era of the fictional blockbuster, a word that is relatively new in the language. I first heard it about 1940 when it referred to the unscrupulous real estate operator who frightens people into selling their property cheap by threatening racial infiltration into neighborhoods, thus 'busting the block.' And my editor Gerry Howard informs me that during World War II, it referred to bombs so powerful they could level a city block.

Now it is applied to large books, as heavy as millstones, as solid as seawalls, as long as tapeworms, which are printed in great numbers because their publishers anticipate that they will be very popular and their sales will be prodigious.

Clearly, a large American audience finds them desirable. They are eminently readable, utterly absorbing. I think it was François Mauriac who observed readers' affection for the long book they could 'live in.' Someone else described them as wraparound books.

But I have no affection for long books. I am not affected by their appeal. If a novel is indeed, as Simone de Beauvoir said, 'a cry for help,' or as Franz Kafka thought, 'an ax to the frozen sea around us,' then long books are drawn-out spells of uncontrollable weeping. The definitive force of the sharp ax breaking the fictional ice in one stroke may not be contained within the dogged results of Brodkey's twenty-six-year-long chopping.

From my shelf I take down the Library of America's collection of Edgar Allan Poe's essays and turn to what I seem to remember he thought about the successful short story or poem. Ah yes, here it is. In 'The Philosophy of Composition,' Poe writes: "If any literary work is too long to be read at one sitting, we must be content to dispense with the immensely important effect derivable from unity of expression—for, if two sittings be required, the affairs of the world interfere, and everything like totality is at once destroyed."

Of course I recognize that this research of mine is an *apologia,* intended to explain to myself, to justify, the short, narrow, dwarfish nature of most of the books I choose to read these days, and all the books I have written. Or it may be that today I look up Poe on the subject because I am hoping to garner some notice for my new book, my pygmy among giants, on the virtue of its brevity. Well no, let me be honest: what I hope for is *good* notice in major places like the *New York Times* and the *Washington Post.* Even if *End Zone* is thinner and shorter than its fellow travelers.

∽

After three days of dailiness on the Cove—the return of the
eider ducks' extended family for one last bout of fishing on the
mud flats, the slight edging of yellow and brown that has begun
to show on the maples (so *soon?* I am dismayed by the
abbreviated summer up here in coastal Maine), the disappearance
from their usual mooring places of two small sailboats—I settle
down to accept the permanent existence of the book out there in
the world. I find it hard to believe in, since the only reality to
me was its presence in my notebook, on the pad on my
clipboard, and then among the incomprehensible bytes of the
computer. In the new life, gone from me, it calls to mind the
story of the American who went to Ireland, and asked an
Irishman there:
    'Do you believe in leprechauns?'
    'No,' replied the Irishman. 'But . . . they're out there.'

∽

Having a book is somewhat like having a baby, as many women
writers have observed before me: the conception, the long
preparation, the wait, the growing heaviness (not of the body in
this case but of the spirit and the manuscript) toward the end,
the initial delight at the sight of the product, fully formed and
seemingly perfect, and then the usual postpartum depression.
What will people whose opinion I care about, and those whose
views I don't value but have weight in the world of readers,
think of it?
    I remember that my second daughter's birth was facilitated
by the use of forceps that left her cheeks badly marked for
weeks. To make matters worse, she was born with crossed eyes.
Her head was bald, shaped rather like a cobblestone. When

visitors asked to see the newborn I would say that the little one
was sleeping or being bathed by her father, or *something,*
anything, not to have to display her. (True, she grew up to be a
good-looking woman, but there was no way of knowing that
would happen from the evidence at first.)

Now I have that same initial feeling. Looking through the
first copy of *End Zone* sent to me, I imagine I can spot flaws,
weak sentences, incompletely developed thoughts, omissions, all
the undeveloped inclusions that critics (persons whom John
Seelye, in his book about a modern, alternate Huck, calls "the
crickets") will surely seize upon. *I* would, if I were sent it for
review. Depression has set in. I have no way of making
changes—or hiding the baby from the crickets. Irrevocably, it's
out there.

↜

Writing one memoir, and then taking these notes for another, I
am struck by the dubiousness of the whole enterprise of
autobiography. The words 'truth' and 'fact' keep insinuating
themselves into every entry I make and into the reviews that
have begun to arrive from Gerry Howard. The more I think
about what I have written, and about what I am writing now,
the clearer becomes what Blanche Boyd once wrote, I think,
about Norman Mailer: "Everything is altered by the observer."
At the moment of retrieval, in the process of recall, the initial,
observer-limited memory is there, incomplete and biased as it
was when first it was stored in the mind. Then it is embroidered
and encrusted over time (I think of the Ladies of Llangollen's
eighteenth-century house in Wales that was replaced in the next
century with Tudor brown wood and "improved," thus
changing the original cottage forever) until it is like a
barnacle-covered shell, with little of the original shape to be
seen.

Then I write about it, giving the memory a literary shape. I leave out what no longer pleases my view of myself. I embellish with euphony and decorate the prose with some color. I subordinate, giving less importance to some matters, raising others to the weight of coordination. I modify. During this literary activity that surrounds the 'germ' of fact, as Henry James called it, I am moving into, well, *style,* and away from, well, let's face it, truth. But I persist, driven by the need to record in readable form what I think about and remember, however unreliable.

⌁

La Rochefoucauld (*Maxims*): 'We work so consistently to disguise ourselves that we end by being disguised to ourselves.'

⌁

This morning I get my two-days-old Sunday *New York Times* in the mail. When first we moved to Maine three years ago, and it was clear that the nearest available *New York Times,* which I was persuaded I could not live without, would require a forty-four-mile drive each morning, I decided to subscribe by mail. At first it came the next day, but now, more often than not, the postal service delays it another day. I have begun to think that 'postal service' is a perfect oxymoron.

Strange, but now I am hardly aware of the paper's tardiness. Nor do I care. It does not matter to me on which day this week Will Crutchfield wrote about an odd relation of the soprano to her voice. He quotes Maria Malibran, the soprano, who used to tell her own voice: 'It is I who will give the orders, and you who will obey.' Crutchfield remarks that 'the voice seems a separate entity to the singer, a different person, even at times, a stranger or an enemy.'

Now I see that it is in the Sunday paper I am reading on

Tuesday. I think about Crutchfield's remarks and find them intriguing because it is the same way with writers. They often regard their fingers and the keyboard of the typewriter or computer on which they work, or the pen they hold, as instruments separate from themselves, taking orders from the disguised self, and demanding to be supplied with words even when that secret self has nothing to say.

For this reason, I remember, I once disliked the electric typewriter. It continued to hum ominously, insistently, even when invention failed me, and I could think of nothing to write.

ꜩ

Having the word 'oxymoron' in my head, I thought this afternoon of the time, a few years ago, when I used to go to the Tuesday-morning liturgies at St. Alban's Church in Washington. Twelve or so of us would gather around the altar at seven-thirty. John Danforth was the celebrant, the Senator from Missouri who was ordained an Episcopal priest at the same time that he was graduated from Yale Law School.

One or another of the little congregation usually gave the homily. Once, when it was my turn, and for some reason I cannot now recall, I used the word 'oxymoron.' At the breakfast-coffee gathering after the service John Danforth asked me what the word meant. I explained that it was two words used together that contradicted each other. An example? he asked. Thoughtlessly, I gave him the first one that came to mind: 'government service.' As I recall, this was followed by a good deal of forced laughter from the little congregation, silence from the Reverend Mr. Danforth.

ꜩ

More reviews begin to come in. Months ago, *Publishers Weekly,* called the Bible of the book trade (sometimes Job, sometimes Revelations, perhaps Exodus?), gave the book a good notice in a short paragraph, and later followed the review with an interview. It was an honest, uncompromising account of my life and work by the historian of the Group Theatre, Wendy Smith. But still, like every other writer alive, I wait out other opinions in a state of acute anxiety. Like the first olive, one good one is never enough. Today there are two more.

Sybil and I are driving on Deer Isle to find Sven Olsen, known as Seven to the natives. We need his repair services for our ailing VCR. As we travel, I read my mail while she searches for his house. There is a letter from Gerry Howard. Two xeroxes drop out. In a state of pure panic I scan them, fast. One is a review to appear soon in the Sunday *New York Times.* It's by Noel Perrin, a New Englander whose book on living in the country, *First Person Rural,* I reviewed years ago. He appears to have liked my book, but he reproaches me for saying I hate travel, and then writing about three long trips I took in my seventieth year.

I find myself talking back to him. It is a matter of definition. To me, and (I believe) to Webster, travel is a progress. It means to go from one place to another, by whatever means. It is the *process* I hate: the proud airlines' contumely, worry about lost luggage and scarce taxis and inclement weather, bad meals and worse airline and train schedules, the race from one plane to its connection two concourses away carrying my luggage because I am afraid to check it for fear I will arrive at an appearance or a speech without the proper clothes, a book to read, or a toothbrush. All of that, I tell Perrin mentally.

Once I arrive, in Paris, in Yucatán, in Key West, in San Francisco, in Columbus, wherever, all is usually well. So I suffer through the unpleasantnesses in order to get there. Then, hours before I am to leave, I sink into a new fit of dread, in anticipation of the ordeal of getting home.

Perrin takes me to task for my 'cranky old opinions.' The headline writer took a liking to that word and topped the review with 'Be Cranky While You Can.' I am taken aback by the repetition of the word, having always, perhaps, I now see, mistakenly, thought of myself as reasonable and good-tempered about my preferences and dislikes. One learns, occasionally, from reviewers to see what one writes as others hear and read it. It is cautionary and useful. But then, if I hide this curmudgeonly inclination in me, I will fall under La Rochefoucauld's warning: 'Our faults are generally more excusable than the means we take to disguise them.'

The other review, in the *Washington Post,* is curious. The reviewer is Anthony Thwaite, literary editor of the *Listener* and the *New Statesman* and now coeditor of *Encounter.* An accomplished Brit. I smile at this, thinking that Nina King, the scrupulous book editor of that paper, who is a longtime acquaintance, must have felt she could not rely on any reviewer in this country who might turn out to be a friend of mine, an enemy, a former student, or a sympathetic fellow writer.

Nervous about this English critic who has been given my offspring to judge, I study his qualifications before I examine the review itself. Then the review. Thwaite confesses that he has never heard of me, has never read 'or even noticed' my novels, and, indeed, has heard of none of the persons who appear in the book. He confesses to being, like me, 'in the later, if not last, stages of life,' and *then,* to my immense relief, admits that he likes me and what is better, my book. 'Whew,' whistled Hal, 'That was close,' as the boy heroes of my youthful reading used to say, stepping back from a precipice just in time.

There is a caveat: Thwaite reproves me for calling Edmund

Gosse *Henry* Gosse, a scriptural error of mine, I'm sure, not caught by the copy editor or proofreader. I am horrified, but what can be done? I am somewhat mollified by hearing from someone that Thwaite's wife is the editor of Edmund Gosse's papers, so he, of course, would have noticed what perhaps only a few Americans will. *I* know Edmund Gosse's name is not Henry, having encountered the chap many times during my graduate-school grind in a course in nineteenth-century English poetry and criticism.

But then I am consoled. I look Gosse up in the index to *The Cambridge History of English Literature,* discover he is listed as GOOSE, EDMUND, and am much relieved that I was not responsible for *that* egregious error.

༄

This morning, a Nicaraguan lady, Ligia, comes to clean house for us. She is an immigrant who taught school in her own country, and then left with her young son when her mother was murdered. I have trouble communicating with her, my Spanish being so rudimentary and her English almost nonexistent. But we get on well, with many smiles and much head-shaking. She has been given succor and sanctuary at St. Brendan's, the Episcopal church in Stonington, a fine little fishing village at the end of Deer Isle. Now she has her own apartment, which she supports by cleaning the Episcopal church in Blue Hill and the houses of some parishioners of both churches. One of them, a charming Southern lady, Mary Lyall Murray, stopped into Wayward Books (the store Sybil built and runs next door to our house) last spring and told her: 'It's good to feel one is doing one's Christian duty and having one's house cleaned, all at the same time.'

༄

This month is the anniversary of Margaret Schlauch's birthday.
She was the professor at New York University who influenced
me to change my major from philosophy to medieval literature,
and then my friend. I continue to think of her. Even up here in
these unscholarly climes, I have met persons who remember her,
who were her students or readers of her work when they did
their graduate work. Hers is the kind of immortality I believe
in, a continued existence in the creative world of scholarship and
learning, a ghostly presence who returns every time *The Gift of
Tongues,* her most readable history of the development of
Indo-European languages, and her other books are opened and
studied. The word for such a return after death, in whatever
form, I have recently learned, is 'revenant.'

⟳

Sitting on the deck this morning, waiting for Sybil to bring the
mail from the post office, which might contain more reviews, I
read the last chapters of the Book of Job. After many long
descriptions, in forty-two chapters, of the terrible trials God
submits him to, there is a happy ending in one sentence of the
epilogue: 'So the Lord restored Job's fortunes and doubled all his
possessions.' And then, at the last (in the *New English Bible,*
issued in 1970): 'Thereafter Job lived another hundred and forty
years, he saw his sons and his grandsons to four generations, and
died at a very great age.'

In its many translations into English, from the seventeenth
century to the twentieth, the Bible moves from poetry to
matter-of-fact prose and rarely back to poetry again. But always
it reflects the patriarchy of the society in which it is written. The
poetry of my more familiar translation, 'So Job died, being old
and full of days,' is gone from the new, 'revised' one, but there
is still the interesting Hebraic insistence on the primacy of male
offspring. Job had three most beautiful daughters who were left

a share of the rich inheritance, but there is no mention of his living to see any granddaughters.

In reward for his fidelity to him, God doomed Job to live on and on (the verbiage here is mine). It is a lovely story, but nowhere is it said that Job suffered any of the usual infirmities of his gift of old age. If his possessions were doubled, perhaps also his age was, which would have made him 280 old. Arthritic? Deaf? Blind? Lame? Toothless? Senile? We do not know. Perhaps God, as an added gift to him, threw in immunity from all such indignities, in which case long time and extreme age would indeed be a gift. But if God did not think to do this, would it not be a further affliction for Job to be made to live on, so 'full of days'?

✑

Bill Henderson, the astute editor of the Pushcart Press who has built a summer cottage on Deer Isle with his own hands ('How did you know how to go about it?' I asked him. 'I read a book,' he said), writes this morning to tell me he likes the appearance of my new book. This pleases me. Ever since another publisher, David Godine, taught me that it is as expensive to produce an ugly book as a beautiful one, or perhaps it was that it is as cheap to make a beautiful book as an ugly one, I have been interested in the subject of book design.

Having no formal training in typography, papermaking, binding, or design, I am usually designated 'the sensitive amateur' when I am asked to judge the appearance of books for the American Association of University Presses, or 'the literary critic' when I write reviews of handmade books for *Fine Print*. But my untutored views are firm enough to make me insist on having a hand in the design of my own books.

The first editor to listen to my complaints about a jacket design was Henry Robbins. I protested that the proposed drawing on the front misrepresented the persons in the text of *Chamber Music*. He laughed, and said that was not an uncommon state of affairs for jacket and copy. 'Some jacket designers do not know too much about what goes on inside,' he said. 'Their instructions are to make something that will sell the book.' Nonetheless, he ordered a change to a nonrepresentational jacket, and so *Chamber Music* appeared in a simple, unglossy 'matte finish,' as it is called, almost puritanical in design.

Another editor, Bill Whitehead, allowed me to specify the type I liked and other small design elements of the body of the text. He listened patiently to my no doubt boring dissertation on how every element of a book—the body type, the design and type of the title page and half title, as well as spine and jacket—ought to be coordinated. If this was done, readers might have a better sense, although they might not be entirely aware of it, of the unity of the whole, the story suitably housed in its pages, jacket, covers.

As for this new book that Bill Henderson writes to me about: the publisher, designer, and editor conspired with me to make, to my mind, just such a satisfying volume. I wanted the right-hand margins to be unjustified, that is, unevenly set to resemble the jaggedness of handwriting in a journal. I like Bembo type for such casual writing. For the jacket I submitted the photograph of a sturdy little Model T Ford taken by a friend in a field not too far from where I live. I hoped the type around it, and the heads and subheads inside, might be in italic rather than roman, to approximate the slant of penmanship.

Then came a surprising, added bonus of goodwill and good bookmaking. Reading the galleys of *End Zone,* the publisher, Donald Lamm, discovered my distaste for the ugly design and tacky production of most contemporary trade books. So he authorized that the book be bound entirely in cloth instead of the usual two-thirds-paper-over-board.

I suppose I would be strung up and eviscerated by the Association of American Publishers if I asserted that writers ought to have a hand in the design of their books. It might be more prudent to suggest that writers spend some time studying the principles of book design, as well as the economics that govern such amenities, and then practice a vast amount of tact in offering suggestions about the kind of domicile they would like to see for their manuscript.

∽

Looking through my good set of what we used to call 'spyglasses,' from my study window, I spot the Cove's many birds. But the view the glasses provide is not always what I want to see. From a distance, and without the glasses, they appear to be a great patch of undifferentiated ducks, the brown female eider melded with the startling black-and-white males. Somehow the view makes me think of fiction, of how Henry James used almost no proper names for objects and places and yet, with the force exerted by his great tissue of words, he created particulars perhaps with the reader's unaware contributions. His unbounded generalities settle in the mind as graphic, detailed singularities.

∽

On a drive toward Route 1 I pass the newly moved Episcopal church, now seated firmly on a hill, still gaunt-looking because the landscaping has not been done or the building painted, but impressive in its architectural aspiration. I think of its six-mile journey, cut into two pieces. Then the parts were put together, the chandeliers and windows and spire restored, and a historic place of worship was once again made whole. . . . Coming back toward Blue Hill, I slow down to see the empty field where the church, then serving a Methodist congregation, stood for so

many years. The site is overgrown, with no sign remaining that
it was a place where hardy Maine Protestants once made their
arduous Sunday journey to worship.

∽

Everywhere in this central coastal area of Maine FOR SALE signs
appear along the roads, some of them the same signs that were
here last year. Real estate, we are told, is being offered at low
prices but very little of it is being purchased. Some older
Mainers who wish to leave the winter cold for the year-round
warmth of Florida are finding it hard to rid themselves of their
(in many cases) ancestral property. Others, who tried to ride the
recent crest of high prices, find that they have missed their
chance for profit, and are held on their land and in their houses
by the very real recession up here.

It is almost unbelievable. This morning on the radio
President Bush claimed that the "so-called" recession is only a
matter of "pessimistic attitudes" on the part of an uncooperative
citizenry. I suppose it is possible to think this if one lives in a
majestic house surrounded by acres of lawn, uniformed guards
holding guard dogs, and a tall iron fence to keep out the
disturbing presence of the homeless and the hungry who camp
across the street in Lafayette Park. Cheerfulness and optimism
are rather easy to maintain under such opulent conditions, but
much harder up here where heating oil and wood for stoves are
expensive, where snow and ice cover the frozen ground for
almost half the year, where there is only seasonal employment
or no jobs at all, and too many people live below the poverty
level. In winter, darkness descends before four o'clock in the
afternoon and remains inexorably until after seven in the
morning. All of this provides a natural culture for pessimistic
attitudes and despair about the economy.

One house, on Route 15, opposite the brave little sign a

neighbor Annie Tobin has had put up at her own expense
(WELCOME TO SARGENTVILLE), boasts a fine view of the
sunset. It has been for sale or for rent for as long as we have
lived here. Recently the sign came down, and now lights appear
in the evening in the living room. A car is parked in front of a
closed barn. I wonder if there are new tenants, or if the old ones
have given up their attempts to leave and have settled back into
residence in sight of the red-gold glory of the evening sky.

ᔕ

The winter enemies of the year-round population are the dark
and the cold. A humorous story is told of an elderly Maine
farmer who lived on the Maine–New Hampshire border. He is
visited by a state engineer who wishes to survey the area. After
he has finished, the engineer tells the farmer that, he is sorry to
report, his farm is not in Maine but in New Hampshire.

'I'm glad to hear that,' the farmer replies. 'These hard Maine
winters were getting too much for me.'

Funny, but also sad. That is about as far as elderly inhabitants
would be able to move, for the most part, to escape the cold.

ᔕ

Right after Labor Day, the Sargentville–Sedgwick–Blue
Hill–Brooksville area begins to divest itself of visitors. The first
sign is the closing of the roadside drive-in restaurant near us
called Milton's Dream, where very good fried fish of every
kind, carbonated drinks, and ice cream are sold from windows
in a long shack. Sybil has discovered that it also dispenses a small
'kiddie cone,' as it is called, for twenty cents. Much as I tend to
rejoice at the departure of tourists and the restoration of the
stores and roads to year-round residents, she mourns the closing
of Milton's Dream for the winter and the loss of her tasty
bargain.

∽

September 23: Lee Eitingon Thompson, a friend since we
worked together at *Architectural Forum* in 1940, telephones to
say they are selling their property in Mahopac. All summer she
has been showing it to prospective buyers. She and her husband
are both 'getting older,' as we say of the elderly when we wish
to be kind. Ed is ill, the place is too much for them, they need
to live in less demanding surroundings. A garden apartment will
be easier for Ed to get in and out of, and less upkeep and
responsibility for Lee.

When first the Thompsons came to New York State from
Washington, D.C., where Ed had founded and then edited
Smithsonian magazine after he had been managing editor of *Life*
for many years, Lee raised peahens on the beautiful estate called
Rock Ledge Farm. I always looked forward to stopping there,
on my way up and down the coast, to swimming in their
old-fashioned pool after a long, hot drive, to sitting beside the
beautiful, acre-sized pond where transient ducks and geese rested
on *their* way north or south, to watching their overpopulated
bird feeder. Then we would have a superb dinner cooked by Lee
in one of her two professional kitchens (she had been a food
columnist for the *Washington Star*), and much good, reminiscent
conversation.

Sadly, places pass out of one's life the way people do. It is
hard to think that my passage from Maine to Washington or
New York and back again will not always be interrupted by a
stopover with Lee and Ed. I don't like to think about getting
acquainted with their new and probably most elegant apartment,
although I will of course always want to see them. But in the
space until the next visit I prefer to imagine them in the long
dusk sitting with their drinks beside the pond on Rock Ledge
Farm, waiting to open the gate when our car arrives.

✍

I pay a bill from Dr. Ramey, a specialist in glandular
malfunction. I consulted him in late spring about possible
parathyroidism (held in check at the moment). While I waited
for him in his office, I read the diplomas on his wall and learned
he attended Yale Medical School.

I ask him, 'Do you know my friend Richard Selzer, once a
surgeon at the hospital in New Haven and now a writer of
fiction and nonfiction, usually on medical subjects?'

'O yes, very well,' he said, and then proceeded to tell me a
rather scurrilous but funny story. It seems that Dr. Selzer was
asked to perform a small surgical procedure, the removal of a
carrot from the rectum of a homosexual man. Afterwards, he
patted the young man on the shoulder and said: 'Sir, learn to
chew your food better.'

✍

I am reading Rose Macaulay's last book, *Letters to a Friend,*
published in 1962. Her friend was an Anglican priest, Father
Hamilton Johnson, and the letters are good, if somewhat strange,
reading, full of the kind of fanatical, absolute devotion to a new
faith that converts often have. Macaulay returned to the
Anglican Church after a flirtation with Catholicism. She writes
that she is reading widely in Anglican texts and yearning to
celebrate every one of the liturgies available to her.

Now, at the end of her life, after extensive travel and
writing about what she saw (I am especially fond of *Pleasure of
Ruins,* perhaps because she shares my fascination with the
mysteries of Mayan civilization) and writing excellent fiction,
she is exploring anew the importance to her of her old faith.
The tone of her letters reminds me of my editor at Doubleday
many years ago, Naomi Burton, who talked of very little but

'the' Church after her conversion to Roman Catholicism.

I think about Naomi. This spring, after a long, almost twenty-year silence, I heard she was in Washington visiting her daughter-in-law, Nora Smith, once a student of mine at American University. Naomi was famed in publishing for bringing her friend Thomas Merton's *The Seven Storey Mountain* to Harcourt, and she edited my second novel at Doubleday, a far smaller (and entirely uncelebrated) accomplishment. My first two novels were 'secretly' published in the early sixties, as the critic John Leonard once said of his own fiction.

Naomi and I talked on the telephone. She told me she had celebrated her eightieth birthday recently, her husband, Melville Stone, had died, she had sold the fine English-style house they had built on the ocean at York, Maine, and was now living in a retirement apartment in the same village. We explored the possibility of meeting again, but, of course, as happens to such plans that are long delayed, it was not to come about. She went back to York, I saw May Sarton there on our way north, but there was no time to seek out Naomi.

One thing from the telephone conversation surprised me. When the subject of the Catholic Church came up (how, I cannot recall), she indicated that her enthusiasm for it was now much diminished, in fact that she (as I did) left the Church because of its inexcusable treatment of women and had returned to the Episcopal Church. I could hardly believe that her passion, which at the time I knew her pervaded every reference she made and every sentence she uttered, had not survived to the very end of her life.

The life history of religious fervor, in those persons whose lives are touched by it, often follows a predictable pattern, I've learned. In direct proportion to its initial ardor it diminishes and disappears, leaving behind a curious bitterness that it ever affected them. Sometimes the contrary conviction sets in hard—passionate atheism or agnosticism. I suppose this might be true of political zealots as well: I recall the number of ardent Communists in my youth who suffered violent revulsion against that philosophy and then became fervent conservatives.

∽

I hear from two of my daughters, who live hundreds of miles apart and yet are suffering the same strange ailment. Kate, who is pregnant with Maya's sister (Maya is a year and a half), has a continuing bad taste in her mouth, and Jane, who fifteen years ago had a benign brain tumor removed, has both the bad taste and a constant unpleasant smell in her nostrils. For them, only eating diminishes the sensation. Kate, a physician, suspects hers is connected to her pregnancy; Jane does not know the cause of hers—it may be the aftermath of a bad eye infection. But she is certain it has nothing to do with the recurrence of the tumor (although she was told by her surgeon that, slow-growing as meningiomas are, they can recur). A small amount of Valium makes things better, she reports. But she agrees to make an appointment with a neurologist to be sure that her own diagnosis ('It's not a tumor. I know what a brain tumor feels like') is correct.

∽

We go to Ellsworth, a shopping town about twenty-two miles from our Cove, to get groceries and household supplies. We pass a roadside drive-in where 'heroes' are offered. I am startled by the term, but Sybil, more learned in fast-food terminology than I, explains that they are long sandwiches, made on pseudo-French bread and filled with salami, cheese, chopped-up lettuce and tomato, onions, and hot peppers, and soaked with garlic-oil-and-vinegar dressing.

  Her description makes me feel slightly sick. But she assures

me that these elongated products are quite delicious even though
biting into one requires a heroic spread of the jaws. The names
for such gustatory monuments are varied, depending on the part
of the country in which they can be found. They are called
'hoagies' in Pennsylvania, so named either for the pork (hog)
contained in them or for the person capable of eating them. In
New England they are known as 'grinders,' the origin of which
is not certain; my guess is that the term refers to the necessarily
excessive use of the teeth. Another title is 'sub,' from
'submarine,' an obviously graphic designation. Add 'torpedo'
(clearly for the shape, not the effect), 'spuky' (for what? I do not
know), 'wedge' in Rhode Island, and 'poor boy' in New
Orleans (called 'po' boy' sometimes) because it contains such a
variety of fillings that it resembles the many courses of a meal
combined into one sandwich.

Are these gargantuan extensions of the modest sandwich
(itself named for the eighteenth-century Earl of Sandwich, who
must have been the first person to insert cheese or meat between
two pieces of bread), and if they are, what was wrong with *two*
mouth-sized sandwiches instead of this one, unapproachable
one?

After we acquire our weekly supply of groceries, we stop at
the place that offers subs. Sybil orders one, I, conservative and
old-fashioned to the end, and feeling unheroic, order a tuna-fish
sandwich.

∽

Today I receive a letter from a poet whose acquaintance I made,
briefly, during a Literary Lions gathering at the New York
Public Library a few years ago. Vartan Gregorian, who headed
the library at the time, had instituted these yearly gatherings to
which wealthy supporters bought tables and invited their friends
to share the table with them. At each table sat one writer, a Lion

for the evening. This elevation was not unlike *Queen for a Day,* the old television show. For most of us it was a great moment. Usually our lives more closely resembled that of mice.

My poet friend reminisced about his table at the affair, taken by Mrs. Vincent Astor, a remarkable elderly woman, very wealthy, who spends her days in volunteer service to the library. He said it had made him realize that if the robber barons had once been both rapacious and charitable, their descendants are often extraordinarily generous with their time and their money. 'Remember all those music halls and the 2,800 libraries that old Andrew Carnegie put up in every state of the union? Well, Brooke Astor is in that tradition,' he wrote.

I remembered the host at my table some years ago, an elderly, chatty man named Milton Petrie, who is a large donor to the library. For much of the time, while we ate an elegant dinner, he proceeded to tell me why.

He was born to Jewish parents in Salt Lake City, where his father, a policeman, was killed in the line of duty. As a teenager he had to leave home to make his living. In Detroit he worked for the Hudson Department Store, having changed his name to Petrie to avoid the company's well-known anti-Semitic hiring practices. But when he discovered he was the only Jew working there, he departed for New York to start his own business, a tiny store on 42nd Street in which he sold women's hosiery and gloves. Aware of his need for further education, he crossed the street in the evenings to the New York Public Library, sat in the general reading room, and called for books on every subject.

From a modest beginning he became owner of a string of department stores throughout the country. Now an extremely wealthy man, he takes a table each year for sixteen thousand dollars and invites eight of his friends to share the evening with him. He regards this as paying the library for his tuition.

Someone seated at his table told me that Petrie provides

funds for families of slain police persons in the five boroughs of New York City. Someone else said he was fine bridge player and every afternoon met with three other elderly men to play at a bridge club. Across the table from me sat Jerzy Kosinski, Petrie's Lion of last year, looking very fit, handsome, elegant, and full of good humor. I recall this only because two years later, Kosinski was dead by his own hand, having become ill and unable to write.

The last time I saw Milton Petrie he was being wheeled in a chair into the great hall at the library for the ten-year reunion banquet of Literary Lions. I think of him often, of his justifiable pride in his Horatio Alger–like business success. Like other Americans who made the same great progress, he was moved to give back to American society a thousand times what he received from it.

ᔕᑎ

Lovely oxymoron on a sign over a furniture store in Bangor, Maine: AUTHENTIC REPRODUCTIONS

ᔕᑎ

Autumn comes early to central Maine. Sitting on the deck facing the water as I work is possible only in the hours around noon, when the sun has warmed the chairs and the wooden boards of the floor, and the wind from the water has died down. By three o'clock I have to move, resenting the cold air that has chased me inside. For a person who likes to write outdoors, this is an unwelcome expulsion.

But today I come in early to answer the door. The UPS man delivers a large box from Norton, my publisher, containing copies of my new book. Seeing all these clones is a jolt, a multiple reminder that all my worries about word choice, sentence direction and structure, exclusions and inclusions, are now immutably settled, set in concrete print, unalterable. Nothing can be done about any of it, no improvement is possible.

The only pleasure I feel now is in looking at the jacket, which contains a photograph, taken by Jim Holdsworth, an acquaintance in nearby Sedgwick. It is of an old car, belonging to another Sedgwick resident, Bill Petry, the agent who sold us our house and later our friend. It sits in a field in Blue Hill that now houses the Episcopal church moved recently from Penobscot. Tall, yellow grass almost obscures its wheels. It looks worn but sturdy and wears its seventy-four years with a certain resignation if not grace. And what is most gratifying, like me who am almost the same age, it still runs.

I regard it as a fitting metaphor for me, rickety but in some ways still somewhat serviceable, of a respectable vintage and a discreet color (black). Both it and the one manufactured a year later, the year of my birth, lack chrome because the Great War was making use of that metal.

෴

The mail brings more reviews. Every time I see those Xeroxes in their fat Norton envelope my heart sinks. Sometimes I have to put them down and compose myself before I have the courage to read the fine print. Today there is one from Dave Wood, a long column that he writes for the *Minneapolis Star & Tribune.* He makes the appropriate admission that he is a friend of mine (from our joint service on the board of the National Book Critics Circle) and then says *End Zone* surprised him because he never thought all this was going on within me.

I understand this comment. It *is* curious to read books written by friends or acquaintances, especially if they are autobiographical, and to realize how little one has really known about the writers, how much one has been unable even to guess about them. Finding their lives fixed strangely to the page by their own hand is something like being in a foreign city and coming upon a married friend from home accompanied by a lady not his wife. Shock. Why is he here? Who is she? What is going on? How is it I never guessed? Did I really know him at all? Truly, we know almost nothing about each other, no matter how close or closely related we are, and what we think we know often turns out to be mistaken.

✐

This is my third September in Maine, the third time I have watched leaves turn abruptly to yellow or occasionally to red. (As early as the sixteenth century, the *OED* informs me, the word 'fall' appeared in the English language for the season in which the leaves drop.) So this season is as properly called fall as autumn.

I sense the water in the Cove growing chilly and hostile to swimmers, seabirds, and summer boats. . . . Working on a new novel, I find it hard to shut out entirely the world of cities, Washington and New York, that I thought I had left behind. The telephone rings often from those places. *End Zone* is making its gallant little way into areas beyond the Cove. People call, or write, or stop by to say they have read it. Norton's Fran Rosencrantz, who handles such things, makes a few plans for me to 'appear.' Radio hosts ask for interviews. These I do not mind doing, since on radio I do not need to worry about having my hair cut or wearing makeup, procedures I had to suffer through the year I did book reviews once a month on *The MacNeil/ Lehrer News Hour.* Oh, the anguish, the shock of recognition, at seeing one's face on a TV screen, looking large, lined, and elderly, even with hair cut and lipstick applied.

A few radio interviews are scheduled—one with Noah Adams at my old home station, National Public Radio. This kind of 'promotion' causes me to wonder: How much more of interest do I have to say that I have not already said in the book? Will not some of the same people hear more than one interview, and be taken aback at the poverty of my replies? Will I not repeat myself, thus sounding somewhat senile? Except to hope that talking about the book may sell a few copies, I can think of no reason for this further indecent exposure.

෴

End of the month: At six o'clock last evening a longtime acquaintance, Morris Philipson, called. He is a good novelist and a fine editor (he directs the University of Chicago Press). He says he is much taken with *End Zone*. I listen with embarrassed pleasure while he goes on about its virtues. He adds that he would like to publish, in paper, two of my novels now long out of print. At this point my pleasure knows no bounds. I ask him to talk to Tim Seldes, my agent. He says he will, I thank him. When we say goodbye and hang up, I have to sit down.

But, as always with me, I cannot accept praise without strong doubts arising at once. I note the time—five o'clock where Morris is—cocktail hour in Chicago. No doubt, I tell myself, his compliments are the result of euphoria engendered by shots of Boodles gin or Johnny Walker Black Label scotch.

෴

I see that Kitty Kelley's biography of Nancy Reagan is on the best-seller list, as predicted. Sybil, my daughter Elizabeth Cale, and I went to the publishing party for her and her book last spring. It was a lavish, Washington-style bash, with wonderful food. The catering is Sybil's department: she cases the food table and directs me to the special goodies, while I talk to the literati and journalists at the party.

But this party was different. There were no literary friends

there, only members of all the media, who followed Kitty
around the room as she walked under a specially arranged
traveling spotlight. I could not get near her after the first
hugging at the reception line. Sybil, Elizabeth, and I ate hugely,
tried not to be trampled by the men lugging TV cameras, and
then watched the antics of the press. Susan Stamberg of National
Public Radio asked me who was important here for her to
interview. I could think of no one. Later I saw her, desperate,
engaged in a serious on-the-mike discussion with another
member of the press. I surmised they were interviewing each
other.

October

A friend asked Yogi Berra:
'Do you know what time it is?'
Yogi Berra: 'You mean now?'

*T*he 1st: This month begins with good weather still holding. All the boats have been taken up, so the water in the Cove is smooth, clear of everything but the vestigial red dots of buoys. We have begun to collect pine branches to cover our bushes and perennials. We are told that the time to spread them is after the first 'hard' frost. The scarlet expanses of blueberry fields, so unexpected a sight to a newcomer to these parts and so startlingly beautiful, make it seem unlikely that winter is almost upon us. Yet local wisdom assures us snow might well fall before this month is out.

∽

I talk to Jane, who reports she is still experiencing the same strange taste and odor sensations. She has a distant appointment with her neurologist, and meanwhile continues to control the unpleasantness with Valium. She inquires about the weather. I say the summer is definitely over.

A mistress of the hyperbole and no aficionada of this state, she says: 'Over? It was over on July 25th. And began on July 23rd.'

Kate, with the reluctance to discuss her own symptoms characteristic, I believe, of most physicians, says she is 'okay,' which probably means she is being typically stoic, at least when she speaks to me. I believe doctors think they will lessen their authority with the lay world if they admit to being sick themselves.

↜

Patty Smith, our friend in Camden, Maine, who is slowly recovering from the loss (from cancer) of her longtime companion, Myrna Basom, is going to Edisto, South Carolina, for a short rest. 'Aha,' I say, 'I've read a fine novel about Edisto and Hilton Head, by Padgett Powell.' She asks me to send it to her.

Before I do, I reread it. The narrator, a boy named Simon, wants to be a writer when he grows up. He says, 'This is my motto: Never to forget that, dull as things get, old as it is, something's happening, happening all the time, and to watch it.'

And the black family servant, Theenie, tells him, 'Sim, you ain't *got* to do but two things. One is to die, and thuther is to live *till* you die.'

↜

Elizabeth, my most iconoclastic daughter, telephones to say she has read 'the book' and finds it unsettling to discover what was going on *inside* her mother in that dire year. I find it odd that no one, including Sybil, with whom I live so closely, seems to have been aware of the depth of my despair at growing old and feeling my age. . . . Barbara Wheeler, oldest of the women who are my daughters, reports that Elizabeth warned her that she would find *End Zone* very, very dour. 'It is like reading through chocolate pudding,' said Elizabeth.

Why do old people so often hide their deepest despair? Is it unpopular, unsociable perhaps, to confess that one hates being old? The more acceptable stance is cheery acceptance, 'The best is yet to be' proclamations, the happy assurances of sanguinity. And if old people do not feel this, they find it more politic to profess it.

∽

The Sunday *New York Times Book Review* arrived today (Tuesday). A biography of the Sicilian novelist Giuseppe Tomasi di Lampedusa has appeared. Vaguely I remember his only novel, *The Leopard,* a large and, I recall, fascinating but difficult book which I read years ago but cannot now remember clearly. It appeared a few months after his death and sold extraordinarily well—fifty-two printings in its first year, I learn from the review.

I have always wondered about big, serious, well-praised novels that have large sales. In their first year, they seem to appear on coffee tables in every literate, well-to-do household. Are they bought and then read? Or are they displayed as witnesses to the fact that the owners aspire to a certain level of 'culture'? Umberto Eco's *The Name of the Rose* is such a book. Two years after its publication it began to arrive among the used volumes Sybil bought for Wayward Books. Copies of the first printing that she acquired were in surprisingly good shape, dust jackets intact, a sign, I believe, that they had served more for decoration or display than reading matter.

∽

Early this morning thick fog from the sea arrived to obscure the wild field in front of our house. Its very existence seemed to be threatened. Death must be an atmosphere like this: the slow approach ('on little cat feet,' Sandburg said of fog, but to me today it appeared more like the claw feet of tigers) of dim, impenetrable, grey-fog light, until it turns into the dark, fills one's throat and ears, closes one's eyes (Emily Dickinson: 'And then I could not see to see'), and then obliterates existence itself.

The fog remains throughout the day, deadening even the activity in my study. I write nothing of interest or use in the novel, and instead of battling my infertility I settle into the old rocker beside the unlit wood stove (fog outside often makes an indoor room seem warm, somehow) to read, as desultorily as I was writing. I pull from the shelf a volume of John Ruskin's *Choice Selections* published by John Wiley in New York in 1884. Out of it falls a leather bookmark I must have put there sometime in the seventies when I was a contributing editor to the *Saturday Review*. It is embossed with a finger pointing upward and contains the admonition KNOW THY PLACE.

At last, after so many years of spiritual wandering, I know mine. It is here, in this study or on this deck, whether in productivity or blockage, in bright sunlight or fog, in autumn/fall, but always in sight of the infinitely varied Cove.

∽

Next day: Surprisingly, I find I am caught by Ruskin. I remember finding him hard to read for any length of time when I was in graduate school. Now I have grown more patient with writing on ethical subjects, a sign of age, I imagine. For instance, he advises me that 'Man's use and function . . . are to be the witness of the glory of God, and to advance that glory by his reasonable obedience and resultant happiness.' I like the adjective 'reasonable' here.

Or again, in a selection titled 'Man's Business in Life,' Ruskin says it is 'first, to know themselves and the existing state of things they have to do with, secondly, to be happy in themselves, and in the existing state of things, and thirdly, to mend themselves and the existing state of things, as far as either are marred or mendable.'

I know why I copy this out, and then sit looking at the sentences. Because so many of the letters I have received about *End Zone* in the past four weeks reproach me for my seeming ingratitude at 'the existing state of things' for me. And this is true in some of the reviews. Joan Dietz writes, in the *Boston Globe*, 'Enjoyment of the present and anticipation of the future came hard for Grumbach,' and Kay Haddaway in the *Fort Worth Morning Star-Telegram*, 'I found myself growing impatient with Grumbach's dark emphasis on the losses in her life.'

There are other reprimands, in print and in correspondence, that I take seriously, and wonder: Was the mood of that time of my seventieth birthday, and so the first half of the book about it, undeservedly, unaccountably bleak? In the light of all that I still had at that age—successful children, a beloved companion, and many friends, a good house in a cherished place, relatively good health, a satisfying occupation from which I do not need to retire because in it I do not grow over-age in grade, as we used to say in the Navy—should I not be cheerful, grateful, optimistic?

The only answer I can give, to myself and to the others who write to rebuke me for my 'acerbic,' 'suspicious,' 'cranky,' 'bitter,' 'grim,' 'bleak,' 'flinty,' 'quirky,' 'crusty,' and 'grumpy' self (this list of adjectives was culled from recent reviews of *End Zone* by Sybil when I could not bring myself to do it), is that sadly, unfortunately, I wrote as I felt. I would like it to have been different. I would have preferred to be, in Ruskin's terms, happy in myself and contented with the existing state of things. I wanted to be honest, and so I wrote of my despair. As Walter Cronkite used to say when he signed off from the CBS Evening News: 'And that's the way it is.'

∽

At eight this morning I drove into Ellsworth to take the Maine driver's test. My Subaru station wagon (so omnipresent that it is often called the State Car of Maine) is now registered here, and I vote and pay taxes in the town of Sedgwick. So it was time to change my license. Last night I studied the thick little manual, memorizing the strict laws about OUI (operating a car under the influence . . .) and all the fines for every kind of minor and major offense.

I was third in line to have my written test corrected. I waited while a young man stalked out in fury because he had exceeded the limit of six errors. Then the girl ahead of me, aged about seventeen, I would guess, left in tears, having told the state trooper she *had* to have her license in order to get the job she had been offered.

The trooper called me to his desk, looked at me carefully, accepted my sheet, and said, before he looked at it, 'Don't worry, ma'am. You're allowed to take it over three times.' I said nothing. He went down my list of answers, wrote o at the top, and said, 'Okay, take this to the photographer in the next room.' Ignobly, I could not resist asking him how many I had missed. 'None,' he said curtly, in what I took to be a tone of disappointment. Then he looked away and called across the room, 'Next.'

There are few triumphs for the elderly in this world. This was my small one for today. I came out feeling very flinty.

∽

Sallust (first-century-B.C. Roman historian): 'All things which rise, fall, and also those which grow, grow older.'

∽

Mid-October: One of my required 'appearances' is in Duxbury, Massachusetts, at an authors' breakfast. The host is Bob Hale, a chap who arranges such things for his bookstore. The place turns out to be a handsome old church and the audience is mainly white- and grey-haired ladies of a certain age. Oh, there are a few brown-haired women, one of whom introduces herself as my student years ago at the College of Saint Rose. I say, 'Oh yes,' but truth to tell, I cannot remember her.

My fellow speaker is a young woman named Mary Cahill who has written a humorous, sprightly novel called *Carpool*, which is exactly what it is about. She is first to speak, and gives a very honest, funny speech about her experiences publishing her first novel. She tells me later, when we lunch together, that she is on a tour of Eastern suburbs where carpooling for the transportation of children is a familiar phenomenon. She is surprised by the elderliness of the Duxbury audience and wonders how many of her listeners know about carpooling. She thinks her publicity agent may have misjudged this stop.

On this leg of her trip she is accompanied by what she calls a 'tour expeditor,' an energetic and attentive young woman who lives in the area, meets her plane, assists her travel from hotel to lecture, and then back to the departing plane. Clearly, writers' tours are a well-organized and profitable business. I have no such person, but no matter: this kind expeditor allows me to ride to Logan Airport with her and Mary Cahill in a blinding rainstorm. By nature she must be kind to itinerant writers, for she races ahead of me to the gate, carrying my bag. I make the plane by four minutes.

To go back to the event: I have difficulty speaking after Mary, because I have almost nothing funny to say. I notice the audience squirms a bit as I describe my views on aging, and certainly, I learn afterwards, when Mary and I sit at separate tables to autograph books, they have not been persuaded by my 'dour' remarks to buy my book. The lines at Mary's table are long. I hear more than one buyer tell her they are planning to send her book to their daughters.

Of my book one elderly lady says to me: 'I am giving it to my daughter's mother-in-law.' She offers no assurance that she intends to read it herself. An old lady walks by, carrying two copies of *Carpool* for her two daughters, I assume. Another lady with a cane does buy a copy of *End Zone* (bless her), and then asks me to inscribe it. I smile happily, write 'For Amy' and my name and hand it back to her. She pats my hand gently and says, 'Well, dear, I do hope you will feel better.'

The flight from Boston to Bangor was accomplished in a plane called a 'Business Express.' It had two propellers and was so small that it was much buffeted by the wind and heavy rain we were 'experiencing,' as the pilot phrased it. It is capable of holding twenty persons, and a crew of three. On this trip there were ten passengers. True to its name, nine of them were businessmen uniformly equipped with briefcases, *Wall Street Journals,* furled umbrellas, and trench-style raincoats.

The Business Express seemed to me to be a somewhat frail, almost rickety, but still jaunty and gallant little plane, a throwback to the forties in style and size. I felt it was more liable to failure or accident than its larger and more robust jet brothers. Should it crash, I suspect a number of large corporations would suffer grievous executive losses. American literature, on the other hand, would not be significantly affected.

∽

I am relieved to be home in Sargentville, weary of being an artificial, public person. Here I feel I become real again, no matter how badly dressed and grumpy, quirky, cranky, etc. I am. *Know thy place.* I find a letter from Patty Smith and a card from a Washington friend. In her letter Patty says she went to a

bookstore in Camden to buy *End Zone.* The clerk could find it
on the computer but not on the nonfiction shelf.

'I know we have it,' she told Patty lamely.

Patty searched and finally found it nestled happily among
more active-type books, on a shelf marked SPORTS.

And Cinder Johanson, a friend and librarian at the Library of
Congress, writes a postcard from Stone Harbor, New Jersey,
where she often vacations. It reads: 'Loved your football book.'

There is a lesson in all this. Mary McCarthy once told me
she was very good at naming books, as indeed she was: she
provided me with the name for the biography I wrote of her,
The Company She Kept, to echo the title of her own book, *The
Company She Keeps.* On the contrary, I have a genius for
misnaming books. *Chamber Music* found itself on the MUSIC
shelves of bookstores, *The Missing Person,* a novel about
Hollywood in the silent days, ended up among MYSTERIES, and
now there is my new football book. . . .

৵

Other mail: A letter from a young man with AIDS who lives in
the Far West. He writes that he was diagnosed several months
ago. Since then, the time has passed 'rather numbly,' from denial
or shock, he is not sure which. He read *End Zone,* interested in
what I had to say about the friends I had loved and lost from
AIDS:

> The dam broke, I've been angry, cried and then started to focus on
> what life means to me, what is important. . . . I hope the rest of
> my life—be it five years or fifty—is lived with some clarity and
> belief in values, in love of friends and respect of self, others and
> the world. I would be exaggerating if I gave your book all the
> credit for helping me past this point. It is at least a wonderful
> coincidence.

He says he has found Oregon, as I have found Maine, a
wonderful change, and that he is planning a garden for next
spring. His lover and he are heading for Mexico in January, he
concludes, because Oregon is very wet and dreary at that time
of year. 'We will think of you when he shows me the Mayan
ruins.'

To receive a letter like this gives me reason to write, to
know that one such reader is out there and, even in a small way,
has been affected by something I said. More than the hope of
monetary reward, or of fame, or of the chance of immortality, I
write in the hope of hearing one person say 'Keep writing,' the
injunction with which Bob Doyle ends his letter.

ᔕ

Sybil asks me to accompany her on a book call to East Blue
Hill, where a lady, who is moving to Tennessee, is selling her
house and her books. Ordinarily I don't go along on these jaunts
because I feel unequal to them. I usually think the books I am
looking at are not worth very much, but Sybil sees value in
many of them, and is usually right. I don't enjoy the dust that
has settled on old collections, and I sneeze and then quickly
grow impatient, reluctant any longer to give up the time it takes
to go through them carefully.

Sybil, a true book woman, is indefatigable, patient, and
generous in what she pays for books, so she is better off going to
see them alone.

But there is one thing about such visits that interests me.
Better than pictures, furniture, clothes, or architecture, books
may reveal the character, the personality, the nature of the
owners. What they bought and collected over the years, or
inherited from parents or grandparents and kept, often throws
light on their lives. In a way, it constitutes sociological data
from which it is intriguing to construct fiction about them, or at

least to raise interesting questions and attempt some answers.

For example: A Maine farmer, whose family has been on its Bucksport land for 150 years, collected books of Japanese prints, mostly erotic (as Japanese art often is). Is one permitted to make something of that? Or, a long-widowed elderly woman is selling her large collection of hard-boiled modern fiction. Or, a Methodist minister is ridding himself of his collection of volumes on the subject of homosexuality.

Recently, very early one morning, we went to Penobscot to buy the books from a family of five, parents and three children. Their collection was varied and indicative. There were many well-used greasy cookbooks, with written-in additions and corrections to the recipes, a good number of Catholic classics by Fulton Sheen, Joseph Girzone, and Andrew Greeley, and William Buckley mysteries, and two old Daily Missals.

In cardboard boxes, under piles of toys and games, there were many paperbacks of good children's books by Robert McCloskey (a master of the genre who lived nearby on Deer Isle), Margaret Wise Brown, Ruth Krauss, Barbara Cooney, Maurice Sendak, Katherine Paterson, and others. They all showed the usual signs of hard wear: nicks, crayon scratches, hot-chocolate spots, and what I took to be saltwater marks. There was an old Hoyle, the great authority on games, Collier's encyclopedia for children, and a few choice books on sailing, birds, gardening, and the seashore.

At once the shape of this family's life appeared to me. I thought I knew them. I asked the young-looking, bearded father why they were leaving.

Regret flooded his voice. 'I've been transferred. To San Antonio, can you believe it?' He looked over at the autumn remains of his vegetable garden and out to the scarlet hillock where his blueberries were, and at the two great balsam firs that framed the entrance to his driveway.

'We all hate to leave,' he said. He was wearing a red baseball cap and a plaid L.L. Bean flannel shirt. He stared at the FOR SALE sign mounted on the road at the edge of his property. A little girl carrying a large, healthy-looking fern asked him:

'Dad, if I sell this, can I keep the money?'

'Sure.'

'How much is it?' I asked her.

'Um. How much is it, Dad?'

'What do you think?' he asked her.

'Ten cents?'

'Oh, more than that,' I said. I, who often bargain for what I buy at yard sales, was seduced by the father's anguish at leaving the state and the little girl's charm. I gave her a dollar. Her blue eyes widened with surprise and delight.

Sybil paid the father for the boxes of books she selected and carried them to the van. I carried the fern. As we drove away I caught sight of a woman's solemn face at a window. We now had some remnants of the past life of a family in the back of our car, residue of the contentment that appears to have characterized the Maine life of this family.

∽

More householders' signs of approaching winter: We stretch the three long hoses to dry out before coiling them and retiring them to the cellar to rest for the winter beside the inner tube, screens, and my granddaughter's baby pool. We empty the flower boxes on the deck and cover the bushes and perennials with pine branches, all to the end of closing out our fine, free outdoor life and retiring, of necessity, to the closed-in, restrictive indoors.

As a sign that I accept the inevitability of the move, I sit in the living room watching the light die over the Cove through the window, and listen to a 1959 Hamburg concert of Maria

Callas singing 'Una voce poca fa' from *The Barber of Seville.*
Her recorded voice is expressive, dramatic, but somewhat harsh
and sharp, 'Italianate,' I always think. Like the air out there on
the deck and blowing through Sybil's rock garden, it has an
absence of summer softness, a crusty edginess.

∽

In a few weeks, DEAN (Down East AIDS Network) will
sponsor a walk in Ellsworth to raise money for its activities.
Sybil volunteers to get donations of food for the workers and
the walkers, and I offer to contact ministers and priests in the
area to ask for their support.

We are both persons who hate to ask for anything, but this
Saturday I accompany her on her rounds, sitting in the car in
cowardly fashion while she goes into pizza places, supermarkets,
and small grocery stores, her heart in her mouth, she says. But
still she goes, and *mirabile,* she is not turned down by anyone,
except by the owner of Merrill & Hinckley, the prosperous
grocery in Blue Hill, who can only offer to sell her, at cost,
what she might need. She is pleased that, with the uniform
generosity of other merchants and restaurant owners, she does
not need him at all.

I call or write a long list of churches, finding each call a trial
because I hate using the telephone but more because I dislike
asking for anything. I devise a mental stratagem to drive me to
the phone. I think of Carlos Calderon, my AIDS patient two
years ago at Capitol Hill Hospital in Washington. When he left
the hospital, I followed him to houses and apartments provided
by the Whitman-Walker Clinic where he was able to stay when
he could no longer live alone. Once he told me he wanted to see
Wayward Books (our bookstore on 7th Street). He climbed
painfully into my car, and I drove across the city and helped
him into the store.

He had no energy left to look at books but I remember him saying: 'I like being in a place where there are books.' His gaunt, handsome face looked happy; he shook hands heartily with Sybil as though she were part of the ambience he liked. . . . Remembering all this (and Carlos's death six months later, one week before we came down from Maine last year) made it possible to make those telephone calls.

Why do I hate to beg? Which of course is what we were really doing. Even in a good cause. Because, I suppose, I was taught 'to pay your way,' never to ask for anything, to live honorably. I think it would be easier, were I in need, to steal than to beg. The act of stealing is private, involves some skill, I would think, and a sense of accomplishment in the face of the danger of discovery. If one 'gets away with it,' a sort of victory over peril is achieved. Whereas begging is public and ignoble, and is only accomplished by assuming a lowly attitude of need and unworthiness.

∽

Last night we had dinner with friends Gail and Celeste. The other guest was John Preston, a writer with whom I had corresponded and for whose books (on AIDS) I have written blurbs. He now lives in Portland and is not entirely well, having had one stay in hospital. But he is full of intellectual (and physical) energy, has contracts and plans for two or three books, and has just taken on the care of a new puppy, an exuberant vizsla dog he tells us is a Hungarian breed, overfriendly, but yet a good guard dog, used in the past to protect the Hungarian border.

∽

Next day: A young woman comes by, accompanied by a photographer, from the *Bangor Daily News*. It turns out she is an entry in my Small World file. After the interview she tells me about herself. She was born into a working-class, German-American, Catholic family, the first of six children. She has Washington, D.C., roots, was a student at American University during the time I taught there, and raised a child born out of wedlock while she studied. She had no classes with me, she says, but used to walk by the closed door with my name on it, and wonder about me. She has battled depression (as well she might have), but now works as a journalist, doing the arts interviews for her paper.

The photographer takes so many pictures that, at last, I put a stop to it. I dread being photographed, more than I ever have. Not being photogenic makes one dislike the camera, the way Sybil, who fears heights, hates bridges. . . . At seventy, I wrote about my discovery before a full-length mirror of the decadent changes in my body, a section of the book that, to my horror, was often quoted in reviews. Interested in what the review had to say, I was forced to read that odious description again and again. . . . Now I am sure his pictures will reveal all the aged ridges, lines, valleys, sagging and blotching of my face and neck, the unreal mask I think my face has become in order to hide the unseemly youth I see in my mind's eye.

ᔐ

New York: Another radio interview, this one from New York by satellite to Philadelphia. Then I go to lunch on the east side of the city with my friend Hilma Wolitzer. She is enveloped in middle-aged contentment, having four good novels 'out there,' her novelist-daughter Meg happily married to a former student of Hilma's (and mine) in Iowa, a first, new grandchild, and a beautiful apartment that looks out, from a saving height, at the glories of the city of New York.

ᔐ

There is something about long blocks of cement paving and horizontal walls of buildings that threatens my stability. Uncertain about how much farther I can walk without repeating my custom of tripping, or turning my ankle, I go into a coffee shop that is kitty-corner from Carnegie Hall. A few young women are sitting alone smoking and drinking coffee. The 'help,' as we used to call waiters and cooks, are all of Central American or Oriental extraction, having replaced, *in toto,* the Irish girls who constituted the help at Schrafft's and Stouffer's and Childs when I was young.

(Suddenly I remember that in Manhattan in my youth, jobs tended to be filled by members of the same nationalities. Janitors in apartment houses were very often German and very exacting. I remember my friend Dolly's father, Mr. Sudermann, who would not permit the tenants of 130 West 86th Street, where my family lived for many years, to come into the basement for fear that 'they will upset it.')

Gallant, ageless old Carnegie Hall is still there, having, from what I can see, not changed at all, except for its newly cleaned facade, from the days in the thirties when I went every Friday afternoon and paid fifty-five cents for a student ticket. I sat on the floor of the second balcony, leaning against the last row of seats with my back to the New York Philharmonic Orchestra, John Barbirolli conducting, often following a score, and always, whatever the music, in a state of uncritical bliss.

In the coffee shop, a waiter drops a tray of dirty dishes into a metal bin from a great height, or so it sounds to me. I am the only one who jumps at the noise, marking me as an outsider, now a citizen of a quieter place who, sixty years ago, gave up her Manhattan citizenship.

In the coffee shop I hear someone behind me begin a sentence with the word 'unalterably.' I cannot resist turning

around. He is a very pale middle-aged man wearing a bowler
hat, a Cambridge University blue-and-white scarf, and a black
velvet-lapeled overcoat. I cannot see the lady he is speaking to;
her back is to me, and they are about to leave. He passes my
table, carrying a rolled copy of the *Manchester Guardian*. It is
chance encounters like this I have left behind in moving to
Sargentville, where the chap seated at the counter in the
Eggemoggin general store will be dressed in baseball cap, plaid
shirt, jeans, and boots, and reading the *Bangor Daily News.*
Unalterably.

෴

I stay in the apartment of my children, the Wheelers, who live
on the sixth and top floor of a Morningside Drive building. Last
evening the sun set over the low skyscape of Harlem, making
that section of the city look quite beautiful: the large windows
facing west took it all in. It made me homesick for the morning
glory of the Cove.

The apartment is a fine example of what New Yorkers can
do when they live in a relatively small space. Sam and Barbara
have replaced their old kitchen with a handsome, useful one,
almost witty in its clever use of space and color (if black and
white are colors). They have covered the walls of the other
rooms with good paintings, a Oaxacan quilt, and rubbings from
English tombs, and built shelves to display Barbara's collection
of Southern folk pottery and their books and records. While he
is away at college, Isaac's room is now arranged for guests, with
a work space for his mother's computer. Sam's small study is
lined with his linguistic-scholarship books as well as hooks for
everyone's outerwear. If you squint through the small window
in this room you can see the spires of Riverside Church and a
slice of Amsterdam Avenue.

Sam grinds and brews fresh coffee very early in the morning (my best hours) and then the two of them take off for work, he to his boys' private school where he teaches Latin, Spanish, and an occasional stint in sex education, and she to Auburn Theological Seminary a few blocks away where she is president. . . . I settle down to write a speech I have to give this evening, luxuriating in the silence (only at a distance do I hear an occasional siren; my poor hearing rules out whatever other street noises there may be), the comfort of this aerie of an apartment, and the solitude.

Although I am enjoying the silence of the telephone I find myself using it to talk to Jane Emerson, who lives thirty blocks away. She is feeling better, but her strange affliction recurs on occasion. Her appointment to see her neurologist is next month.

∽

In Barbara's well-lighted bathroom mirror I see, close up and clearly, my wrinkled face. So seldom do I look in a mirror that, for long periods, I am unaware of unsightly changes. Sometimes when I do look to see if I have remembered to comb my hair that morning, I am in such a hurry that I fail to notice very much. I have come to believe that wrinkles must be far more evident (and horrifying) to women born with beautiful faces than to those of us who have never had a reason to inspect closely our plain visages.

∽

In the cab to the airport to return to Maine, I notice how skyscrapers now affect me. I feel the need to withdraw from them in order to protect myself, to move inward and away from their confining, narrow, vertical menace. Recently, when we were driving through the Berkshires, I noticed that mountains act upon me the way Billings Cove does. They decrease my self-centeredness, they draw me out, elevating and extending what I daringly call the soul.

∽

Thinking about the Berkshires reminds me of something I learned the other day: People who drive through these lovely mountains in the fall to see the foliage (and those who do the same thing in Maine) are termed 'leaf peepers' by the natives. They are welcomed for their trade but scorned for their obstruction of the highways.

Other nomenclature: At Dartmouth at the beginning of this month, where I went to give two talks to a breakfast (and then a luncheon) audience about the fictional nature of memoirs, diaries, and journals, we were served a dish which I could not identify. Turned out to be a local favorite, made with blended cold beets, and called 'Red Flannel Hash.'

∽

News reaches us from southern California that our friends Diana and Mary, both librarians at UCLA, have won the state lottery. Their share is seven and one-half million dollars. Sybil, an inveterate buyer of lottery tickets in whatever state she happens to be, gloats. She telephones the winners to congratulate them. What will they do with their prospective riches? Diana says she will buy, first thing, an electric pencil sharpener for her office, something she has always wanted.

Having never known anyone who won money in a lottery, even a small amount of money, I am amazed, and, for the moment, silenced. I have always scorned investing in such enterprises, claiming that they are a fraudulent and seductive way of parting the foolish and the poor from their money. And still . . . but now . . .

Sybil decides she will buy tickets when next she is near a

state that has a lottery. I decide I will not be moved by Diana
and Mary's incredibly lucky strike. I already own an electric
pencil sharpener.

∽

Almost no one in Sargentville or surrounding areas knows about
the publication of *End Zone,* and that is a good thing. I am
egotistical enough to enjoy being 'known,' but only beyond the
radius of about one hundred miles from where I wish to live in
peace. Once in a while, someone 'from away' brings a copy of
the book into the store and asks Sybil if I would sign it. I do,
but always I remember the story of Sophie Tucker's
autobiography, which she published herself. We once bought a
signed copy of it for the bookstore and asked Bob Emerson,
who owns a theater bookstore in New York, what it was worth.
    'Almost nothing. The trick is to find an unsigned copy. *That*
might be worth something.'
    If one is concerned for posterity, there is a moral here.

∽

Coming back to Sargentville after the speeches, the bookstore
visits, the signings, and the speeches at breakfasts, I am depressed
by the thought that everything I have done for more than a
week was, somehow, ignoble. Selling, signing books: why does
it matter to a reader if the writer has put her name in the book?
Parading from place to place, always in behalf of a book that
should be making its own way in the world without all the
peripheral folderol of 'appearances,' feels unworthy. The
English have a nice word for it: 'hedge-born,' meaning what it
says, I suppose, and in general referring to activities that are low
or demeaning. Today I feel hedge-born.

∽

I am home. The Cove has waited for me, calm, patient, the last thing I looked at before we drove south to the cities, the first think I sought out when I came back to where I started from. . . . This morning, two-thirds of the way through the month of October, is heavy with fog and the promise of rain. I watch a crow make her royal progress across our uncut, rough field. Decorously, she acknowledges her constituency, a flock of smaller birds that seem to live in the woodpile we are preparing to burn. She walks on, as somber, black, and erect as a funeral-home director, having made a long ceremonial advance out of Rebecca Peterson's woods, across our field, and then onto Jeannie Wiggins's land, out of sight.

I realize how seldom I look for very long at large birds. I tend to be interested in tiny, multicolored visitors to our feeder and to the boxes on the deck, especially purple and gold finches, chickadees, and hummingbirds. Of course I exclaim with pleasure over the presence in the Cove of large water birds like egrets, cormorants, and an occasional osprey. But the crow, with its lustrous black plumage (in some light as iridescent as the hummingbird's), I take for granted, registering its appearance as a sign of approaching rain, instinctively denigrating it for its murkiness, dismissing it, and then looking at something else.

I had forgotten that Edgar Allan Poe immortalized its cousin the raven, and Wallace Stevens recorded 'Thirteen Ways of Looking at a Blackbird':

> I do not know which to prefer,
> The beauty of inflections
> Or the beauty of innuendos,
> The blackbird whistling
> Or just after.

Gone from sight, the crow's raucous cry still hangs in the air, reproaching me for my avian prejudice.

∽

There was a pile of mail and books waiting at the post office
where Frances, our omniscient postmistress, had saved it in a
large box. She handed it out through the door. 'Glad to be rid
of it,' she said.

There is a letter from Linda Pastan, a poet I have known in
Washington for many years. She sends me another story about
Tom Victor, the excellent photographer of writers who died a
few years ago of AIDS. 'The day he spent with me taking
photographs may have been the most "romantic" I have ever
spent. We walked the streets of Manhattan, and he kept running
ahead, kneeling down, and snapping pictures. It felt like *La
Dolce Vita.* Tom had a way of making his subjects feel utterly
beautiful. "Those cheeks!" I remember he said to me. It was a
terrible letdown to travel home, look in the mirror, and see my
usual plain face.'

Mixed in with a few commendatory letters there is a good,
give-it-to-her-straight note from a lady in Maine (Scarborough)
whom I do not know. She informs me that the 'slow delivery'
of my book reviews on National Public Radio 'drove me up a
wall.' She read *The Ladies,* she said, and 'did not think I would
read anything else by you,' a neat way of expressing her opinion
of that book, I thought. She lets me know that she read an
interview with me in the *Maine Times,* and so borrowed *End
Zone* on interlibrary loan. Clearly she did not wish to be
saddled with it permanently if it turned out to resemble my
aired remarks or *The Ladies.* Finally, she admits that, to her
surprise, she enjoyed it and has even gone so far as to order a
copy for a friend. Against all reason and anticipation, I gather.

A long letter from Frederick Manfred, with whom I used to
correspond regularly in *New Republic* days. I remember him as a
Siouxlander, a white-haired, unusually tall and handsome

Minnesotan whose novel *The Manly-Hearted Woman* I reviewed enthusiastically. He comments on *my* comments in *End Zone* about Brenda Ueland, a Minnesotan, and another correspondent from those days, whose long, active, loquacious life I admired. He knows much more about her than I do and offers the fascinating suggestion that Sinclair Lewis (another citizen of Minnesota) was the father of her born-out-of wedlock daughter.

I no longer own a copy of Mark Schorer's life of Lewis, an enormous, detailed work as I recall, so I cannot look Ueland up in the index. It would be interesting to know if this is true. Ueland was a free spirit long before it was fashionable and socially correct to be one. She went to teas at Willa Cather's apartment in Greenwich Village, wrote for New York magazines, and produced at least two books, one on writing that was reprinted recently, just before her death. She lived on a health-food diet most of her life and climbed mountains after she was eighty.

Manfred himself must now be 'getting on,' as they say, but he is still very active. He is reading galleys on a new book, and writing still another. I seem to recall a long list of novels in the front of one of his books. He writes: 'It's funny but I have the feeling that I'm only now learning how to do it.'

∽

Birth and death in a day: Wanting to see the last of the afternoon light yesterday (it begins to grow dark here before four), I went out on the deck and caught sight of a black, diaphanous mayfly, a very late comer to the fall lawn scene. I remember that the mayfly's life span is a day. It was born this morning and now, in the growing afternoon darkness, is on its way to its death.

The sight sends me back to my study, where I search until I find a copy of Thomas Boreman's *Moral Reflections on the Short*

Life of the Ephemeron. First published in London in 1739, my
copy was made by David Godine early (1970) in his notable
career as publisher and designer of elegant letterpress books. It
has delicate, colored etchings by Lance Hidy, is printed on fine
Amalfi paper, hand-bound, and put up in a cloth-covered box
made, I think by Arno Werner. I handle it with pleasure. In
every sense it is an example of a book that suitably houses its
contents.

The introductory paragraph reads this way:

> The Ephemeron, or Mayfly, is a common freshwater insect. The
> nymph grows for two years before it surfaces, sheds its skin, and
> emerges as a delicate, transparent fly. It is unable to eat, and can
> only fly and mate during its day of life. . . .
>
> Trout fishermen and philosophers have both written about the
> Mayfly. . . . Aristotle established the Mayfly as a symbol of the
> shortest-lived animal. Philosophers use it still as a reminder of our
> vanity and mortality.

I look through the study window to the deck that is now
entirely obliterated by the dark. The mayfly I saw must now be
dead, or moribund, as was the one Boreman contemplated in the
eighteenth century, the 'dying sage' who speaks to her fellow
flies of her youth in the morning:

> What confidence did I repose in the fullness and spring of my
> joints and in the strength of my pinions! But I have lived enough
> to nature, and even to glory. Neither will any of you whom I
> leave behind have equal satisfaction in life in the dark, declining
> age which I see is already begun.

Tonight I am unaccountably sad. I feel as if I were possessed
of what in Hebrew folklore is called a *gilgul.* The soul of the

mayfly seems to have entered into me, and I can think of
nothing but the ephemera of time and the permanence of death,
of bright life and then the dark, like the blackout at the end of a
skit in an inconsequential revue.

∽

Today we planted more bulbs, and accompanied them with
mothballs, one ball to a bulb. It may be that the odor will
discourage the avaricious squirrels. The ground is cold but very
dry. I think of Gerard Manley Hopkins's line: 'Mine, O thou
lord of life / Send my roots rain.'

∽

I am rereading parts of Hermione Lee's excellent life of Willa
Cather. It is full of original, useful insights, so good that I
despair of ever going back to my notes to do the book I once
planned. Perhaps it is as well. In the ten or more years that I
have been thinking about Cather, I seem to have taken on some
of her personal characteristics. Lee remarks upon her 'grumpy
repudiation of the modern world.' The adjective has now grown
familiar: Helen Yglesias, my good novelist friend who lives a
few miles away from us in Brooklin and who provides me with
much of the literary talk I sometimes crave, calls me 'grumpy' in
her *Women's Review of Books* piece, and I must be, because
readers and reviewers detect something of that tone in my book.

Hard as it is to do, I take up *End Zone* and review my stated
dislikes. Now, three years later, the edges of my discontents
seem to have softened, perhaps because I am protected against
the noise, pollution, crowds. I go, with reluctance, into the
world and then come back, full of relief that this place is still
here.

Sometimes I worry that I rely too much on this place for my
salvation. Have I made a fetish of it, am I obsessed with it? Yet

when I am here, I am content, protected, free, less grumpy, I
think. . . .

∽

And then, this morning, as I wrote these last words, there was a
knock on the door. A lady who owns the house on the edge of
the Point, within sight of the front of our house and across the
Cove, asks if Wayward Books will be open today. I tell her
Sybil has gone to look at books in Surry and should be back
soon. I invite her in to wait.

She tells me that she and her husband occupy the grey house
close to the edge of the Reach. They are there a few weekends
in the fall and spring, and in the summer. We talk about closing
houses for the winter and then she tells me that their house was
vandalized last winter. Some young boys from the area (one
from Deer Isle) broke in, for some reason decided to trash all the
photographs on the wall, broke things but stole nothing, and
left. The photographs were old, valuable ones of the Cove, the
Point, the Reach, nineteenth-century views of Sargentville and
Sedgwick.

So. I have been deluded. There is no absolute safety, even
here. Twice trashed in the District of Columbia, we came to the
Cove to escape the threat of the destructive city, only to have
our neighbor's house on the Point damaged. I should keep in
mind what I once knew but seem to have wanted to forget, that
Shakespeare's Henry VI told his soldiers: 'In ourselves our safety
lies.'

∽

Looking through a reprint of an old book, *Divine Poems* by
Francis Quarles, I am reminded that faith offers another security,
echoed in Martin Luther's hymn:

> Great God! there is no safety here below;
> Thou art my fortress, thou that seem'st my foe.

∽

Resolved to be more cheerful (and not to fall back into the desolation and despair of my seventieth winter), I read my mail. There is a letter from a woman with whom I went to summer camp when we both were teenagers. Helen Mandelbaum has an incredible memory and recalls that I thought up charades for her 'bunk.' A camper appears with dirt smeared on her forehead: Soily Temple. And a girl named Ann stands crying. The rest of the bunk touches her slightly as they pass her by: Presbyterian (press by teary Ann). How terrible. No wonder I opted to forget such things. But her memories cheer me up.

∽

After a hasty trip to Washington for bookstore business, we are back in Sargentville. In the short time we stayed in the cool city, we combined our craving for Oriental food with a reunion with Jeff Campbell and Gene Berry, neighbors on the Hill and friends from the days when Sybil ran her shop on Seventh Street. Gene works at the Library of Congress and, until recently, collected first editions by living American authors he had read and admired. Then he would write to them, such charming and beguiling letters that they agreed to sign the volumes he sent. Anne Tyler, M.F.K. Fisher, and Eudora Welty are three I recall his having corresponded with.

But at the Queen Bee, our favorite Vietnamese restaurant across the river in Arlington, he tells us his new passion is collecting antiques. He does not mention any further correspondence with writers, even antique ones, and I am saddened by his defection. . . . Jeff, his architect friend, is always very patient, very quiet, during Gene's description of his enthusiasms. It's hard to know if he shares them, but I think it would be hard not to. Gene's eyes glow with that peculiar light common to all avid collectors when they talk about their pursuits.

∽

Sleeping in the apartment the first night was strange. Neither of us could remember where we were when we woke at our usual early hour. Sybil remembered first, shot out of bed, dressed, and went for the papers ('Imagine,' she gloated, 'having the *Post* and the *New York Times* at seven o'clock on *the same day* they appear!') and what she calls *etwas* and coffee from Bread and Chocolate on the corner.

The pleasure of cities—*das gewisse,* that certain something—cannot be denied. Thus far I have been able to identify five: reunions with friends we have reluctantly left behind; the presence of a physician, Amiel Segal, whom I admire and trust; the morning newspapers; buttery scones from the bakery across the street; and daily Mass at St. James, five blocks away. Try as I might, I can think of no others.

Oh yes, one other: the flea market on our block, every Sunday morning. Last week we bought a photograph of the sculpture at Hain's Point. Jim Culhane took the picture of Charles Johnson's remarkable work. A furious prophet lies half buried in the ground; only his arm, one leg, and his John Brown–like head can be seen. The photographer says there is talk of removing the wonderful piece and replacing it with a park. So I bought his photograph in case the sculpture disappears. This morning we decide we will hang it in Maine near the woodstove in the living room and not far from the nineteenth-century colored drawing of the Capitol.

ᔕ

Graffiti spotted on a fence at Dartmouth College during a visit
to Hanover:

'Why worry about tomorrow when today is so far off?'

ᔕ

Jane calls to say she is still having her unpleasant health
problems, although Valium continues to help. Her appointment
with her neurologist is not far off. I am anxious for that to take
place, although she seems quite sure nothing is really wrong.
Her confidence calms me. I notice how willing I am to accept
reassurance for my worry, as though I am glad to be rid of it, no
matter how flimsy the grounds for its dismissal.

ᔕ

A rainy, windy, misty Sunday. I worry about driving across the
bridge to church in Stonington, and even more about a power
failure (as common as weeds in this area. Sometimes a cloud
passing overhead seems to cause the power to go off) while I am
using the computer. So I abandon both enterprises, put on my
heavy jacket and gloves, take the ash cane that Richard Lucas,
my friend who died of AIDS, sent me in the last month of his
life, and walk across to the bookstore.

Sybil has a fire going in the woodstove, and is happily
selling books to a dealer from away, and to our favorite
customer, the potter Charlie Hance, who lives and works on
Deer Isle, and is a serious (and yes, avid) collector of editions of
modern poets. Sybil says he makes her feel secure in her business,
because there is always a stack of his books 'on hold' on the
shelf, almost as if he were investing in Wayward Books' future.
A few days after we first arrived to take up residence in Maine,

Sybil showed her books at a fair in Bucksport. She had one customer, Charlie, who bought a first edition of Wallace Stevens, I think it was. After that, she says, she felt reassured about the future of Wayward Books Down East.

∽

Next day: Ed Kessler writes from Washington (and American University) that *End Zone* struck him as 'a sea-level book, a stoical book.' He says he senses no rage against the dying of the light and asks: 'has the Hound of Heaven lost your scent?' and sends me a poem by William Carlos Williams called 'To Waken an Old Lady.' I've never read it before:

> Old age is
> a flight of small
> cheeping birds
> skimming
> bare trees
> above a snow glaze.
> Gaining and failing
> they are buffeted
> by a dark wind—
> But what?
>
> On harsh weedstalks
> the flock has rested,
> the snow
> is covered with broken
> seedhusks
> and the wind tempered
> by a shrill
> piping of plenty.

Ed advises me: 'Don't be too resigned; keep some shrillness in your piping of plenty.'

❧

The postscript to Ed's letter is a scene he witnessed in his bank
the other morning. A large black lady waited at the front of the
line before the cashier's station. Further back on the line stood a
man with a little boy. The black lady's beeper went off, and the
boy said to his father: 'Is she backing up?'

❧

Another correspondent, Dagmar Miller, a woman of about my
age, I surmise, delineates the many similarities between her life
and mine that she noted in my book. She too loves the water.
For her, too, it serves as a recuperative element. She grew up in
New York City, 'in the Washington Heights area and
remember its good days,' was elected to Phi Beta Kappa, had a
photographic memory, was going to join the WAVES but 'the
War ended too soon,' worked in Washington as a journalist,
spent time at the Villa Serbelloni in Bellagio, knew my friends
Howard Simons and Jim Boatwright, both now dead, one of
cancer, the other of AIDS.

In her youth, she memorized the same astronomical facts as I
did.

'Every so often I, too, silently recite the names of the
planets. But over the years, Pluto has become Plato.'

She liked my book, she writes, and I enjoy reading her
praise. My pleasure reminds me of Mark Twain's remark: 'Oh, I
do love compliments—we all do, humorists, congressmen,
burglars—all of us in the trade.'

❧

Yesterday I heard of an old lady who was driving out the Main
Line after an afternoon concert of the Philadelphia Orchestra. A
young driver, under the influence, crossed the median line and

crashed into her. She died instantly, while her head was still
filled with fine music. Or so I imagine. From that single point
of view, I consider her a lucky woman.

᷑

A book Sybil picks up at a sale: an intriguing history, published
in 1971 by Robert Reisner, of graffiti. It contains a photograph
of drawings found on the wall of a cave in a prehistoric
Egyptian tomb (they can be read) and advances through time to
the present. It is full of quotations. I liked two modern graffiti
found on walls in universities.

—At Cornell University: 'I think I exist, therefore I exist, I
think.'

—At the University of Michigan, Ann Arbor: 'It often
shows a fine command of the English language to say nothing.'

Norman Mailer wanted us to believe that graffiti were an
important form of popular culture. This book at hand, by
exploring their history, takes the phenomena very seriously,
turning them into literary art. Anytime now I expect to see a
graduate thesis that connects subway scrawls and graffiti with
the mainstream culture of our time.

Mailer saw in graffiti the desperate expression of
disenfranchised young persons putting their mark on cities. For
our time this may be true. I always feel a pang of sorrow when I
pass a great rock formation at the edge of a city and see painted
on it something like ROB LOVES LUCY. JUNE 1953. Did they
marry? If they did, does he love her still? I think (with my usual
misanthropy), probably not. If they didn't, and if Rob is still
alive, does he look back with longing to that June graduation
night almost forty years ago when, full of beer and high spirits,
he climbed a steep cliff and immortalized himself and his high
school sweetheart with red paint on white rock? However it all

turned out, there is always an unexplainable grief for me in the sight of such graffiti.

◡

People stop me in Blue Hill to say they too are planning to write their memoirs. Some write to say they have led a truly fascinating life, and surely I would like to hear about it and then commit it to writing for them.

Of course, it is true: everyone who has lived for a while has within them wonderful memories, events that only they are privy to. But often the expressed desire is followed by the sentence: 'I would write it myself, if only I had the time.' To them, the writer is someone who is not doing something more important, like them, and therefore has the time.

◡

Simon & Schuster sends me its new catalogue. Dutifully I read through all such mailings to see if there is something of interest to me that I should watch for in the months ahead. I am stopped halfway through the announcements of new hardback books by a title: *A Look Back from the End Zone.* This turns out to be a genuine sports memoir about fathers and sons, football and competition, a book that didn't borrow the idea for a metaphor, the way I did.

November

The time on either side of now *stands fast.*

—*Maxine Kumin*

*R*ain today, and a light coating of frost over everything. The Cove has taken on the look of steady menace. Blue water is gone, turned to grey, and no longer extends a shining welcome to the visits of birds, boats, or swimmers. At six this morning when it was fifty-eight degrees in my study, I had trouble starting a fire in the woodstove. After much futile paper-shredding and smoke I gave up, and resignedly turned on the furnace. It caught with a roar, echoing my own fury at having to burn expensive oil.

Failure with the stove repeats itself at the clipboard. There I am working on a novel which I have called, as a convenient joke (after the title in the contract), *Unnamed*. Nothing comes. I go to the computer on which I edit the work of yesterday, for this memoir. Nothing works. I walk aimlessly about the house, stowing things which do not need putting away in already jammed kitchen cabinets. Desperate, I decide to change the location of pictures on the walls.

I am of the opinion that doing this brings them back to life. They are dissolving into oblivion, I reason, when they stay too long on one wall, in one place. They seem to sink into it. Changed, replaced, they rise up and out, demanding that 'attention must be paid,' as Willy Loman's wife required for her husband.

So I put *The Prophet* where *Three Sirens on a Rocking Horse* hung. The Sirens are a pen-drawing acquisition from New Orleans last winter. Funny and startling as the three nude ladies are, especially astride the horse and stared at by a lascivious, mustachioed gentleman in the bushes, I have not really *seen* them for a long time. Perhaps, in their new location . . .

I go back to my study (now warmed), sit at my desk, and stare out at a red squirrel busily engaged in digging up the bulbs we have just planted in the rock garden. By now, too indolent to consider going onto the cold deck to chase him, I dial Helen Yglesias's number, feeling guilty because this is Helen's writing time too. There is no answer. Then I remember why: Helen is not answering her phone because she is in New York for the month.

I decide I am hungry. It is ten o'clock. I cannot be hungry. I've eaten a good breakfast.

But of course I know what is wrong with me. My affliction is creative drought, another oxymoron. Today I am a dry well, a milkless breast. Diagnosis: an aridity of words, an absence of ideas, a lack of verbal vigor. Nothing for it but to water the indoor plants that, by now, are as needy of moisture as I, put a CD of Frederica von Stade on the player, and, when that is over, go out and shout at the marauding red squirrel if he, at least, is still at work.

I had planned to revise the first, sticky section of *Unnamed*. 'Nothing doing,' as we used to say. I give up. For some reason, Paul Valery's dictum comes into my head: 'A poem is never finished, it is abandoned.' Equally true of a novel.

Sybil comes back from the bookstore for lunch, bringing the

mail and the newspapers. A welcome distraction. She is very
cheerful and tells me of her profitable morning. She priced
books, vacuumed the store, rearranged the remainder table, sold
a book via the telephone. Barren and unproductive, I say
nothing. When she leaves, to return, presumably, to a profitable
afternoon, I go through the Simon & Schuster catalogue again,
and am amused to see that it is publishing *The Birdcage Book*.
Birdcages, the copy reads, are the 'new, new, popular collectible
of the '90s.' I ought to send for it so I can shelve it with another
absurd volume I have kept precisely because it is so ludicrous:
Robert Gottlieb's big, glossy book on plastic handbags.

I go upstairs to take a nap.

༄

Next day: The sun, at long last. True, it is a pale cast of itself,
somewhat sickly. But it lights up the faces of the few pansies
still clinging to life in the round flower bed, and illuminates our
white rowboat lying upside down in the rough field, looking as
though it is huddled, like the green canoe nearby, against the
cold.

Feeling mentally alive once more after the sterile disaster of
yesterday, I settle down to work, and then waste good time
searching in the manuscript for my lost place where I stopped
correcting the day before yesterday. Losing things . . . Elizabeth
Bishop has a poem about that:

> The art of losing isn't hard to master;
> so many things seem filled with the intent
> to be lost that their loss is no disaster.

Bishop catalogues all the things she has lost—door keys, places,
names, her mother's watch, houses, cities, a beloved person—and
ends with a fine couplet:

the art of losing's not too hard to master
though it may look like (*Write it!*) like disaster.

L'envoi: Working well again is the process of finding what one
thought one had lost. It is discovery of what one did not know
one knew. The sun, thin as it is, shines indoors, on the words
that emanate from my clipboard, on the screen of the display.
Warmth rises from the unlit woodstove, and all seems well with
the world in my head.

In today's mail, I find three more adjectives to take careful note
of. Alan Cheuse, critic and acquaintance from National Public
Radio and Washington, writes to say he liked the book all right
but found it a little 'testy' here and there. Good friend Joseph
Caldwell, filling in at Yaddo for the director while the board
tries to find a new one, and putting the finishing touches on his
novel *The Uncle from Rome,* thought it 'melancholy.' And Joyce
Thompson, a student at Florida's Atlantic Center for the Arts a
few years ago, author of two published novels, says it is good, if
somewhat 'bleak,' company.

Next day: After some desultory shopping in Bangor, one of
Maine's three large cities and the nearest one to our peninsula,
we lunch at Olsen's, a favorite restaurant for natives in the
Brewer area (Brewer is on the edge of Bangor). It is the habit of
many retired persons to have their big meal of the day here,
around noon. The waitress informs us, with a genuinely pleasant
smile, as though we had been waiting a long time for this news,
'We have turnips today.' We look blank. She goes on, as if to
enlighten us further:

'With white-meat turkey, gravy, mashed potatoes, salad, and coffee. Five ninety-five, *and* a senior-citizen discount.'

I decide to settle for a tuna-fish sandwich. But Sybil loves this kind of food and decides not to disappoint the expectant waitress. Looking around, we see that almost every couple and single diner has turkey, with turnips heaped up beside the thick white slices, mounds of mashed potatoes covered with thick brown gravy, and little white fluted paper cups of cranberry sauce. I gulp and look away.

Sybil grins and says to the waitress:

'I'll have the turkey. Could I have dark meat, please?'

'Sorry,' she says, 'We only serve white meat.'

Sybil looks startled. She asks: 'What do you do with the dark meat?'

The waitress has grown noticeably cooler. 'I have no idea,' she says, and leaves.

∽

While we were in Bangor we looked into a bookstore to see if it had copies of *End Zone*. The clerk said they had none. In fact, she had not heard of it. Should she order it for us? We hasten to say no, and depart quickly. Outside, I tell Sybil that Nadine Gordimer once said: 'The best way to be read is posthumously.' There is some cold comfort in thinking that might happen to me.

∽

Today I manned (wrong word now. Personed? Terrible-sounding. Womaned? Worse. Staffed? Well, maybe) the store while Sybil went to a book sale. A bearded young man with a knapsack came in, not to buy a book or even to look around, but to ask me about getting his novel published. Where could he find an agent? Did he need one, actually? Who are the good,

stable publishers? I told him I had no answers to his questions. I
have been on the fringes of the publishing world for a long
time, I said.

Then he wanted to know about my writing methods. I told
him enough, clearly, to make him decide I must be a very dull,
untypical, orderly writer. I wanted to add that I was of the
quill-pen generation, but he rushed on.

'Oh, I am very different. I write anywhere, anytime, on
anything, whenever the spirit moves me, sometimes not for days
or weeks, and then again, for three days running. I am a writer
of very irregular habits,' he said proudly.

I refrained from pointing out that 'irregular habits' was an
oxymoron, and went back to the book I was reading. He made a
little show of fingering a book on the remainder table, and then,
clearly disappointed by me, he left. I could hear the disgusted
roar of his motorcycle as he turned onto the main road.

∽

I have been receiving advice in the mail about ridding our
garden and deck boxes of red squirrels, from persons who read
of my failure in the afterwords to *End Zone.* One woman says
to put cayenne pepper on the flowers in the boxes. A man
advises placing mothballs around the roots. A longtime gardener
says that drops of cooking fat will rid us of the little pests if
they are applied in melted form: Squirrels don't like the odor.

Perhaps aware, through intuition, that I am now receiving
good advice aimed at their discouragement, the little red fellows
have vanished before I had a chance to try out these various
schemes.

∽

Tracy, our carpenter and friend, is almost finished shingling the
back side of our house. Now it has that new, raw, unweathered

look that I hope will turn grey before long. She lunches with us on the screened porch she built last year. We use it in all seasons since we put up both plastic curtains *and* Plexiglas panels. The sun cooperates by providing solar warmth in the middle of the day. We feel privileged to have acquired, at moderate cost, a new room.

When she goes off to Bangor (she has decided that carpentry will not sustain her as she grows older and less fit so she has gone back to the university to get her degree) Tracy leaves behind her copy of the *Bangor Daily News*. The front page has a story about the fight between the merchants of Ellsworth, who oppose the use of the old, abandoned Federal Building, and a group of nuns who wish to shelter homeless persons there. One forthright city council member refers to these persons as 'dirty bums' who will desecrate, by their very presence, the fine Main Street of the city where the building stands.

An ugly story, made especially unpalatable by another story in a glossy section of the same paper, this one reporting on Jackie Kennedy Onassis's housing arrangements. She has 'retained her weekend home in Bernardville, New Jersey, because of her membership in the Essex Fox Hounds Hunt Club nearby.' She has another weekend and vacation home on 425 acres in the village of Gay Head on Martha's Vineyard, an estate worth $4.5 million. It has nineteen rooms, heated toilet seats and towel racks, and a two-thousand-foot circular driveway. Paul Mellon's wife, Bunny, visits her here on occasion. For those times, Jackie keeps, just for her, a suite of rooms, and Bunny does the same for Jackie in the mansion on her Middleburg, Virginia, estate.

There is also Jackie's twelve-room New York apartment at 1040 Fifth Avenue. . . . Homelessness will never be a problem for the glamorous ex–First Lady and others of her class, only for the unemployed, the battered, and the destitute, the runaways and child prostitutes, the 'dirty bums,' the newly impoverished middle-class sufferers from the recession, and, of course, the hunted red foxes.

∽

Our local library has reduced its hours for the fall, winter, and spring season. It is now open only on Saturdays, from two to four in the afternoon. Whereas the video store in Blue Hill is open seven days a week, from ten in the morning until eight in the evening.

∽

We are in the deer-hunting season. In this state, it lasts a month. No one dares to venture out of the house, even onto one's own paths or woods, without being decked out in an orange cap, an orange vest, even orange gloves. The gloves have become important. Three years ago in southern Maine a housewife wearing white mittens was shot to death by a hunter within a hundred yards of her back door. He was found not guilty of involuntary manslaughter after he explained that he thought the mittens were the rear end of a deer.

Despite all the reasonable explanations advanced for the need to eliminate the deer (overpopulation, the destruction they wreak on vegetable gardens, fruit trees, and ornamental bushes), I hate this season. I dislike the sound of guns being fired nearby, and the sight of carcasses slung over the hoods of cars or the rear ends of pickup trucks.

Somewhere I have a clipping from the Bangor paper that describes the successful moose-hunting season last month. It lasted a little more than a week. On the first day (when only natives, not hunters from away, are allowed to pursue the moose) three hundred were killed. It was gleefully reported (or so it seemed to my biased mind) that this was one hundred more than last year, and the season was expected to double last year's 'kill.'

Now I remember why Helen Yglesias has gone to New York for the month. Native Mainers who are her neighbors have parked their cars and hunted on her land for generations. At first, thirty years ago, she gave them permission to continue. But after a while she grew to abhor and fear the constant explosions near the house. The hunters would drain and clean their kill near their cars. Then her dog would drag the bloody entrails to her front steps. She asked them to stop hunting on her place, and they agreed. . . . But still, she hates hunting season and goes to New York for the month of November, to see her friends, to see plays and hear opera, to talk to her agent about book business, and most of all, to be away from the sound of guns.

∽

Yesterday, in the bookstore, a young customer told me she is writing a novel about her sixteenth year when she was rejected as a cheerleader for her high school and lost the chance to go to the Rose Bowl. She experienced extraordinarily violent emotions that have affected the rest of her life. So she has a great deal to write about, she said.

Serendipitously, after she left, having bought two paperback volumes of Ann Beattie's stories, I picked up a book that quoted the composer Charles Ives. He is talking about what he calls the Byronic Fallacy: 'that one who is full of turbid feelings about himself is qualified to be some sort of artist,' the mistaken notion that these feelings are as genuine an impetus to art as sympathy for others. I'm glad I found this after the young woman left because, ignobly, I would have been tempted to quote it to her.

∽

Later: A dark, melancholy afternoon, so I abandon the clipboard
for my little copy of volume one of *Hard Times.* I've learned
that reading Dickens requires the presence at hand of a
dictionary. Example: he uses the word 'whelp' again and again
for one of his young male characters. I had thought whelp
meant the young of an animal. No, it is that, but also, in the
nineteenth and early twentieth centuries, a youth, especially a
despised or impudent one.

In a few pages, I learn this meaning for whelp, and then
putto, from an Italian word for boy, a drawing of a cherubic
infant. And 'herm,' a four-sided shaft with a statue of Hermes
whose erect penis passersby stroke for luck. All this explains
why I am so slow in getting through a Dickens novel. I use it as
a vocabulary-building device.

∾

Vachel Lindsay: 'A bad designer is to that extent a bad man.'
This sentence, written on a piece of torn newsprint that fell out
of a book I am donating to the Blue Hill Library, perplexes me.
To *what* extent? For some time I've been disabused of my
girlhood belief that a good writer must be a good person, and
the reverse. Sadly, I now know better.

∾

Is anything, no matter how well-intentioned, without its biases?
The *AARP Bulletin* arrives today, full of concern for the rights
of the elderly. I inspect the masthead of the *Bulletin* and note
that the executive director, the publicity director, the editor,
three senior editors, and the managing editor, all of the top
personnel, are men.

∾

Today, perhaps because of a letter from a former student, and two from elderly but still-active nuns, I spend some time thinking about my dead friend Richard Lucas, whom I met at the College of Saint Rose, my first college-teaching experience.

Thirty years ago, when I first taught there, Saint Rose was a small, quiet, church-related girls' school. Its curriculum was heavy with theology and Thomist philosophy courses. All the rites of the Catholic Church were observed with role-model gentility by a well-educated order, the Sisters of St. Joseph of Carondelet—Cee Ess Jays, as they were called by irreverent lay faculty and students.

I enjoyed my teaching, having started with evening classes in English composition and world literature while two of my children were still at home. When they were well established in a nearby private school with their older sisters, I taught full-time, four courses a semester for a small salary. Usually my first course was at eight o'clock in the morning. Harried and incommoded by getting a gaggle of little girls to their school before I arrived at mine, I would arrive at the classroom building, passing the composed, sedate Sisters returning from Mass.

None of these difficulties seem to have been important to me, because the Sisters, from the grimmest and most doctrinaire to the freer spirits, treated the lay faculty well and what was more, gave me a chance to teach all sorts of singular courses (for that time, the early sixties, and in that place, a Catholic girls' college) such as Black Literature, Proletarian Literature of the Thirties, the Novels of Henry James, Nineteenth-Century Humor, and Mark Twain. I had designed these courses, not because I knew very much about the subjects, but because I wanted to educate myself in them.

The campus, set down in the middle of a large capital city,

Albany, New York, suggested the intellectually and socially
isolated nature of the college. The school consisted of a rectangle
of buildings, fronting on two broad avenues. In the center were
fine stands of trees, bushes, and grass, crisscrossed by walks to the
backs of classroom and dormitory buildings. A statue of Our
Lady, lovingly planted with flowers, stood near one of the
entrances to the campus. The buildings were named for saints,
respected clerical founders, and, of course, St. Joseph.

Once inside this enclave I felt safe, embraced, even hugged
(some felt stifled, almost suffocated, but not I) by the secure
warmth that omnipresent priests, nuns, and rituals engendered.
We were all, Catholics and freethinkers alike, prayed for at the
Sisters' early Mass every morning. Mary was crowned Queen on
the first day of May and students marched down State Street
carrying religious banners on her feast day. Classes opened, *de
rigueur,* and closed with a prayer. Since its founding at the
beginning of the century, Saint Rose had been a haven of
classical studies (Latin was a required subject; medieval history,
rhetoric, Greek were offered), feminine strength and friendship,
and (at least on the surface) undisturbed faith.

I go into all this in detail because much of it came to an end
in the late sixties after Vatican II adjourned. When Pope John
XXIII opened a window to air out the must of unexamined
doctrines and ancient practices unchanged since the Council of
Trent, the college, like most Catholic institutions, began its slow
but unstoppable journey toward change. It was not simply that
the curriculum was scrutinized and then 'renewed' and revised.
The very atmosphere on the grounds and in the classrooms and
library seemed to change. Male students were admitted, more
lay persons assumed positions of authority as chairmen and
administrators, the requirements for theology and philosophy
were reduced to a minimum, and, after a long, unbroken line of

presidents who were always Sisters of the Order, the college hired its first layman.

I had served on the search committee for a new president. I had expressed my doubts about the enthusiastic choice (after three other men had turned us down) of the board of trustees and some of the nuns on the committee, but in the end, as we were then schooled to do, I voted with the others for the candidate.

Alphonse Miele, possessed of a rather unfortunate name (I remember thinking), came to the college from an executive position at the Air Force Academy. He was a genial-appearing but authoritarian fellow who enjoyed the power and unilateral sovereignty of his position. He made *pro forma* moves toward confraternity with the faculty senate and then settled in happily, issuing edicts about matters the faculty believed (but very recently, of course: Saint Rose was slow about matters of academic freedom) were in its purview.

The faculty knew almost from the beginning of his reign that it was going to have trouble. At his installation, which came months after his arrival, and as president of the faculty, I remember reminding him that a college was its students and its faculty, and the administration was there merely to hold their coats. At the reception afterwards, Miele and I eyed each other warily. I suspected his absolutist inclinations; he quickly knew me to be what one of my grade-school daughters said her teacher called her, 'a scurvy elephant,' that is, a disturbing element.

The climax came close to the end of Miele's first year as president. Word reached the faculty senate that he had sent terminal contracts to two very popular priests in the theology department (which then had four members, all clerics). Sent to interview Miele on this clear breach of the recently established procedures of the rank and tenure committee (the committee itself was only two years old), I learned that a member of the theology department had reported to him that the two priests were gay.

It is hard, at this remove, and with all the changes in the society's (and thus academe's) treatment of such matters, to reconstruct the repugnance in Miele's voice when he told me about this. He said he had discussed his decision with the chairman of the board of trustees (a local banker) and had been affirmed in his view that the accusation should be accepted as true, without further question or notoriety, and the priests dismissed. He said he had told me about the unsavory matter in confidence and relied on me to talk to no one about it.

I did not need to keep the secret. The two threatened priests told a friend on the faculty, who, in the way such things go, told another. Indignation flooded the campus and reached the students. We were about to witness what no one had ever heard of before on that decorous campus, a full-fledged rebellion. Seven-eighths of the faculty and staff (some untenured) signed a petition for Miele's removal to be sent to the board of trustees. Most of the innocent nuns signed, appalled by the accusation. They did not believe in the possibility of its truth, and thought a terrible injustice had been done to their beloved priests. Students abandoned classes to sit in the halls protesting the president's act. Banners reading REMOVE MIELE and AFTER YOU, ALPHONSE appeared on the well-kept lawns of the campus and in classroom windows.

The board of trustees, at an emergency meeting, reaffirmed their faith in the president. Matters then got worse. Miele found it difficult to enter his office over the outstretched legs of striking students, who said they were resolved not to take final examinations if the president remained. But of course, not everyone was with us. I received a number of anonymous letters, one of which accused me of being the Antichrist. One irate parent standing behind me in line in the bank one day blamed me for her daughter's unaccustomed sedition:

'I sent her to Saint Rose so she wouldn't turn out like all those hippies at Columbia and those places, and now look,' she said.

The events had a happy, and then an unhappy, ending. The board of trustees, stunned, I think, by an insurrection it believed could only happen on secular, godless campuses, asked for Miele's resignation. He left the campus, students went back to the classroom for their finals, faculty members settled back into the routines of grading and commencement. Except for Father Lucas, one of the priests accused. He decided not to sign his contract because, I believe, he could not bear the strain of hiding any longer what he knew he was.

Richard Lucas left the campus, the city, the Church, went to New York, became a respected editor at Doubleday, and then a successful sales manager on the West Coast for Harper & Row (in its religion department) and finally, until his death of AIDS three years ago, for the University of California Press. He had been a good priest at a time when there was no acceptable place for him in the Church.

I hear that the college now flourishes, with new buildings, new computer equipment and courses, a whole new secular face as the number of available teaching nuns and priests fell off. The outside world, I am sure, with its accepted revelations about the varieties of human sexuality, now has affected those once-protected acres. Mary's chaste spirit may well be somewhat in retreat and Richard's unconventional soul may walk the protected lawns and scrubbed corridors of the college.

The world of pre–Vatican II is firmly rooted in my memory. As Yogi Berra, my resident sage, is alleged to have said: 'It is a case of *déjà vu* all over again.'

$\wp$

Jeannie Wiggins, our over-eighty, sharp-witted, humorous, and active neighbor, comes by our place on occasion walking with her dogs, looks around at our gardens, the new porch, the deck, and always says to us: 'You kids have done a great job here.'

Last evening we kids had dinner at her house, together with some other elderly folk. Sybil, aged sixty-two, said she enjoyed being the youngest guest there. Someone told us the story of a friend, now ninety-five years old. She has rolled up all the rugs in her house to make sure she will not trip, like so many of her friends. Recently, she told her granddaughter, whom she was visiting:

'Can't stay long. I've got a ticket for a revival of *Jesus Christ Superstar.*'

Another story garnered from the dinner party, I think from Connie Darrah. She is a descendant of the founding family, the Sargents, of our village, and gave us a fine old photograph of Ella Byard and her friends. (It was Ella who built our house.) She told us about a woman in central Maine who was driving her Subaru when she collided with a moose. She was injured and is suing the manufacturer of the automobile, claiming the company did not provide her with sufficient protection.

$\wp$

Later: I enter these stories, and realize that keeping a journal thins my skin. I feel open to everything, aware, charged by the acquisition of interesting (to me) entries, hypersensitive to whatever I hear, see, guess, read, am told. Matters that once might have gone unnoticed are no longer lost on me. I may sue my publisher for not providing me with sufficient protection against assault by whatever sensations are out there.

∽

La Rochefoucauld: 'Death and the sun are not to be looked at steadily.'

Yes. At seventy that was what I did. I looked at death too steadily and too long. I held it aloft and reviewed it from every angle, like a potter with his pitcher mounted on a rotary stand, like Hamlet with Yorick's skull. I inspected its terrors, and saw its threatening effects in my body, in my diminished hearing and unstable gait.

Now, having passed that melancholy landmark and looked more steadily at my fears, I take heart from this small victory and no longer stare at death's imminence with so cold an eye. Having been reproached by people who read of my anguish and scolded me for it, I find I have taken note of their rebukes (sample: 'I am eighty-one and damn glad I've made it thus far,' and 'What are you whining about? Have you considered how lucky you are?') and vow to try to sin no more in that direction. I've been trying to turn what seemed tragic into what it would be nice to think of as comic:

Woody Allen, twenty-seven years younger than I: 'I'm not afraid to die. I just don't want to be there when it happens.'

But still, death is the great mystery, life's great puzzle. To be present at the solution requires that we not exist as we have come to know existence. It must be what James Joyce meant when he asked on his deathbed, 'Does nobody understand?' It was not the enigmas of *Finnegans Wake* he was referring to, I suspect, but the meaning he saw at the moment of his death. No one but he, at that moment, understood.

∽

Word from Jane in New York that the first neurosurgeon she consulted thinks she might not need an operation for what is a

slow-growing tumor, at least not yet. She is relieved. But she
says she has an appointment with a neurologist to make sure of
the diagnosis. Then she will decide what to do, and how soon.

〜

The body of a finch on the roof outside our bedroom window
has been there since the late spring. Now it is gone. Blown away
or resurrected? I cannot tell. The little corpse had lost its color in
death, so I have no way of knowing whether it was a gold or
purple finch that had crashed so recklessly (I assume) against the
glass of the window, broken its neck, and fallen a few feet to the
roof of the screened porch.

The thought of resurrection and an afterlife is central to my
faith. I have always been able to grant those supernatural
certainties to the Christ whose entire life, from his virgin birth
on, was so extraordinary. But I've had some trouble assuming
they would be part of the end of a life as ordinary and
sin-ridden as mine.

Still, some wise unbelievers have granted the possibility of
these occurrences to themselves. On his deathbed, the brilliant
cynic and atheist Voltaire saw a lamp flare up. 'What, the flames
already?' he asked. When agnostic Disraeli lay dying, the
mourning widow Queen Victoria proposed to visit his bedside.
'Why should I see her?' he told his attendant. 'She will only
want to give me a message for Albert.'

And another: One of my recent correspondents, one of those
who scolded me for my pessimism, sent me a sentence, said to be
Goronwy Rees's last words, in 1979, to his son Daniel: 'What
shall I do next?'

She did not tell me who Goronwy Rees was.

〜

Telephone report from Ron King about the Down East AIDS Network walk last month. Six thousand dollars was raised, many people participated in Ellsworth, the food that Sybil solicited from area merchants and two groups of friends gathered was sufficient for the walkers and volunteers, and very good. This success marks a significant change in awareness of the need for concern and care on the part of a hitherto indifferent community.

ᓆ

I have finished *Hard Times* and moved on to *Bleak House*. My cherished set of Dickens, in many volumes because each novel is separated into three or four small books, bound in blue cloth with bright gold stamping, once belonged to a woman named Mary S. White. Her name is neatly stamped on the flyleaf of every one of the thirty-six or so books. I think she read them all, for there are minor blemishes on some pages, here a light thumb mark, there a trace of tiny bits of food that have dropped into the gutter.

There is a pleasure in reading books that belonged to someone else. Clearly, Mary S. White enjoyed these books before me. I fantasize about her life: She was an elderly spinster, a New Englander (I found the books in the Owl Pen, a bookstore outside of Greenwich, New York) who lived alone after the death of her parents, whom she cared for during their long lives. Delicately built, she favored small books that fit comfortably into her tiny hands. I see her seated alone at five in the evening, in an upright chair at her small, round dining-room table, drinking tea and eating a buttered scone, a few crumbs of which have dropped into the margin of, say, *Pickwick Papers*. When I get to it, I will surely find them.

Out of volume three of *Bleak House* falls Mary S. White's

posthumous gift to me, a yellowed clipping. It is undated but seems to be from a New York daily newspaper at the turn of the century:

> A lady lately visited New York city, and saw one day on the sidewalk a ragged, cold, and hungry little girl, gazing wistfully at some cake in a shop window. She stopped, and taking the little one by the hand led her into the store. Though she was aware that bread might be better for the child than cake, yet desiring to gratify the shivering and forlorn one, she bought and gave her the cake she wanted. She then took her to another place, where she presented her a shawl and other articles of comfort. The grateful little creature looked the benevolent lady up full in the face and with artless simplicity said, 'Are you God's wife?'

BEAUTIFUL INCIDENT is the story's headline; it is a sentimental little tale that might be written today, made linguistically contemporary, if the little girl were to ask the kind lady: 'Are you God?'

∽

The plea for the use of plain words when writing English prose is common, not limited to William Strunk's popular *The Elements of Style.* Among Sybil's purchases yesterday for the bookstore was a 1988 paperback of a book, *Plain Words,* on the subject by Sir Ernest Gowers, first published in 1954. Gowers advised writers to prefer 'get' or 'buy' or 'win' to 'acquire,' to use 'rich' in place of 'affluent.' 'Near' he finds preferable to 'adjacent.'

About 'adjust' and 'alter' he says, 'If you mean "change," say so.' He derides 'analogous'; it is a starchy word for 'like.' He instructs us to substitute 'clear,' 'plain,' 'obvious' for 'apparent,' and 'find out' for 'ascertain.'

This list is chosen from the list for the letter A in Gowers's dictionary of short verbal preferences. Fifty more pages follow, for the rest of the alphabet. But I fear that if we forcibly removed fancy words from the speech and writings of most people (including me), we would leave them almost speechless, and certainly unable to compose a letter, a term paper, or a review. For 'compose' here I should have used 'write.'

I must take this good advice more often. For 'linguistically contemporary' in my journal entry before this one I should have said 'up-to-date.'

∽

Last night we had a small dinner party for friends. There was much good, witty talk, in which I tried to participate but found it hard. When I am alone I find I can go days without needing to say a word to anyone. Talking is clearly social mucilage, silence a threat to sociability. Recently, I looked through Aleister Crowley's *Diary of a Drug Fiend* in the bookstore and copied out: 'People think that talking is a sign of thinking. It isn't, for the most part; on the contrary, it's a mechanical dodge of the body to relieve oneself of the strain of thinking.'

∽

Coming back from a brief visit to May Sarton in York: We found her weak, thin, in pain, but gallantly working on a new journal to be published on her eightieth birthday and determined to *live* and write despite her dismaying infirmities. We stop off Route 1 at Moody Beach where my family and I spent many summers when the children were young. We pull into the Hazeltines' driveway. Their house is closed up and shuttered—they have gone to Florida for the winter, we are told. We walk out onto the great, flat expanse of a most beautiful beach and a boundless ocean.

Sybil observes that it looks huge after the relative limitation, almost confinement, of our Cove. Our water is bounded by the rough meadow in front and green banks on either side. It is usually calm; the coming and going of tides are hardly audible. . . . But here at Moody there is almost no end to the vast carpet of sand and blanket of water, except at the horizon that joins the sky at a great distance. It is the difference between mortality of the Cove and the immortality of the ocean, between backyard and continent.

For me, Moody, which lies between Ogunquit and Wells at the southern end of Maine, is the Ur-beach. It was where I renewed my love of the sea, which had been lost or buried in my memory from the time I was six and went with my family for the summer to the ocean at Atlantic City. Then, without warning, in the next summer I was sent to a girls' camp in the mountains, beside a lake, and learned, I remember keenly, the disappointment of limitation. After a few years at camp, I was able to swim about one mile to the far bank of the lake, a feat common to most of the 'intermediate' swimmers, as we were called, but one that, to my mind, fatally diminished the glory of Crystal Lake. If I could swim it, it was too small.

Reluctantly, I came away from Moody Beach. It was like leaving the immeasurable cosmos for a two-foot yardstick at home. Thinking about May on the journey north, I realized how fortunate she is, in a way, to have a lovely pond at the right side of her property, where herons and egrets come regularly, and the wild ocean at the foot of her meadow. Her place is endowed both with the pleasure of the closed circle and with the infinite immensity of the sea.

I have always loved Moody and, as well, its name. There is a story by Nathaniel Hawthorne, 'The Minister's Black Veil,' about Parson Hooper, whose sad history, Hawthorne tells us in a note to the story, is based on 'another clergyman in New England, Mr. Joseph Moody of York, Maine.' Without too much substantiating evidence, I like to think that Moody Beach is named for the clergyman who wore a black veil over his face to cover his guilt ever since his early life when, by accident, he was responsible for the death of a beloved woman. Or so the story suggests.

∽

Outside of Wells, we go to a yard sale, one of hundreds held all over Maine on weekends. We stop at every one we pass, looking for books and, at the same time, inspecting all the artifacts of Mainers' lives spread out on rickety card tables and boards and trestles: odd pieces of chipped porcelain, old burned pots and pans, plastic wall decorations and knickknacks of every description, as well as rusty, interesting old tools, kerosene lamps, ships' parts, and always, used clothes of every size, clean but very worn.

I find a small, battered Peter Pauper 'gift' book copy of La Rochefoucauld's *Maxims*. I buy it for fifty cents to read during the four hours we have yet to drive, ignoring Sybil's reminder that I already own two copies, one in Maine, the other in the apartment in Washington.

Sybil is driving (as she usually does, because of her profound, but justifiable, distrust of my poor reflexes and absentmindedness), so I read aloud to her from the book:

'Youth changes its tastes by force of passion; age retains its tastes by force of habit.'

We debate the truth of this aphorism. I am of the opinion that it is certainly clever but, to my mind, like much else that is clever, in error. I have retained my passionate, youthful tastes throughout my life, *regrettably*. But my physical capacity to enjoy them diminishes and then leaves me, with age. Rich food and hard drink are no longer easily digestible, music and theater are less available because of the failure of my ears, of becoming 'hard of hearing,' as we used to say. Reading is more difficult as my eyesight weakens. My old love of swimming is not enough to overcome my body's debility. And the joys of sex? They are gone when opportunities and hormones diminish; they join the dubious pleasures of nostalgia and memory that we all must settle for.

I read the rest of the book to myself while Sybil listens to a country-music station, and I try my best not to hear it. La Rochefoucauld's maxims are like acupuncture, small stings on the skin, producing a modicum of pain and some subcutaneous pleasure.

∽

We are home. A light, powdery snow has fallen during our two-day absence, turning the roughness of the meadow into a smooth expanse. We watch the evening news, listening to reports of Anita Hill's testimony before a Senate committee. We want to find out if her accusation of sexual harassment against a Supreme Court nominee, Clarence Thomas, will stand in the way of his appointment. Who has lied? Why? There are no answers, only a growing sense, for both of us, that Thomas is not a suitable or credible candidate for so high, so important, a position.

The news moves on to other Senate business. I grow bored and find myself meditating on a frivolous observation: Senator Paul Simon's earlobes. They seem uncommonly large buttons of flesh that descend from his ears, almost organs in themselves.

This trivial matter sends me into the bathroom to inspect my own ears, something I cannot remember having done since my

girlhood. Ah, there I see: mine too are now changed. Instead of
the small, smooth globes I remember, now there is flabby flesh
scored by vertical lines, to accompany, I suppose, the vertical
lines that have worked their way into the flesh at the sides of my
mouth, marks of disillusion and pessimism now echoed in aging
earlobes. I remember that my friend Kay Boyle has worn large
circular white earrings ever since she was a girl. On the jacket of
her latest book, written at eighty-five, she is still wearing them.
If I had thought of doing this earlier, I would have been
prepared to hide my newfound defect.

∽

This morning's mail brought the Knopf catalogue for next
season. In it I find that Deborah Digges, a student at the Iowa
Writers Workshop when last I taught there, has written a
224-page memoir. How *old* can she be? Is it easier to write a
memoir when one does not have to go back very far for one's
memories?

∽

My niece, Laurie Danziger, writes to ask if I will collaborate
with her on a book about children of agoraphobic mothers. Her
mother suffered from this illness, from the time she was eighteen
until she died of cancer at forty-two. Laurie, now almost forty,
has had serious psychological problems ever since her mother's
early death, and she must see a causal connection to her mother's
agoraphobia.

I wish I could help her, but the truth is, I cannot conceive of
collaborating with anyone. I tell her I am the most hermitic of
writers, finding it hard to write if anyone is in the next room to
me, or even in the same house. After I mail the letter, I seem to
remember that Evelyn Waugh said something about this, and go

to my Waugh shelf to find his remark: 'I could never understand
how two men can write a book together; to me that's like three
people getting together to have a baby.'

⌒

The gulls have disappeared from the Cove. Do they migrate? I
realize how little I know about the lives of gulls, those beautiful
shorebirds that are my neighbors all through the spring, summer,
and fall. I walk over to the bookstore and borrow Frank
Graham's book on the subject, published in 1978. It begins by
describing an expedition that went out to Eastern Egg Rock
Island, Maine, in order to poison a portion of the black-backed
gulls there. It seems that a colony of puffins, who were killed or
driven off the coast of Maine by 1907, is to be reestablished on
that island. But now it is overpopulated by gulls, whose growth
was encouraged by 'a careless civilization's wastes.' When the
book was written the gulls had reached 'pest proportions.'

I'm uncertain what wastes he is talking about. I'm sure he
does not mean the leftover fried clams that used to feed the gulls
at McDonald's near Wells, Maine. How big is 'pest
proportions'? Who is being bothered?

Ornithologists went ashore at the island and destroyed the
eggs in a hundred nests. Then a tragic scene was played out. 'The
first of the gulls began their descent on spread wings, eager to
resume brooding on the eggs they had abandoned as we came
ashore.' Graham does not describe what follows, but I can
imagine: The returning parents find only desolation and
destruction. Their unborn offspring have been reduced to an
unsavory mixture of albumen, yolk, and embryonic feathers.
. . . Terrible. Coming to the book to learn about life, I discover
death and destruction.

Henry Beston, the naturalist, is quoted by Graham on wild
creatures: 'They are not brethren, they are not underlings; they

are other nations, caught with ourselves in the net of life and time, fellow prisoners of the splendor and travail of the earth.'

Laws protect gulls, like other birds, I have always thought. But not always so. We devise ways to trick them. Graham says waterfowlers mount carved gulls on their boats as 'confidence decoys.' Ducks and geese seem to know that gulls are not shot, so they cultivate their company 'under the delusion that that they too will come under the protective umbrella.' Artificial bird facsimiles are sometimes intended to alarm and chase away other birds, like the metal owl Barbara and Sam Wheeler mounted on their New York windowsill to discourage the pigeons. The omnipresent New York birds are back, I think, having conquered their fears and discovered that the owl was a sham menace.

Man can kill protected creatures, it would appear, or their unborn progeny, in order to give the opportunity for life to another variety of bird. Perhaps unfairly, it reminds me of euthanasia as urged upon us by those who believe the chronically ill and very aged ought to 'give way,' the euphemism for 'allow themselves to be put away,' in the interests of the young.

Should it not also remind me of abortion, a practice that, in theory, I support?

In Graham I learn that e.e. cummings said of penguins: 'Their wings are to swim with.'

All these details are very interesting in themselves, but I come to the end of Graham's book on gulls without finding out if they migrate. I *have* acquired some very fine phrases like 'prisoners of the splendor and travail of the earth' and 'confidence decoys,' as well as a nice image of swimming with wings, but no answers.

Washington: Under silent protest, even though it is only for
four days, I have had to leave Sargentville to go to Washington
for a Phi Beta Kappa meeting. Alone in the elaborate hotel the
night before the gathering, I turn on all the lights in the
Madison Hotel's two-room suite because of the unfamiliar
corners and doors and pull the drapes against the sights and
sounds of Connecticut Avenue.

Before the meetings begin, I decide to have a solitary dinner
with the *Washington Post,* at a K Street Chinese restaurant. I
walk through the broad, almost empty downtown streets,
deserted by their hordes of daytime workers, and now occupied
by a few homeless men who have settled down for the night in
doorways.

An elegantly dressed man with a furled umbrella he is using
as a walking stick passes me. He looks exhausted and wary,
determined not to look to the right or the left and carrying his
newspaper rolled under his arm. He seems vaguely familiar to
me. An employee of Dean, Witter where I once invested some
money? The headwaiter of a restaurant I once frequented?
When he comes close he lowers his head as if to avoid any
possible contact, and pushes on.

An old black man huddled in an Army blanket in a doorway
laughs, in a mad sort of way, as I pass him and says, 'Hy-yuh.' I
say 'Hi' and manage a weak smile.

The distraught, the frightened, the senile, and the mad are all
around us on the streets of this city, making me think of all the
possible paths to being sick and old I have thus far been spared.
On the plane this morning I sat across from an elderly couple
who, as the plane took off, and again when it landed, held
hands. Her hands were disfigured by hugely swollen knuckles;
when the attendant came by with 'a snack,' she was not able to
lift the tray from the arm of her seat. Throughout the trip her

husband was mute and stared ahead unblinkingly. Something
was clearly wrong with him.

She was a pleasant, cheerful lady. She wore a gold cross on a
chain around her neck and little white pearl earrings and a
white-beaded Indian bracelet. 'He has sinking spells,' she
explained to me. They are from New Orleans and are going
home after visiting their daughter in Boston. Their daughter is a
registered nurse with two children and a husband who works
'for the city.' She chattered on to me. I realized she was glad to
have, for the moment, someone to talk to who could listen and
respond.

We landed in Washington, where they had to change for a
plane going south. I asked if she needed any help in making the
transfer. She said no and then added proudly, 'My son is coming
to meet us. We'll go to a restaurant with him in the airport. He
works for the government.'

We said goodbye. She added politely: 'If you're ever in New
Orleans . . .' although I do not know their names. It was a *pro
forma* airplane farewell. In the airport, waiting for my luggage, I
saw their son moving them toward the terminal, holding each
one carefully by the arm. The old man was still staring ahead,
his wife was talking happily to her son. . . . Now I know why
the business-suited man with the umbrella on K Street seems
familiar. He looks exactly like the dutiful son meeting his
parents in the airport. Or so I imagine.

⟳

Almost alone in the Chinese restaurant (it is six o'clock, and
Washingtonians, I remember, dine late, usually after eight,
while many Mainers, intimidated by the early dark and tired
after their early rising, eat 'suppa' as early as four-thirty or five),
I am seated by the maître d' in an inconspicuous corner to which

single customers are usually consigned. It is as if there was
something almost shameful about having to appear alone in
public without a proper escort.

I order a Boodles gin on the rocks with a twist of lime. No,
make it a double, I say, and spread out the morning's
Washington Post, which covers almost all of the tiny table. Oh
yes, I see. I am back in civilization. I read that two women,
threatened by eviction from a Connecticut Avenue high-rise
apartment house, jumped, hand-in-hand, from the twelfth floor.
One died 'on impact,' the other before the ambulance reached
the hospital. . . . Of every thousand infants born in the District
of Columbia, 20.1 die within their first year of life. . . . Five
young black males died last night in the southeast section of the
city from gunshot wounds; three were engaged in the drug
trade, the other two were innocent bystanders.

Further afield, yesterday, in central Texas, a young man
smashed his pickup truck into a restaurant window at one in the
afternoon, killed twenty-two people, wounded two hundred;
then he shot himself in the head. . . . In Old Bridge, New Jersey,
a twenty-year-old college student gave birth to a seven-pound
baby in the bathroom of her parents' house, stabbed it many
times with a nail scissors, and then threw it out the window.
Her parents did not know she was pregnant. Her father found
the dead baby in the bushes and thought it was a discarded
doll.

After I read about the former mayor of this city, Marion
Barry, who has now been sent to a more secure prison as
punishment for allegedly performing a sex act in the visitors'
room of the jail he formerly inhabited, I close the *Post.* The
chicken in plum sauce has not yet arrived. I order another
Boodles and think about what it might be like to live in
Ushuaia on the coast of Tierra del Fuego, the southernmost city
in the world.

◯

In the early morning I call for breakfast. A pot of strong coffee
and the newspaper are to arrive before seven. While I wait for
it, I explore the fifty or so channels on the television provided
by cable. I note, as I have many times before, that even with all
these channels available, there is very little to watch. In Maine,
we are not provided with such vast choices, the cable people
having decided that too few people live in Sargentville to make
it profitable for them to bring it to us. With the four channels
we have, there is *still* very little worth watching, only a little
less than with the fifty-five available here.

Outside the window of the hotel suite I hear the constant
roar of traffic, the clatter of garbage trucks, the sirens of fire
engines. Altogether, it is like being subjected to the high whine
of a dental drill.

◯

Scheduled for tonight is a large gathering of delegates and
senators to the Phi Beta Kappa triennial meeting, a buffet supper
and speeches, to be held at the National Archives building. I've
been to so many of these affairs in federal buildings that I
anticipate interminable standing on marble floors in dress-up
shoes (my Nike running shoes are not suitable, I realize, for the
occasion) and small, 'finger-style' sustenance. So instead I ask the
hotel's concierge to get me a ticket for the Kirov Ballet at the
Kennedy Center. He does.

In the Great Hall of the center, the area before the entrance
to the Opera House, I buy a sandwich and a cup of espresso, and
sit on the red-carpeted steps to the theater to eat and drink,
because no seats are provided. I think about the past, when the
center first opened and one could purchase only wine by the
plastic glass at the little stands.

During an intermission of a Wagner opera, Sybil and I,
struggling to stay awake, asked the center's then director, Roger
Stevens, whether coffee would be sold in the near future. 'Never
will be,' he said with some show of irritation. 'It would be
spilled on the new carpet and ruin it.'

Now I look around for spots in my immediate area and see
none. . . .

But what a treat live music and ballet turn out to be. The
Kirov is an athletic company. The men leap high and land
loudly, the ballerinas are somewhat more hefty than the
anorexic Balanchine ladies I am used to. The corps dancing in
Act II of *Swan Lake* is perfection. This is a ballet I usually
avoid, especially in its complete form. But tonight there is just
enough of it to remind me of how beautiful are the
Tchaikovsky music and the accompanying movement. . . .
Anthony Tudor's *Lilac Garden,* done as an Edwardian love
quartet, is dull, as the Edwardian age itself may have been, and
the Petipa ballet, *Paquita,* seems to make dreary, heavy progress
despite the expert dancing.

In the intermission, when people walk about in desultory
fashion to stretch their legs and see each other, I think of the
stately, formal Promenade we watched at an interval in the
Vienna Opera House. To the eyes of a foreigner it was an
entertainment in itself. Perhaps conscious of their elegant dress,
men and women in formal clothes proceed in a well-defined,
elliptical path, marching in almost discernible Germanic time, as
if they were exercising or performing some military drill.

During the disorganized meanderings at Kennedy Center, I
hear a young couple discussing the last time they saw the Kirov,
'in Leningrad,' the young woman says. 'No, now it's St.
Petersburg,' says her companion. 'Isn't that wonderful?' she
replies. 'Like in *Anna Karenina.* Maybe now they'll bring back
the Tsar and that beautiful royal family.'

◌

Next evening I was supposed to attend a grand-ballroom
banquet for Phi Beta Kappa delegates. I decided there would be
too many people in attendance (how my three Maine years have
unsuited me for the social life of cities!), so I escaped and went
back to the Kennedy Center to see Robert Morse give his
one-man portrayal of Truman Capote. The concierge had
obtained for me a seat in the presidential box of the Eisenhower
Theater.

It was a spacious, luxurious place. I had it to myself and was
amused by the number of people in the orchestra (in the 'pit'?)
who looked up during the intermission, wondering, no doubt,
who the high executive-branch official was up there. I felt I
should acknowledge their lowly presence with a slight queenly
or papal wave. I resisted the temptation.

The box was so comfortable I did not leave it during the
intermission. So I had time to study the curtain, which
contained a huge reproduction of the November 1975 issue of
Esquire. The caption under the photograph of Capote, paring
his nails with a knife, read: 'More from *Answered Prayers*. The
most talked-about book of the year.' This was the book, years in
the writing because by now Capote has become a society gadfly,
that satirized his wealthy friends. When it was published, they
all abandoned him permanently.

What interested me was the description of it as the most
talked-about book of 1975. Think of that. Seventeen years later,
I wager, no one in this audience, or in this city, and few of the
literati of the country, have read this book, or even remember
that it appeared. The 'most talked-about book' may be the
kiss-of-death label for the endurance of the written word.

◌

From Washington I call my daughter Jane. The news is less
pleasant; in fact, the tumor has taken a new turn into the sinus
cavity and must be removed. One neurosurgeon adds 'quickly.'
There is some danger that the optic nerve has been affected,
putting her sight in question if the tumor is removed in entirety.

Jane says she will go to Philadelphia with her sister Kate,
who is a physician, to talk to neurosurgeons there: Kate feels this
is a very good place, so Jane will make the visit. But she seems
to prefer having the operation performed in New York, near
her home, her husband, and her friends.

A heavy shadow falls on my days and nights. The threat of
mortality to a child is far worse than the thought of one's own
death. It is terrifying—and unnatural.

∽

A light note. Back from Washington and in the haven of
Sargentville, I spend half a day sorting through and reading
mail. It is full of bills, catalogues, advertisements, and some
good letters from readers. But the most interesting piece of mail
is an invitation from a lady in Richmond, Virginia, to subscribe
to her service for devotees of historical romances. It is published
quarterly and divides the huge genre into convenient
subdivisions, listing the authors of each. For example, if I
subscribe, I will receive the names of writers of romances in
every period of history: the Civil War, the Age of the Cowboy,
the American Revolution, the Middle Ages, Western Expansion
(different from books about cowboys, apparently),
highwaymen, pirates and privateers, Indians (different from
those about Western Expansion and cowboys?), the
Renaissance, Victorian England, Tudor England.

Most of the writers listed are women, many with romantic
names like Jude Devereaux, Linda Ladd, Thea Devine, Robin
Leigh, Katherine Deauxville. I suspect these are pseudonyms,

perhaps for the same prolific writer of historical romances, whose real name may well be Mabel Butts.

The circular ends with an imperative: 'TELL ALL YOUR FRIENDS!' I decline to do this, and the invitation to subscribe, by throwing away the circular.

∽

Leaving all the catalogues, circulars, and junk mail for Don Hale, our weekly trash collector, who is, in the way that Mainers are often more than one thing, also a sail maker and repairer, a substitute mail-delivery man, and volunteer fire chief for Sargentville, I light my woodstove, coax it into burning, and sit near it to read a chapter of *Barnaby Rudge*.

As usual, I am stopped by a word I have never heard before, 'link-boys.' I resort to the *OED,* and discover they were lads who accompanied gentlemen through dangerous, dark-night streets in the time before street lighting. But why 'link'? I take the heavy L volume over to a stand and learn that a link was a torch made of tow, pitch, or tallow, carried by the boys who . . . Pepys, in his *Diary,* says he was lighted home by a link-boy.

But then, what exactly is 'tow'? I haul out the T volume, to learn that it is the fiber of flax prepared for spinning by scutching. Or it may be the shorter, less desirable flax fibers separated from linen fibers by hackling.

'Scutching'—what is that? It is, I find (in the S volume), dressing flax by beating. I would like to know exactly what 'hackling' is, but it will appear in yet another volume, and my arms are too tired to lift it from its place. I shall probably never know.

I am making my usual, Dickens-slow progress through *Barnaby Rudge.*

∽

The first hard freeze. Twenty-six degrees at six in the morning.
The short grass has taken on its shredded-wheat look. I sit at the
kitchen table to read morning prayers and watch the sun rise
over the subdued-by-ice landscape. Then I celebrate the event by
slipping on the back steps on the way out to the garbage pail.
Nothing is hurt, *mirabile dictu.* I attribute this to the wearing of
so many layers of clothes in Maine in winter that I am protected
from injury by padding.

We decide to provide all the entry steps to the doors of the
house with tar-paper strips, provision against further such
mishaps.

ᔕ

Mademoiselle, the magazine in New York City I worked for
briefly in my early twenties, just out of graduate school, is
having a reunion. Someone sends me a list of more than four
hundred names, persons who have worked for it since 1935. I
recognize five. One, with whom I am still in touch, Dorothea
Zachariah, always called Zach, is here mistakenly listed as
'Zeke.' She has been an editor of *Gourmet* magazine for many
years. Barbara Probst I think of as a friend, although our contact
has been somewhat spasmodic over fifty years. Jean Condit's
name is followed by an asterisk, meaning 'We are missing her
address.' So am I: I have not seen her or heard from her since I
left the magazine, although I have often thought about her. I
remember a few raucous evenings we spent together in 1940.
We went to a French restaurant on the East Side where sailors,
pompons rouges, right off the *Richelieu,* gathered to drink, and
we joined them, imbibing so much vermouth cassis that the way
those nights ended is not entirely clear to me. Geri Trotta is
listed. I believe she is still an active and productive journalist,
writing about travel. And I am there; however, my name is
misspelled.

Maggie de Mille, Betsy Talbot Blackwell, George Davis, the other contemporaries I remember, are dead. I do not know about Bernice Peck, who later wrote wonderfully chatty fashion pieces for the *Playbill,* distributed in New York theaters. The whole staff in 1940 I remember as talented in maintaining the proper respectful tone toward the world of fashion. Mrs. Blackwell, editor-in-chief, was a member of New York society who lived in Tuxedo Park. Her young son was a member of the prestigious Knickerbocker Blues regiment, and his picture, in full uniform at the age of twelve, sat on her desk. She was small, dark, elegant, smart. She sat at the kidney-shaped antique French desk hardly big enough for an opened book, always wearing a hat. This was because the millinery industry, members of which advertised in *Mademoiselle,* had reported to her that women were abandoning this practice. For good financial reasons, Mrs. Blackwell was determined to respond personally to the complaint, and asked the whole staff to follow her example.

I remember arriving at the office on 57th and Fifth Avenue wearing a tam, the only hat I owned. I had bought it the year before when I was a graduate student at Cornell to protect my hair from the rain and snow. By now it looked pretty tatty. Mrs. Blackwell stared hard at my head, I remember, at my penny-loafer shoes, at my omnipresent Peck & Peck plaid skirt, turtle-necked wool sweater, and tweed jacket, and said nothing.

Almost from the first day, being in the habit of removing both my hat and my shoes as soon as I arrived at the proofreading desk and took up the day's page proofs, I knew that I was not destined to be long for the fashion world. I was advised politely by fashionable Maggie de Mille, the footwear editor, who wore a stylish, broad-brimmed black hat and bejeweled pumps, that it might help my career if I bought a pair of 'real' shoes. That I never did, together with the ratty tam, the Peck & Peck uniform, and irreverent, undiplomatic,

tongue-in-cheek wisecracks, accounted for my rapid
disappearance from the masthead.

Six months before I left, at Betsy Talbot Blackwell's
unsmiling request, I had been elevated to the rank of assistant
copywriter. In this capacity, and because my new office was
across from the fiction editor's, I got to know George Davis,
rotund, brilliant, amiable, tragically blocked fiction writer (after
a great success with his first, and only, novel, *The Opening of a
Door*). George was the owner of a large house in Brooklyn
Heights on Middagh Street, where Wystan Hugh Auden and
Christopher Isherwood, Benjamin Britten and Peter Pears,
Carson McCullers and Gypsy Rose Lee, and other literary and
musical persons all visited or stayed, from time to time.

On occasion, during the year and a half I worked at
Mademoiselle, I was fortunate to be a silent, awed young dinner
guest at the Davis ménage. I remember wild, exuberant,
contentious talk at ten o'clock in the evening when we finally
got around to eating the dinner composed of whatever everyone
thought to bring, usually what each one preferred, with enough
for one or two other portions. I was so intrigued by the
interests, plans for the future, and intelligence of the persons
who inhabited this cosmopolitan world that I ate almost
nothing, and felt, as I rode back to Manhattan on the subway
after midnight, that my ears ached from trying not to miss
anything that was being said.

Once, the ecdysiast, Gypsy Rose Lee, came to the office to
have lunch with George. At the last minute he was summoned
to an important editorial meeting (the tyrannical editor-in-chief
excused no one, *no one,* from such a gathering). I, being so low
on the editorial scale as to be entirely unnecessary to
decision-making, was the only one available to take Miss Lee, as
George introduced her, to lunch. I had met her once before, in
Brooklyn, but she did not remember me. Terrified, I agreed.

That day, Gypsy was a sight to behold. She was swathed (one could almost say, in the Old English use of the word, *wrapped*) in black satin, low at the neck, high at the knees, and everywhere very close to her handsome body, revealing a fine décolletage and excellent, long legs. A straight black line went up the back of her flesh-colored nylon stockings. Her black hair was piled high on her head, and in it (or so I seem to remember) were tall black ostrich feathers. She wore elbow-length black kid gloves and black patent-leather pumps with heels at least three inches high. Gypsy was a very clever businesswoman: she dressed to call attention to herself, to advertise her profession.

I, of course, expecting to eat my homemade sandwich at my desk, was underdressed. That is to say, I was wearing my usual graduate-school outfit. In my scuffed loafers I must have been a foot shorter than Gypsy; without makeup and sporting a badly cut short hairdo, I felt like a pale, insignificant shadow of this glamorous vision.

George decreed that we would lunch at Stouffer's, a classy tearoom across the street from the office building. He said he would join us when his part of the meeting was over.

I doubt if too many persons remember the ambience of the old Fifth Avenue Stouffer's. It is fastened to my memory with all the painful glue of youthful embarrassment and an unbearable sense of social inadequacy. At noon the large, pleasant restaurant was filled with matrons from Westchester and white-haired dowagers from New Jersey and the East Side of the city, sipping iced tea and eating peaches-and-cottage-cheese salad. The redolence of Chanel No. 5 filled the sedate air as young Irish waitresses, their accents lilting and sweet, moved energetically among the tables.

Into this serene, feminine sea of diners strode Gypsy, with me several steps behind her. The hostess stared, recovered, and then said, 'This way, please, ladies.' I tried by whisper and gesture to indicate we wanted to sit somewhere near the wall, but she ignored me and waved Gypsy toward a table at dead center of the room.

The next hour was, for me, pure, unrelieved torment. Gypsy ordered a double martini in a voice that shook the Jell-O-with-whipped cream on the dessert table near us. The waitress, all smiles, said they did not serve liquor. I cannot remember what either of us ordered or ate. It does not matter. What I do recall is that an audible silence had settled over the restaurant. Gypsy, seemingly unaware of it, carried on an enthralling soliloquy in response to a foolish (I realized almost at once), low-voiced leading question about life in burlesque that I managed to ask; I could think of nothing else to talk about.

Everyone in the room seemed to me to be hanging on Gypsy's every word as she described to me, in vivid, earthy language, how runway shows were conducted and what it took to qualify for, and then last in, the art. At this distance I remember very little of her monologue, so sunk in confusion, so red-faced, was I. But I do recall one graphic piece of lingo. She told me that burlesque queens placed their bare breasts in pots of ice water just before going onstage to guarantee the elevation of those appendages when they danced. In the trade, this was known as 'icing the bordens.'

Toward the end of lunch I watched the door, praying for the appearance of George Davis, so that I would not have to walk the gamut of the floor eyed by the enthralled customers. George never came; it all went on and on as I dreaded it would. I could feel the gaze of the gathering on my neck as I struggled to open the door just ahead of Gypsy. I almost fell out into the street.

I think it must have been the longest lunch I was ever to eat. It taught me lessons in the pain of self-consciousness I would never forget. I admired Gypsy's magnificent self-possession (was she aware that we were the cynosure of every eye and ear for an

hour? She gave no sign of it) and the richness of her colorful
vocabulary. I yearned to have her 'command,' her 'presence,' but
I knew, in my twenty-one-year-old, stammering, blushing state,
I would doubtless never acquire it.

As long as I lived in New York City, I could never again
bring myself to enter a Stouffer's, even alone. The restaurants,
once all over the city, now have vacated their familiar sites and
shrunk down into packaged TV dinners of that name. The
memory of that lunch is still strong. I've never been able to buy
one.

One other memory, another New York expression, is still
with me. I used to have breakfast in a coffee shop near the
Mademoiselle office. When I ordered an English muffin, the
counterman would call back to the cook: 'Burn the British!'

౭౧

My old acquaintance Kurt Vonnegut, newly divorced from his
second wife, someone tells me, is quoted in a book of
'outrageous' sayings titled *The Natural Inferiority of Women,*
which arrived in this morning's mail from Poseidon Press. He is
said to have told an interviewer, in 1985, 'Educating a woman is
like pouring honey over a fine Swiss watch. It stops working.'

The book is a mine of evidence of how old and deeply
embedded is misogyny. I am not surprised by the proverbs: 'If
wives were good, God would have had one' (Georgian), and
'Bigamy is having one wife too many. Monogamy is the same'
(nineteenth-century British), and 'The woman cries before the
wedding and the man after' (Polish).

But modern man! Dr. Benjamin Spock, the hero of my
generation of parents, female and male: 'Biologically and
temperamentally, I believe, women were made to be concerned
first and foremost with child care, husband care, and home care.'

The respected black leader Stokely Carmichael: 'The only

position for women in the Revolution is prone.'

Lech Walesa, who became president of Poland, and said in 1981: 'Women are to have fun with. In politics I prefer not to see a woman. Instead of getting all worked up, they should stay as they are—like flowers.'

Henry Miller, thought to be the originator of the movement for sexual freedom through literature, said he could not understand why the women's liberation movement disliked him so: 'I adore women as a whole. I enjoy them as a breed, like a dog. They're another species that you become endeared to.'

I am pessimistic about reform in men's view of women. After all the years in which some small change might have been expected, Patrick Buchanan, a candidate for President of the United States, was asked by someone if he still believes, as he did in 1984, that 'the truth is that women's income, on the average, will always be a fraction of men's, so long as America remains free.'

December

*Each age of life is new to us; no
matter how old, we are still troubled
by inexperience.*

—Source Unknown

*D*riving back from Camden this morning, I notice a heartening change on the roads. There are no more dead deer in the backs of pickup trucks. Instead, I pass a number of cars and trucks carrying large Christmas trees.

∽

Copper Canyon Press sends me a copy of Kay Boyle's new *Collected Poems*. I am familiar with almost all of them. Kay is now eighty-nine and can no longer answer letters, but I write at once to tell her how much I've enjoyed rereading her work. I copy out a line I want to remember, from 'Advice to the Old': 'Have no communion with despair.' I take this personally, as we used to say. In another place I find: 'Let it be courage that our tongues compose / There being no refuge from the hurricane that blows,' from a long work titled 'A Poem on Getting up Early in the Morning . . . When One is Old.'

I miss Kay, although I have not seen her for many years. I miss seeing her fine, readable, backward-leaning handwriting on envelopes, and her courageous voice in letters urging me to participate in one cause or another—Amnesty International, black students' rights at California State, concern for a woman she knows in prison who is being badly treated. S.I. Hayakawa, former president of the college at which Kay taught, died a few months ago. He had tried to force her out of the school when she sided with the students during the Vietnam War and burned draft cards for them on the steps of the San Francisco Federal Building. In every sense, she has survived and overcome her old adversary.

∽

I have noticed that some correspondence from readers of *End Zone* is in the form of portmanteau letters, that is, they are composed of two distinct halves. They begin with something like 'I read your book and liked it,' or 'Your book meant a lot to me.' There follow various reasons, some effusive and, as it turns out after reading the second half, not to be entirely trusted or believed.

The second half of the letter consists of one or more of the following:

1. I too am a writer and . . .
2. I am having trouble getting my book published.
3. I need an editor (an agent, a publisher). Could you recommend . . .
4. Can I send you my manuscript?
5. Under separate cover I am sending you my manuscript.
6. I have a book, somewhat like yours, being published next year. Would you be willing to write a blurb?
7. I am applying for a Guggenheim.

Of course there *are* genuine fan letters, and one hugs them to one's breast with gratitude, and forgets the portmanteau self-seekers.

✑

Kippers: in all the years I read about kippers for breakfast in
English novels I was never quite sure what they were.
Rereading a collection of Evelyn Waugh's short pieces today, I
am forced look up the word and discover they are smoked
herring. Simple as that.

✑

My final issue of *Harper's* arrives. I had decided not to renew
the subscription, finding too little in it that interests me. But
there is one exception. *Harper's* contains the most fascinating
classified section published in this country. Under 'Personals'
there are *twelve* advertisements that contain offers to meet
marriageable Oriental women. One claims it is 'the World's #1
Service,' proffering 'Asian women [who] desire Romance.
Overseas. Asian Dreamgirl introductions.'

There are other curious ads: one for an Anarchist Cookbook,
one for Literature for Skeptics, one for 'Anti-Religious Classics
that refute Christianity,' and another for 'Dix, a publication of
Spanish Dirty Words.' Three ads address persons who wish to
obtain degrees (including Ph.d.s) by home study, one will print
your book, and another will 'write everything for you,
including papers and books.' Nudist videos are available as well
as something called 'Xandria . . . sensual products . . . plainly
and securely wrapped . . . designed for both the timid and the
bold.' Even Xandria's catalogue must be tantalizing. It costs four
dollars.

Now that I think of it, maybe I will renew my subscription.
I would miss the classifieds.

✑

It has grown cold. I wear three layers of clothes, wrap my legs
in a blanket in the evening when I sit to read or watch the news
on television, and wear a hat to go out. At noon it is a little
warmer. I think of the variety of temperatures a day in Maine
can have. In summer, I've noticed, it is spring in the early
morning, summer at noon, autumn in late afternoon, and winter
at night.

And yet, when I am working well in my study, it always
seems the right temperature, the true climate. Balzac, when he
left a party to go to his study for the night, used to say: 'I must
rejoin the real world.'

〜

A very elderly lady stops me in church on Sunday to tell me she
is writing her 'memories.' She says a writer she knows wanted to
put her in his book, and asked her permission to use parts of her
life. She was very indignant at this suggestion, and said if
anybody wrote about her, it would be she, not he. Elizabeth
Taylor had the same reaction to others writing about her. She
decided to write her autobiography and announced: 'I am my
own industry.'

〜

While Sybil is away at a book fair, my friends and neighbors
Ted Nowick and Bob Taylor and I decide to visit Grand
Manan, a Canadian island in the North Atlantic that one reaches
by boat from Canada's St. Stephen. To my mind this will
always be Willa Cather's island; she spent about twelve summers
there, the last time in 1940. In the only story she wrote about
the place, 'Before Breakfast,' published posthumously, she
described the difficulties of reaching the place she loved: 'The
trip up to Boston was long and hard, by trains made up of the
cast-off coaches of liquidated railroads, and then by the two

worst boats in the world.' This is a condensation of her own
laborious trips. They were actually longer and harder. From
Boston she took the train to Lubec in Maine, and then a small
ferryboat to Campobello Island, and then another, larger boat to
Grand Manan, the place she chose because at that time it 'wasn't
even on the map.'

Fifty years later, we drive to Calais, then to St. Stephen
(here you cross the Canadian border), and thence to Buck's
Harbour, where we take a luxury liner, complete with
restaurant, lounges, and room for a hundred cars, across the Bay
of Fundy to the island. We stay at a curiously named inn, the
Compass Rose. We are the only guests—all the summer and fall
visitors, Maine citizens, and 'snowbirds' have long since gone
south.

The next morning, in the deep fog that lingered on the
island for our entire three-day visit, opening up now and then
to allow us a glimpse of the harbor and the sea, we set out to
find Cather's cabin. Most people we asked did not know of its
existence, but eventually we were directed to an obscure dirt
road going through woods to the water, and there it was. In her
story Cather says:

> The cabin modestly squatted in a tiny clearing between a tall
> spruce wood and the sea,—sat about fifty yards back from the
> edge of the red sandstone cliff which dropped some two hundred
> feet to a narrow beach—so narrow that it was covered at high
> tide. The cliffs rose sheer on this side of the island, were undercut
> in places, and faced the east.

The story that follows is slight, taking place in the very early
morning. After his first, bad night in the cabin, an elderly man is
filled with despair at the closeness of death and his love for the
wooded, glacial-rock island 'off the Nova Scotia coast.' 'Why

bother to put his eye drops in,' he wonders. 'Why patch up?
What was the use . . . of anything? Why tear a man loose from
his little rock and shoot him out into the eternities? . . . A man
had his little hour, with heat and cold and a time-sense suited to
his endurance.'

He takes a walk 'to the edge of the spruce wood and out on
a bald headland that topped a cliff two hundred feet above the
sea.' The sight of a young girl (a 'plucky youth,' Cather calls
her) taking a quick dip in the 'death-chill' of the water cheers
the old man. His appetite for life is renewed. He walks back to
his cabin eager for his breakfast.

Old inhabitants of the island report that in all those years,
from 1925, when she had the cottage built to her specifications,
until 1940, when she stopped coming in summer because of the
war, Cather remained secluded, unfriendly, encouraging no
visitors, making very few friends. She had Edith Lewis, her
longtime companion, proceed her on the narrow path to the inn
to discourage unwanted encounters. We follow her path along
the top of the cliffs, careful to stay ahead of her shade, through
heavy woods. We find the footpath she and Miss Lewis must
have taken to get to the hotel, the Whale Cove Cottage Inn, at
which they usually dined. A vestigial path is there, much
overgrown. I sense Cather's lingering presence.

We search for her little garden, the wild-rose-bush hedge she
writes about. Only the 'patch of lawn' in front of the cabin is
there, now gone to rough-cut weeds. We look through the
locked windows to see that her heirs have redone the tiny sitting
room (how she would have despised that, she who railed against
anything 'modernized'). It would be nice to climb up the
narrow stairs to her bare study, with its handmade desk, but of
course the little cabin (disconcertingly small) is locked securely,
having twice been vandalized, the caretaker of the local
historical museum tells us later. (Her typewriter is displayed in

the entryway to the museum.) In this study she worked on what turned out to be lesser works, *Shadows on the Rock, Lucy Gayheart,* her collection of essays, and *Sapphira and the Slave Girl.*

The study is the only upstairs room. I remember that Cather's first, minuscule bedroom was in the attic of the tiny Red Cloud house. Ever since that time she seems to have hated being 'underneath,' at the mercy of sound and interruption by footsteps and noise over her head. I seem to remember that when she lived on Bank Street in New York, she rented the apartment directly above her to prevent hearing what Myra Henshawe, in *My Mortal Enemy,* was so plagued by: 'We are unfortunate in the people who live over us,' Oswald, her husband, explains to Nellie, the narrator. And the dying Myra adds: 'They tramp up there all day long like cattle . . . beating my brains into a jelly.' Cather loved her cabin for its 'great quiet, in this great darkness.'

There was no telephone line in her time; now, of course, the wires are there. Once there were 'four waterfalls, white as silver, pouring down the perpendicular cliff walls.' Now we see only one, thin and almost tentative. But the weir she wrote about still stands in the water, within sight of her window had the trees not grown up so much. Weirs, I learn, are fishing traps, made of huge, pointed tree trunks, driven into the water and holding what is here called twoine (from twine?), nets into which herring swim and then cannot escape. At high tide the sticks are barely visible through the fog, reminding me of Whistler's watercolor *Southend at Sunset.* Although I suspect the vague sticks in that work are a distant pier.

(I am always struck by how the memory of a work of art often shapes, indeed determines, what I come to see in the natural world. Would Cather's weir have looked the same that fog-filled day had I not known the Whistler?)

When we leave, Ted educates me about the trees on Cather's

land, tamaracks, which are pines with red-brown bark and
needles that turn lacelike and bright yellow in the fall when
every other pine remains green, and the scrubby shrubs on the
headlands that are pygmy, speckled alders. Then he walks to the
rear of the cabin, where there is a crumbling stone wall. I
fantasize, seeing Cather's heavy white hands (or Edith Lewis's
more delicate ones) building that low wall from the stones
everywhere on the beaches and headlands. When we go back to
the car, I find that Ted has carried away a small cobble-shaped
one for me. I demur but am secretly pleased, having thought
about 'liberating' one myself but being too cowardly to do so.
Now it sits, solid and reassuring, on a corner of my desk,
reminding me of a fine writer productively at work fifty years
ago in a secluded, quiet, and beautiful place. Like mine.

Odd. I had the curious feeling Cather was still around there
somewhere, resenting our intrusion on her privacy, waiting
impatiently for us to leave.

On our way back to the inn, we stop at a small grocery store
and buy some canapés to have with our evening drink. Herring,
of course, is the major catch on the island and the main contents
of its small canning industry. I buy a can of kippers, feeling
smug about my newly acquired education.

ॐ

I am reprimanded by an eighty-year-old correspondent. 'Let me
set the record straight,' she says. 'You are badly mistaken about
the nature of old age.' Her view differs from mine in many
respects. She writes that she never thinks about the slow,
inexorable decay of her body, as I seem 'obsessively' to do.
Unlike me, she does not despair at losses and decline, but instead
rejoices in what remains to her, and daily celebrates the gift of
time she has been granted.

What shall I reply? That I could not write of her fortunate

experiences in growing old, only of my own. I needed to be
honest about what I felt, not dishonestly cheerful. 'I needed to
set my own record straight, unpalatable as it might be to some
readers,' I wrote to her. I have written this, in different words,
to other protesters against, to them, my unjustified pessimism.
Some of her words echo in my mind. I go to *The Writer's
Quotation Book,* published by Bill Henderson's Pushcart Press in
a neat, small, pocket-size book, and find what I thought I
remembered. Gloria Swanson (married numerous times) said:
'I'll be eighty this month. Age, if nothing else, entitles me to set
the record straight before I dissolve. I've given my memoirs far
more thought than any of my marriages. You can't divorce a
book.'

∽

Vocabulary I acquired on Grand Manan: Fishing boats of
whatever size are called dories there, never dinghies, as in Maine.
Dulse: purplish seaweed that is edible, gathered on the rocks of
the west coast of the island in Dark Harbour, dried on the beach,
and then packaged and served as a snack, like peanuts. Some
people do not like eating it but chew it and then spit it out, like
tobacco. I look at it but do not buy it, being, as I have become
in old age, loath to try anything new, sure it cannot possibly
taste good.

∽

Information about Cather's summer cabin that I found in my
file of letters at home: In 1963 the New Brunswick government
wanted to make it an historical site so that visitors could view
the place, 'reverently.' Miss Lewis, Cather's long-time
companion and executor, replied to the request that Miss
Cather, as she always referred to her, 'was so opposed to any
publicity on Grand Manan—she so wished to keep the little

cottage unadvertised and unknown—that I do not feel that I
can give you permission for any sort of lease for viewing the
site.'

I was right. Miss Lewis wanted the place kept private for her
friend, sixteen years after her death. Cather is still there, hostile
to our presence, forty-five years later.

༄

The prospect of months ahead in Sargentville, cold, icy, and
tempestuous as they might have been, has been dimmed and then
wiped out. Jane's operation is the third of next month, so we
will drive down about that time.

I had looked to January and perhaps February here to try out
my theoretical love of solitude. Cato: 'Never am I less alone
than when I am by myself.' The test will have to wait until next
year.

༄

Sunrise in winter is far redder, far more brilliant, than at any
other season. It starts early and by six has filled the sky over
Deer Isle with a color not unlike fire. . . . I think of the news
recently that the Berkeley hills were caught in a great sweep of
fire, leveling a hundred homes. On television, standing in front
of a sky still burning, I saw old acquaintances, the McClungs,
and listened to them tell of the total destruction of everything
they owned. They are book people, he an editor at the
University of California Press and she, I think, active in the
University Press bookstore in Berkeley that we visited years ago
when we went book-hunting in California. I have a horrified
vision of the hundreds of books that must have inhabited their
house reduced to grey ash.

༄

I cannot escape constant worry about my daughter. When I look out over the winter-roughened water of the Cove I see her face. What makes this operation especially harrowing for her, and for the rest of us, is that she had a benign brain tumor removed fifteen years ago. It was a long and terrible experience. She has a vivid memory of the pain she will have to endure again, of the difficulties and indignities that accompany having one's head opened and foreign matter removed from it, and the long, slow, pain-filled recovery.

Having been through all this, she is understandably in an acute state of nerves. The Wheelers and her husband, Bob, are trying hard to help her through these next weeks of waiting, but it is not easy for anyone, especially not for Jane. . . . Her younger sister, Kate, a physician who is very pregnant, has come up from Baltimore to assist her in conversations with the doctors who will do the seventeen-hour surgery. Another sister, Elizabeth, will take leave from her Lake Placid job to stay with her when she comes out of intensive care, thus putting to rest at least one of Jane's great worries, being alone in a hospital room, as she was last time when an emergency arose. And she is promised a private room, another of her concerns: she doesn't feel up to bearing the pain of anyone else, unreconciled as she is to the prospect of her own.

It is good to see how concerned these sisters are about each other in an emergency. I am filled with pity for Jane, and find it hard to concentrate on what I had planned to do. How selfish writers are. Full of concern for a child I love, still, a morsel of resentment sticks in my craw that anything should happen to distract me from putting words on the page.

⁓

Three years of occupation of what I once considered a most spacious study, and now there is hardly room to get into it.

Books and folders are piled everywhere. It makes me think of the visitor who was shown through Mark Twain's study in Hartford. He asked the great man why it was necessary to have so many books spread and piled so untidily over the floor. 'Well, you see,' Twain said, 'it's so very difficult to borrow bookcases.'

My greatest difficulty is finding what I need. The old, original classification scheme, installed by my librarian-housemate Sybil, seems now to have been completely broken down, by me. Books are stuffed in everywhere, on their sides, flat on their backs. Next time I arrange them I will resort to the most absurd system I know of, like the one I read of recently in *Lunacy and the Arrangement of Books,* a small Christmas book published by the bookseller, Oak Knoll. It was a crazy scheme suggested in an etiquette book of the Victorian age: 'The perfect hostess would see to it that works by male authors and female authors were properly segregated on her bookshelves. Unless (like Elizabeth and Robert Browning) they were married.'

The telephone rings. I tell this story to the caller. She laughs. 'That system is still in use,' she tells me. Elaine Showalter, the feminist scholar at Princeton, admits only women writers to the shelves of her dining room.

∽

I welcome a day away from the difficulties I am encountering with the novel to drive down the coast to visit May Sarton. On the way I stop to see what damage has been done by Hurricane Bob to Moody Beach. Seawalls have been broken and steps washed away; the Hazeltines have had water driven in under their porch. But on the whole the beach has survived well and is still as vast and as beautiful as ever.

Standing at the top of the seawall in front of the Hazeltines' cottage, which adjoined ours, I imagine I can see Sam Wheeler, then a Roman Catholic priest, visiting us. It is early morning, and Sam is a sight to behold. He is dressed in his long, black cassock and is playing long-distance Frisbee with my husband and Mike Keating. Five years later he will be my son-in-law. I wonder what has become of his cassock.

And I recall another scene. We are sitting around a campfire built very close to the Keatings' cottage up the beach. It is growing dark; we are all about halfway through the evening's drinking and feeling fine. The children are bedded down. The grown-ups decide to stay up as long as the fire lasts. We build sand barriers against the encroachment of the tide, and watch it with inebriated interest as it creeps closer and closer. Then a miracle: the water breaks through the sand wall, parts around the still-burning embers, and comes up to the steps, avoiding the fire. It is close to three o'clock in the morning. Still we sit, celebrating our victory over the force of nature.

At this point my memory fades. But Kathy Keating tells me the next morning that we stayed to see the tide turn and begin to retreat, as if discouraged by the noise of our intoxicated hilarity. At that moment, we put out the fire, I am told, and went down the beach to our cottage, walking in the black water. The Keatings went skinny-dipping, as we called it then. The sky was beginning to lighten, that I recall. It was one of the great moments at Moody Beach.

Another: On Labor Day, beginning at noon, we would build a great bonfire, composed of every broken object, every scrap of wood and driftwood we could find. One year it rained, so we mounted a broken umbrella over the built-up high point, and it protected the fire most of the day until it too succumbed to the flames. All day, neighbors emptied their refrigerators into the fire; the odors that resulted were terrible, especially when Kathy disposed of a huge pot of decaying turkey soup into it. In the evening, we held a sort of bacchanalia around it, with music, drunken dancing, and folk singing to Mike Keating's guitar. The drinks of the night consisted of the remains of every wine and liquor bottle of every description left over in the cottages.

The high point of the evening came when we gathered in the dying firelight to review our summer's collections of sea glass, deciding which pieces were not sufficiently 'done' to be retained. Sea glass, as every walker of the edge of the sea must know, are bits of glass washed up by the sea, blue, green, brown, white, and colors in between, which are remnants of bottles caught in the sea wrack.

We had decreed, in our first year on Moody Beach, that the discards had to be thrown back into the sea by a virgin, in order to be further seasoned by the pious action of the waves. For some reason we saw the ceremony as religious in significance. The selection of the person to perform the rite became the night's pinnacle of hilarity: who was truly fit for the task? It was thought we might have to go as far as York Beach, or Wells Beach, to find a truly qualified candidate. At last, after much debate, Martha Keating was settled upon as the only sure celebrant along the mile-and-a-half stretch of beach: she was four years old.

Today, standing on the edge of Moody's empty expanse, I thought I was watching a shadowy volleyball game, played every afternoon between the Keatings, the Grumbachs, and their friends. Mike Keating and my husband were fierce competitors. Once, when the Keatings were a point or so behind, Mike reached for the ball in the air, hit small Martha, and knocked her out. Perhaps I remember it wrongly, perhaps it never happened, but what I see and hear is Mike shouting to Kathy to pull her out of the way without taking his eye off the ball on his side of the net. The game went on, goes on still in my memory, played hard by absent sportsmen and children, in a time half a century in the past.

∽

Vita mutator, non tollitur. My friend LaSalle, writing to me about a sentence I quoted in *End Zone* ('There is no death. Only a change of worlds') sends me the version of it from the Tridentine Mass of Requiem: 'Life is changed, it is not taken away.' In whatever version, I continue to find it very hard to think of death as anything but oblivion, the bottomless abyss, life's light obliterated, the unending dark. Perhaps that is the 'change' the proverb and the liturgy describe.

∽

Elizabeth Cale, my sports-loving daughter, is going over her huge collection of clippings, in an apartment where she has finally been able to have a room just for her collection. Twelve years ago she clipped an article from the *New York Times* about the Mormon Nation (a faith in which she was, for a time, deeply interested). She sends it to me. For a moment I am puzzled, not understanding its pertinence to my interests. But on the back she has drawn an arrow pointing to a headline: 'Rare Cancer Seen in 41 Homosexuals.' The date of the clipping is July 3, 1981. The article begins:

> Doctors in New York and California have diagnosed among homosexual men 41 cases of a rare and often rapidly fatal form of cancer. Eight of the victims died less than 24 months after the diagnosis was made.

The article, the first, I think, in newsprint on AIDS, appears far back in the paper, on page 20, and goes on to say that diagnosing doctors have alerted other physicians 'to the problem' in an effort to reduce the delay in offering chemotherapy treatment. The cancer is given a name, Kaposi's sarcoma.

Just that long ago? Beginning so simply, so inauspiciously, seeming so containable. A little thing, a problem, another variety of the Big C. Would that it had been, and that thousands more had not followed those first forty-one men into that good night.

∽

The Christmas season: All our tree decorations are on a shelf in our apartment in Washington, so we decorate this house with a plain wreath on the door. A Spartan holiday for me, but Sybil, who never cares much for transforming the house with Christian symbolism, is content. On Thanksgiving she told me this was her favorite holiday because it had no religious connotations. I too have my partialities about holidays. I don't like the patriotic ones, the often-bogus display of flag and bunting, uniforms and marching-band music, war-praising speeches and gun-and-cannon firing.

I also have an aversion to sentimental displays, Mother's and Father's Day, and other such plastic celebrations. Subtract religious, patriotic, and sentimental holidays from the calendar and what do we have left? I yield to Sybil: Thanksgiving.

∽

Two days before Christmas, St. Brendan's, the little church in Stonington, finds itself without a priest. Cynthia, who has served the Episcopal congregation well for two years, has decided she must be at a retreat house in the West, her whole sacerdotal profession now being inner-directed. She regrets her need to be absent, she tells us, but she wishes to continue her 'spiritual journey' under the leadership of Father Keating, a

Catholic priest, whose films she has been showing us for some
time.

Cynthia is a deeply spiritual woman, with strong mystical
(and Catholic?) leanings. We all express our understanding, to
an extent, of her choice between our needs and her own. But we
are angry, resenting the prospect of a bleak Christmas Eve Mass.
We can go to the church in Blue Hill, of course, not go
anywhere, or hold our own Mass without the Eucharist.

We decide to stay together, to use the whole liturgy of Rite
One, except for the words only the priest may say, and to ask
Cynthia to consecrate and reserve the sacrament so that we can
receive it and celebrate with the wholeness that Christmas
requires. That evening (Maine churches hold their midnight
services at nine because of the cold and the icy-road threat), a
saving remnant of us met in the Catholic church, which always
allows us to use its sacred space when it is not otherwise
occupied, and celebrated Christ's Mass. There was an eerie
suggestion of the very early church rites about it. Without a
priest, the royal priesthood of the people, as Martin Luther
termed it, had assumed the celebratory role.

〜

Less than two weeks until Jane will undergo her ordeal in New
York. Last evening at the Christmas Mass, during the prayers of
the people, I spoke her name, without saying why I was asking
for prayers for her. It is perhaps naive of me, but I have faith in
these communal requests for the Lord's help.

〜

Almost daily, on Route 172, we pass a huge barn, built very
close to the road, that is in the process of collapse. It once
belonged to our neighbor Abby Sargent's great-grandfather,

whose children operated the farm for many years. Now almost eighty years old, the barn served for a time as a 'hen factory,' and began to fail in 1979. Everyone, most of all Abby, worried about it. We watched it age, grow more feeble, threaten to fall into the road, much as we would watch a beloved old person go into a decline, as we used to say. It was Abby, I believe, who spoke to the road and town authorities to see if something could be done to hasten its safe demise.

Finally, by what agency I do not know, the beautiful old building fell down entirely this week. Now it is a flattened pile of grey boards, done in, I would like to believe, by a kind of joint civic euthanasia. The old die late and well in Maine.

∽

This morning, because I am feeling very good in the presence of the beauty and snowy elegance of the buried gardens, the meadow, the edge of the Cove, the silence and the solitude of the house as I work, the name Miss Schaff suddenly entered my mind. I searched my memory for the reason, could not find it. Then I spent an hour going through a notebook from five years ago. *Voilà,* here it is. I remembered it, I believe, because of the headline 'The Long, Unhappy Life of Miss Schaff.' Stories appear regularly in the newspapers about obscure persons, seemingly of low degree, who die and leave a fortune. Katherine M. Schaff's life story is both odd and prototypical; it has remained in my mind.

The headline writer was correct in one respect: she did live long, ninety years. The assumption that her life was 'unhappy' is what I question. She was born in Pequannock, New Jersey, and left school at thirteen to work in nearby Union as a jewelry polisher, leaving home before dawn, taking three buses, and coming home long after dark. Her father and two sisters died in her early childhood; she lived with her mother for forty-five years, supporting and caring for her, and then, for the next twenty-five years, with her brother, until he died. Except to go to work, she left her house only twice in her lifetime: once to take a pleasure trip for a day to Asbury Park, and at the end, after a stroke, to enter a nursing home, where she died in 1982.

She worked overtime at every opportunity, building her many savings accounts. In 1978 she began to collect social security, $270 a month, which she lived on. Her reclusiveness was abetted by her fears: of bugs (her house was always spotless, and in the nursing home she rose at four-thirty every morning to clean her room), of thunder, and of men (a terror she inherited from her mother). She hated having children enter her yard, yet she planned two weeks ahead for Halloween. She had had one suitor, whom she turned away because of what she said was her duty to her mother. After her retirement, a kindly neighbor did her shopping for her, and checked on her by telephone each morning. Miss Schaff would reply, 'I made it through the night.'

Her only visitor was her neighbor, who came by on New Year's Day for pickled herring. She had a radio and a telephone, made her aprons from old dresses, her blouses from her dead brother's shirts. Only her neighbor, a minister, and the driver of the hearse attended her funeral. To Pequannock's Rescue Squad, which had once taken her to the hospital, to the Fire Brigade, and to the Youth Recreation Department she left the contents of her five bank accounts: over one hundred thousand dollars. Her neighbor eulogized that Miss Schaff had led 'a hard, very unhappy life. I don't think I ever remember her laughing.'

Unhappy? I wonder. I think I understand her life. She loved routine and sameness. They made her feel safe against her fears of invasion by dirt, the elements, the opposite sex. Her hermitic life was further protection. She had shut herself away, pulled in the boundaries of her existence, so that the walls of her life sheltered her against everything she could not bear. She must have preferred her own company, solitude, to the company of others, which may be what loneliness is. The radio was her connection to the world, as much of it as she wanted to hear about. To her, 'doing without' must have seemed both normal and satisfying, and her money lying secure in her banks was a safety net she was never to use. Buffered in this way, expecting nothing, never disappointed or rejected, with nothing to lose and nothing to be concerned about gaining, must we assume she was unhappy?

She rarely laughed, we are told. So somber an outlook on the human affairs of our time seems entirely appropriate to me. But I am puzzled by one small biographical detail: Why did she choose Asbury Park in which to spend her one outing? Had she once an affection for the seashore? Did she know it had an amusement park, that it was, even then, noisy, crowded, and full of the tinny sounds of the merry-go-round and the high, panicked shouts from the Ferris wheel? I do not know why she went, but I can guess why she never went back.

∽

The *New York Times* reports this morning that George Rapee, 'one of the world's great veteran bridge players,' is playing (at the age of seventy-six) in Indianapolis at a national competition. I learn that he held three world titles in the fifties. I remember him clearly, seated cross-legged on a table in the editorial office of the *Washington Square Review,* of which I was editor in my senior year (1939) in college. He had very black hair combed straight back; he never said very much. Someone told me he was the son of Ernie Rapee, the orchestral conductor, 'one of those sons of famous people who never come to anything,' I remember someone saying.

〜

A wonderful letter from a man in Texas who wishes to augment my stories in *End Zone* about absurd military discipline and behavior during the war. He served in the Medical Corps at a base hospital in the Pacific which cared for severely burned sailors. An order came through that a very important member of 'the brass' was arriving to inspect the installation. All patients who were able were to stand at attention beside their beds as the general passed through. All others, too severely wounded to rise, were to lie at attention, and salute, during the inspection.

〜

Jane calls daily, or I call her. The time of her ordeal is close. Yesterday, Christmas Day, was her forty-fifth birthday. She celebrated with her husband, her sister, and her brother-in-law in New York City, where they all live. It must have been a less than festive day, like the prospect of New Year's Eve when more of the family will be together. I cannot believe that the level of hilarity will be very high.

Sybil and I are packing to go to Washington, closing the house slowly, talking to Mr. Snow about turning off the water, checking to make sure that everything we hope to see turn green and bloom again is covered, the bushes secured under blankets of boughs or hemp, the whole living organism that is a house put into hibernation, cold storage, for the long winter.

〜

I call Abigail McCarthy, an old friend from *New Republic* days, to ask her to introduce me at the Woman's National Democratic Club next February. She says she will try to change her Florida plans to visit her sister and move them a few days ahead. I think

this is remarkably good of her. She says, when I tell her about
the sad decline of my Catholic faith, 'I don't know that I have
much of the old faith left, but I still behave as though I did.'

The club asks for a title for my speech. I have no idea what I
will say, so far from the day, so I use Red Smith's *mot:* 'There's
nothing to writing. All you do is sit down at a typewriter and
open a vein.' I decide to call the speech 'Opening a Vein,' and
hope it fits whatever I think up to say two months from now.

ᔌ

Winter thought: You grow old, and the older you grow the less
you are known as a person who has done this or that, and the
more your name is prefixed with the fact of your advanced age.
Or, if you have a small accomplishment, it is enlarged in the
eyes of the reporter, it never stands alone, your age is always
attached to it: 'At the age of seventy-five she won a senior
marathon,' or 'At seventy-three, he taught himself Greek.' Josh
Billings knew that living a long time was its own single virtue:
'I've never known a person to live to 100 or more, and then die,
to be remarkable for anything else.'

January

'My children,' said an old man to his
sons who were frightened by a figure
in a dark entry. 'You will never see
anything worse than yourselves.'
—quoted by Ralph Waldo Emerson
in Spiritual Laws

*L*ast month, on the 11th of December, Berenice Abbott, the distinguished American photographer, died. She was in her mid-nineties, I believe. I knew Susan Blatchford, her companion, slightly (she had twice visited Wayward Books). We made indefinite plans for me to visit them in a town only about an hour from Sargentville, but nothing ever came of it. I kept thinking there was still time, put off calling again, next summer, I thought. . . . So I never got to tell her how much her photographs of New York City in the thirties shaped my memories of the city of my birth.

I remember one thing Susan told me about her friend. She said that Miss Abbott never complained about old age. Every day was an enjoyment to her; she woke each morning with a sense of delight that she was still alive. I found this amazing, in the light of my feelings each morning that nothing good can come of the day ahead. I told Susan I would like to acquire some of Berenice Abbott's *joie de vivre,* but I never traveled to Munson, to catch from her the enviable contentment with

which she lived her life. Once more, as if I were not already
aware of it, I learned that there is never 'still time.'

∽

In Washington, preparing to go to New York to see Jane, who
is enduring the first hard days after her operation, and waiting to
hear if her vision has survived it, I discover how bleak is my
interior landscape, how much like the view from the apartment
I have now, of an alley, of the windowed wall of a public
school, of another, new building with all the charmless features
of modern architecture. It is some consolation, or perhaps
reassurance, when what you see matches so well the way you
feel.

On the last morning in Maine, we were treated to a vision of
sea smoke, as it is called (or steam fog, some say). It is a lovely
white haze clinging to the edges of the Cove, caused by cold air
flowing over a body of relatively warm water. The resulting
vapor condenses in small columns near the surface of the water.
It resembles steam, and takes on very delicate tinges of color as
the sun rises over what looked like grey mountains, but of
course there are no mountains, only a stationary bank of fog, or
cloud, which then turned white and melded with the sea smoke.
The Quakers have a useful expression for what I felt as I
watched this phenomenon: it 'spoke to my condition.'

∽

From the business section of the newspaper this morning I learn
that in merchandising there are persons known as 'factors.' They
guarantee payments for 'receivables,' especially when those
accepting the goods may not be able to pay for them
immediately. Macy's department store and Burdine's are in such
unfortunate positions, and the factors (who sound to me more
like entities in a mathematical equation), I gather, stand between

them and the manufacturers, the middlemen between debtors
and creditors for large transactions. Such curious and almost
anonymous occupations must be necessary in the complex
business of capitalistic enterprise. But I would have trouble
owning up to such employment:
  'What do you do?'
  'I am a factor.'
  The anonymity of that word makes me think of the time
I first encountered, in some mystery story or other, the
description: 'He is a fence.'

༄

From our balcony I see a cloud of pigeons light on the roof of
the garage. They seem to have been rendered almost colorless by
the dirt and smog of the city. . . . I am put in mind of the family
of small, black-backed white ducks that moved into the Cove
just before we left. I had not been aware of their presence since
the spring. It was fine to have them back. I felt honored, as
though they had explored all the other possible habitats during
the long summer, decided Billings Cove was superior to them
all, and returned.

༄

National Public Radio holds a contest to find the best collective
nouns that listeners could invent. The winner, and my
preference:
  A staph of doctors.

༄

We go to New York, take a taxi to a hospital at the top of
Manhattan Island, about twenty blocks north of where I was
born, and find Jane's private room, into which she has just been
moved, this day, from the intensive care unit. She is badly

bruised, one eye swollen shut, her forehead, nose, lips, and parts
of her face and head blue and swollen. Her fever indicates that
some slight meningitis is present, so a tube connects her to
antibiotics. She is in much pain and asks for Demerol long
before she is due to receive it. Her hair is shaved around her
face; a brutal-looking scar crosses her head from ear to ear.

To my maternal eye she is a sorry sight. Yet I am filled with
gratitude that she is alive, that she has not lost her sight during
the operation that removed a fortunately benign tumor that had
wrapped itself around the optic nerve and intruded into the
sinus cavity.

The prediction is that she will be entirely well in a short
time.

The family takes turns staying with her during the day,
especially her sister Elizabeth, who is there almost the entire
time, feeding her, cheering her, holding her hand during the
unpleasantnesses that follow such a massive invasion of the head:
spinal taps, hypodermics in the forehead to remove excess fluid,
tests and shots of every variety. Her husband, Bob, comes early
in the morning and then again as soon as he closes his bookstore.
He is a cheerful and encouraging chap who is, even more than
the rest of us, sensitive and sympathetic to her pain. Isaac
Wheeler, her nephew, comes down from Yale on the weekend
and reads Molly Ivins to her. She smiles weakly at the lovely
wit, but tells him her mouth is swollen on the inside so the
humor hurts. Sam Wheeler is there every day after his school
closes, full of his customary good humor and priestly calm, and
Barbara Wheeler, her older sister, brings in well-cooked dinners
that Jane makes an effort to eat. Only Kate is absent, the family's
doctor, who telephones every day but cannot come because she
lives a good distance away, has a young child, and is pregnant
with another. Her father calls nightly from Albany.

Often at odds, a pride of highly individual women and

supportive men, sometimes turned away from each other by a word or an act, nonetheless, a family like ours is at its best in adversity. It becomes a single defensive unit against whatever threatens to diminish it, cemented by a kind of disparate love that is as fierce as its occasional animosities.

∽

One virtue of coming away from Maine earlier than I had planned (besides the relief of being close to Jane) is that I will get to see small Maya, my granddaughter, who will celebrate her second birthday this month. She arrived twenty years after my sole grandson, Isaac. I would have settled for the pleasure of watching (at some distance) him grow from a humorous, curly-haired, loving, intelligent, and thoughtful whelp (a besotted relative's adjectives, and I am probably misusing the noun), interested in everything, into a very tall, intelligent, socially aware, short-haired lad whose love for his family, his friends, and the rest of the human race is his most endearing characteristic.

But then his cousin Maya arrived, a smaller-than-average infant born, to the obstetrician's surprise, with her eyes wide open. In the two years I have been acquainted with her, seeing her only occasionally, I have recovered some of my affection for being alive. Before Maya, I had many unaccountable, often very disturbing flashbacks to the decades of my childhood, youth, adulthood, maturity. Now I am more inclined to sudden hopeful, forward flashes, fantasies about what might be:

A small, blue-eyed, blond child demonstrates to me her ability to read.

I show her a saltwater tidal pool and watch her delight at the sight of scurrying sand crabs, mussels, barnacles.

I see her splashing in Billings Cove or (if the Cove proves too cold for her until she grows up and acquires some body fat) in the low waves of Moody Beach, or *some* beach, or the warmer waters of the pond on Deer Isle. Like her grandmother, I fantasize, she will love water more than land, and feel the same rush of extraordinary freedom in it. There are already signs of this: At a year and a half she could stay afloat, put her face in the water, even jump in from the side of the pool. I hope I am still around to induct her into the Gertrude Ederle Society, my girlhood invention for high-school swimmers who aspired to that great Channel swimmer's achievements.

I see her, almost grown, her solemn, round blue eyes wide open to the possibilities of artistic or intellectual pursuits and still unaware of society's pervasive corruption, of atmospheric and water pollution, of the failures of government and church, in a depraved world I and my contemporaries have left to her.

೧

In this Sunday's *New York Times,* the argument rages over Kurt Masur's plan to conduct the Israel Philharmonic in a program of Wagner's music. It concerns not just the use by the Nazis of Richard Wagner's martial-sounding music, but the newly uncovered strain of anti-Semitism in Wagner's prose. Defenders of Masur excuse him by claiming that 'Wagner's prejudice was shared by many other artists and intellectuals of his time.'

This time-sharing alibi is very common. Writers like Edith Wharton, Scott Fitzgerald, Ernest Hemingway, and Willa Cather are exonerated from the charge because, in their time, anti-Semitism was in the very air they breathed. To some people, this seems to be enough to excuse their unpleasant portraits of Jews in their novels.

In this year, an aspirant to the Presidency of the United States, Patrick Buchanan, was accused by conservative William Buckley of having made some blatantly anti-Semitic remarks. An editor of the liberal journal *The New Republic* offered an

ingenious defense of Buchanan: 'Pat is the kind of guy who likes
to overstate his case. And in his own heart Pat believes he is not
anti-Semitic and that counts for something.'

These unconvincing absolutions from the charge bring me
back to the time, a few years ago, when the book critic for the
Washington Post, Jonathan Yardley, and I engaged in a nasty
verbal interchange in the pages of that newspaper. He had
reviewed the recently opened *Diary* of H. L. Mencken and
disagreed with its editor, who had declared flatly that 'Mencken
was an anti-Semite.' Not at all, wrote Yardley. 'We do well to
bear in mind that his prejudices were those of his time and class.
We do no man of an earlier time justice if we judge him by the
standards of our own more "enlightened" age.'

In a response to this, I wrote a piece for the editorial page of
the paper, listing twenty-four very nasty examples from the
Diary of Mencken's bigotry. I noted that 'his time' was not a
century ago, but the years (of the diaries) 1930–1948, when the
worst acts against humanity in centuries were being perpetrated
against Jews and when a responsible journalist committed an
unforgivable crime by contributing to the atmosphere of
prejudice.

In the last paragraph of the piece, I moved in a direction that
Yardley, who had been a literary friend of mine for many years
(I introduced him to his present wife, published him often in
The New Republic, and recommended him for his present job),
could not forgive. I speculated about persons who defend
obvious anti-Semites, and concluded that only someone
insensitive to the evidence, indeed, someone possessed of 'an
anti-Semitic sensibility,' could overlook it and defend the
writer.

In a few days Yardley devoted his long column to calumny
of me, my 'self-righteousness,' my McCarthyism, my lack of
reasoning (I 'would earn an F in Logic 101'), my 'private spitting

match' against him, proving that only among little 'insignificant' literary people like me was such an attack interesting or important. Out of our sense of our own insignificance we (the insignificant literary people) engage in attacks on each other because 'the world out there doesn't give a farthing.'

Now, a few years later, I look back on the yellowed clippings and think: I would now put it somewhat differently. I would assert that many people, Yardley among them, are unconscious of anti-Semitic slurs and statements, do not, in fact, even hear them, and therefore are able to assert, with assurance, the absence of them entirely. Perhaps it is too strong to say such people possess 'an anti-Semitic sensibility.' Too strong, yes, I suppose, but time and much further thought have not fully convinced me it is not true.

And, let us face it, the world out there *does* give a farthing when the issue is not literary gossip but the great concerns of man's inhumanity to his fellow man.

∽

Thinking today of my love for Isaac and Maya, I embarked on a fanciful dissertation. Those grandchildren are bound to me not by proximity or frequent contact, but by ineffable psychic connection. In my long life, I've learned there are pluralities to love, not one LOVE, varieties of the emotion called by that name and composed of diverse elements.

For example, I loved my mother, I thought. But, with the lofty scorn of the young for a parent, I treated her badly. I was indifferent to her needs, her sorrows, her disappointment with her narrow life. She yearned, I now believe, to learn something from the classes I took at college and the reading I was given to do. She had to settle for late-morning lectures at Town Hall, given by popular pundits with three names like William Lyon Phelps, Raymond Gram Swing, John Mason Brown, and A. A.

Brill, who, with great self-assurance, told their all-female audiences what to read, to see, to think about.

My college-student contempt for these fashionable servings of pap was profound, I who was reading Franz Kafka, Thomas Mann, André Gide, and Marcel Proust while my mother went regularly to Womrath's lending library to borrow the latest novel by Warwick Deeping or Hervey Allen. But when I needed her, for encouragement, comfort, affection, she overlooked my superior pretensions and provided me with them. She asked nothing of me but my imperfect, puerile 'love.' I had the mistaken notion that this was enough.

Another example: first love, sometimes phrased as 'first true love.' This is perhaps the most passionate we are ever to know, and the most unforgettable. Catullus tells us: 'It is difficult to lay aside an old passion.' For some, first love may be akin to childhood parental love. For others, like me, it was the first time the whole self responded to another, like the action of a catherine wheel, an emotional sweep so intense that one is powerless to describe it to anyone else.

Scenario: One sits at a bar, young, alone, say, unprepared and unexpecting. One looks up and sees in the doorway of the place the man one is to love, in this way, for the rest of one's life. One may marry another, even happily, live a long, contented, connubial life, see the object of this first passion only occasionally over half a century. And yet, its force is never diminished. I believe that in the long run, as they say, one's marriage may be saved by this parallel existence, by the endurance of an underlying passion never entirely laid aside.

For marriage is a condition that is severely tried by duration. Cemented by sacrament and official decree, more often than not it wears thin, its first, fine affection attenuated, much like raw cotton spun into fine thread. . . . On the other hand, first love endures over time, because, if it is not tried by marriage, it is never subjected to the stresses of daily life. It thrives on absence, and on the distance which is said 'to lend enchantment to the view.'

Or consider marital love itself. It is not very different from any alliance of long duration, between members of the opposite or the same sex who are engaged in the endurance contest of diurnalness. It takes the form of a right triangle standing on its base with the left side high, a side of decline, the right angle at the bottom. Hope and expectancy are the peak, but blind to reality, as justice is said to be, and rose-colored as optimism.

Time and the strains of family life tend to erode connubial love. It is changed by custom, and rushes down the declining slope of the triangle. A lasting marriage is often held together by the glue of inertia, usage, consuetude. In the view of those who wish to maintain the shape of society as we know it, marriage is a necessity, determined not by the passionate needs of the human spirit and body but by preservative and reproductive instincts that are stronger than desire. Theocratic notions rule our lives; marriage is their ineluctable decree.

And then we come to *amour propre*, self-love, the basis of all the other kinds of love. At our core we are beings whose seamless skin contains all the machinery for generating self-love. We may feel great sparks of passion, but they will move out of us only so far and then, halted subcutaneously, they return to our center to warm us, to act as selfish fuel for the fires of our inner being. Self-love is the hidden cistern that waters us from within, a kind of secret stream which attracts us to others. We say we love them, or admire them, as the result of the overflow of those egocentric waters. But oh, how conservative we are, how seldom we open the dike of ourselves to quench the thirst of another.

There is the love we feel for the dead, for those who have gone from our lives. It begins at the moment 'the distinguished thing' (Henry James's designation for his own approaching death) appears. Its first moments are full of show, an outward display of sorrow so powerful it is often said by others that 'he will never get over it,' or the widow's declaration: 'I will love him until I die.' But time is an effective analgesic, a consummate painkiller. You may think this a cynical view, and of course it is. Certainly it has its notable exceptions. But few people die of love for the dead. Most survive to make a complete recovery, to experience another 'love,' to marry again.

After the spectacle of grief is finished, postmortal behavior often turns into sentimental memories, verbal tags, and clichés, memorial tablets and services, anniversary notices in the newspapers. The dead we once believed we loved so ardently sometimes disappear from our real world to become conversation pieces, touchingly recalled at an appropriate time. Very often, sadly, that is all there is to it.

And then of course there is the kind of love that is usually accompanied by the awkward adverb 'arguably': sex, arguably a form of love. The intense, unique, private enjoyment of it, unlike the more respectable and public acts in our lives, causes prigs and puritans to think of it as noisome, messy, illicit, offensive, and disgusting. Some say it is not love at all but lust, a word they use with a sneer; others (I incline to this view, looking back over more than fifty years of pleasurably engaging in it) regard it as the main event, the *Ding an sich,* one of the few moments of light and heat at the end of torpid, humdrum days. When sex fails to animate the body, it leaves behind only scorched earth.

Doubtless there are fifty-one other varieties. These are the six I can testify to, either from close observation or from experience, whichever came first.

I come upon the name Thomas Higginson attached to a sage reflection on women. Is this the same Higginson to whom Emily Dickinson sent a few of her poems and enigmatic descriptions of herself in letters? No, I think this Higginson was an editor, and the one whose sentence I admire was clearly a clergyman. He wrote: 'I never performed the marriage ceremony without a renewed sense of the iniquity of a system by which man and wife are one, and that one is the husband.'

At the Library of Congress I look them up and discover, to my delight, that they are one. Thomas Higginson was a Unitarian minister, an abolitionist, the colonel of the first black regiment in the Civil War (about which he wrote *Army Life in a Black Regiment* in 1870), author of a novel and three biographies (of Margaret Fuller, Whittier, Longfellow), and the correspondent of the then-obscure American poet. After her death he edited, with her niece, two volumes of her poetry. And in addition to all this he was responsible for that perspicacious piece of feminist wisdom.

∽

I sit at my improvised desk, a slab of heavy black plastic mounted on two metal legs in an alcove of the living room (probably in the floor plan for the apartment it was called the dining room), and remember that Helen Yglesias told me her friend Lisa Baskin possessed Virginia Woolf's writing desk. Can this be? And if it is so, is Mrs. Baskin able to write at it? Would it not be so formidable, so awe-inspiring, that a letter composed on it would seem frivolous, a laundry list an insult, a book review a desecration? Would not a kind of sclerosis of the creative impulse take place in the presence of that redoubtable ghost seated beside you, or looking over your shoulder?

∽

There is an advantage to having as companion a bookseller who is also a constant and attentive reader. In the fall, Sybil showed me another of her 'finds,' a thick, beautifully bound, gold-stamped, gilt-edged (on three sides) volume called *Our Home* by Charles E. Sargent, M.A. Two ministers assisted him in putting down these chapters of advice on influencing children 'from the hearth.' The book was published by subscription only, and proclaims with some pride, I thought, that it was not for sale in anything so ordinary as a bookstore.

Why not? I wondered. It is full of fine advice to parents and should have been widely available. Most notable are the pages headed 'The Education of our Girls:'

> We are pained when an eminent writer gives weight to expressions like 'the great vocation of woman is wifehood and motherhood.' Would the author object to a slight change in the latter part of the phraseology so as to make the expression applicable to man? [thus]: 'The great vocation of man is husband and fatherhood.'

Another laudable (and unexpected) sentiment:

> We hope the world has heard the last of that sickly sentiment concerning 'woman's sphere,' 'the hand that rocks the cradle rules the world,' etc. If the hand were permitted to take hold of the world a little more directly, it would not at all interfere with its ability to rock the cradle.

Contemporary, radical feminist propaganda? Not at all. The book was published in 1900.

∽

Today I start my rounds of what is now called one's support system, an image conjuring up the outmoded, sagging physical structure that I have become. Internist, gynecologist, otologist (and hearing-aids supplier), but first of all, dentist. For a tooth is about to fall out and needs costly replacement, and I require the services of his accompanist, the tooth cleaner.

Driving up to 19th and N from the Hill, I remember a recent dental experience in Maine. Like most people, I have been going to a dentist since I was twenty, and taken to one by my mother, against my wishes, since I was about eight. In the last thirty years the entrepreneurial dentist has taken to himself one or more assistants who do his dirty work, that is, clean teeth. She (somehow it always seems to be a 'she') is called, euphemistically, a dental hygienist. What she is, actually, is a kind of spelunker, a scaler of mountains, a mine excavator.

On Deer Isle, the new operator (an accurate designation) began by addressing me, in every sentence, by my first name, a practice I am notorious for disliking on first acquaintance, especially by a young woman at least forty years my junior. She then proceeded to dig. It turned out she has the curious habit of grunting as she passes each badly tartared place, with disgust or satisfaction I could not tell. During one interruption to the operation, I had to make a general confession to her: I had let the process go for six months, instead of the usual four. She grunted. After one unusually hard spell of gouging, she said, 'Okay.'

Now, I am well acquainted with all these teeth. As she advances around the gaping cavity of my mouth, I anticipate her approach to the one I expect will hurt when she probes: I think it may have a hole in it. I try hard not to give any sign of pain in hopes she will not notice my weakness and say 'Aha,' proclaiming the need for something radical to be done.

What I dread most is the announcement which has come from every hygienist I have ever encountered: 'You need to have deep, periodontal scraping done,' she says. I tell her, to prevent her from inflicting even more damage than she has already done, that my gums have bled for more than fifty years. Four times I have been dispatched to periodontists. Each time I have been informed that if I did not submit to violent, surgical treatment ('one quadrant of your mouth per visit'), I would certainly lose all my teeth. Each time I preferred not to, as Bartleby phrased it in Melville's story. I opted to ignore the first prognosis when the dire warning was issued, and I went on doing so for thirty-five years.

(I have a clear memory that when my former husband came out of the Army after World War II, he was told by an early practitioner of the art of deep delving that he too would lose his teeth unless . . . He too refused. He is now almost eighty and, as far as I know, has a sufficient number of his own teeth for all practical purposes.)

That day in Maine the hygienist was in the by-now-familiar tradition. As I sat down she informed of her intention to apply Novocain and do some deep scraping. It was the first I had heard of this plan. I disabused her of her purpose and instructed her to proceed normally, to clean my teeth. She grunted, but she did it. In half an hour the ordeal was over. I was discharged, a new, soft toothbrush in hand, and my gums bleeding a little as a result of her retributive ministrations, I believed. Once again, into the breech, I have saved my teeth from the Visigoths of dental hygiene and periodontia.

∽

While I waited in the dentist's office on Deer Isle, I read *Woodworking,* a slick, glossy magazine on fine carpentry. (In Maine you find a publication like this in the reception room; in Washington, D.C., it is more likely to be *People* or *Fortune.*) From its subject matter one might expect something less coated, more homespun-looking and workmanlike, with a brown paper cover perhaps. But no matter. In its pages I learn a new meaning for the word 'distressed': wood purposely blemished or marred to give it an old look. 'Country furniture is enhanced by physical distressing,' the article says. Last week in the hospital, having watched Jane suffer extreme distress in the accustomed sense of the word, I have decided that only varieties of country furniture, not human beings, are enhanced in this way.

✑

Maya's second birthday: Sybil and I drive to Columbia (a manufactured community south of Baltimore) to be present at her party, an elaborate affair, with a live Mickey Mouse, a Mickey Mouse cake baked in the morning by her mother, games, a mound of presents, and an assortment of friends and relatives, all centered around the little curly-haired, blue-eyed moppet.

She was admirable in her composure, in her solemn demeanor during all the hoopla and photography. So camera-conscious is she that she has a special, fake smile she produces whenever she sees one. But I see her genuine smile of delight when she catches sight of Mickey, when he (actually her mother's best friend, Martha) picks her up and she touches his huge ears.

'Mickey,' she says fondly. 'Hello, Mickey.'

I have never understood the appeal of Mickey Mouse to young children. Every child at the party displayed the same fascination for the homely, grinning rodent. Maya delighted in having 'Mickey' carry her about, while she firmly resisted the efforts of infatuated adults (like me) to hold her.

✑

The city is united over the success of its football team, the Redskins. Today they won the National Football League

championship. Black and white, natives and transients, young
and old, everyone here seems to care about winning the
Superbowl. The Skins are the only thing that holds this disparate
population together. Right now it is violently divided by the
sad saga of its black former mayor, who is in jail for cocaine
possession. His supporters among blacks believe he was set up
and railroaded by the media and the white community. Marion
Barry himself is firm in this opinion. He has had stationery
printed for his letters from prison. It is headed: MARION BARRY.
POLITICAL PRISONER.

⟡

I try not to think about the view of the Cove as I sit in my
abbreviated apartment study. No, that is not honest. I do think
about it, every time I look up from the keyboard. On the wall
over the display there hangs an enlarged colored photograph of
the meadow and the Cove: green lawn, blue water, dark
shadows of elm and horse chestnut trees. I am still overcome by
knowing that I have that scrap of land and water and sky to go
home to.

⟡

Waiting for me among the apartment mail, amid galleys, book
catalogues, and publicity releases, I find a biography by Judith
A. Roman that interests me. It is about Annie Fields, the wife of
publisher James Fields (of Ticknor & Fields), and the great and
good friend of regional writer Sarah Orne Jewett. I have come
upon Fields before while studying the life of Willa Cather, who
visited her in her apartment on Beacon Hill in Boston.

But what fascinates me is the care, almost what one might
call the scrupulous avoidance, with which the biographer
explores the 'partnership' (as she calls it) of the widowed Mrs.
Fields and Jewett. Admitting that Jewett was inclined to love

women, that her important friends were women, and that 'the
conventional destiny of heterosexual marriage was not suited to
her,' the biographer still avoids any conclusion about the nature
of the relationship between the two women. It is termed a
'romantic friendship,' a 'Boston marriage.'

Jewett was a sophisticated stylist. But to Annie Fields she
wrote daily letters when she was in residence in Maine and
Fields was in Boston, using pet names like Fuffy and Pinnie, and
baby talk that is often embarrassing to read. Jewett said she had
no intention of marrying; further, she must have been one of the
first women to declare that she 'had more need of a wife than a
husband.'

ᔐ

Ralph Waldo Emerson ('Spiritual Laws'): 'Not in nature but in
man is all the beauty and worth he sees.' To me, the terms of this
aphorism should be reversed. Later, in 'Self-Reliance,' and
following the famous definition of consistency, he says: 'If you
would be a man [or a woman, is it not proper now to add?]
speak today what you think today in words as hard as
cannonballs, and tomorrow speak what tomorrow thinks in hard
words again, though it contradict everything you said today.'

ᔐ

Today, Sunday, I went back to St. James, the Anglo-Catholic
church I like so much. On Eighth Street off Massachusetts
Avenue, in the heart of a diverse Capitol Hill population, it is a
small congregation of whites and blacks, heterosexuals and
homosexuals, single persons, couples, and families, all of whom
must enjoy, as I do, the whole panoply of religious rite that the
Anglican Church offers. The grounds are beautiful, the church is
a model of small, grey-stone English architecture sitting in the

midst of flowers, trees, and bushes maintained by a devoted parishioner.

There, I pray for Jane's complete recovery, at noonday Masses, and Saturday and Sunday. I pray that Kate will carry her second child, a daughter, to full term in April and have a safe delivery. . . . And suddenly, my mind wanders away from the Prayers for the People. I think of Dorothy Day (exactly why I don't know, unless it is that religious rites and concern for others always brings her to mind), the acquaintance of my youth, and the only saint I've ever known. She's been dead about ten years, I believe. Yet for me she is often present when I worship.

Dorothy Day was a convert to Catholicism from the Episcopal Church. Before her conversion, she led a free, bohemian life, never married the father of her daughter Tamar, and was a dedicated socialist whose social views came close to anarchism in her mature years. She was a passive war resister who opposed the authority of the state on every matter of social justice and treatment of the poor, the homeless, the hungry, but was a complete conservative when it came to the rites and practices of the Catholic Church. Still, she was deeply aware of the Church's shortcomings, of 'the scandal of businesslike priests, of collective wealth, the lack of a sense of responsibility to the poor.'

She took a private vow of poverty and chastity, but never became a religious. She lived the rest of her life with the poor, believing that the Sermon on the Mount was a law to be lived, not 'an ideal to honor.' At every point, except ritual and the sacraments, she ran counter to the American Catholic Church, believing with Romano Guardini that 'the Church is a cross on which Christ was crucified.'

Words as hard as cannonballs.

∽

Louise Nevelson's sculpture comes close to serving as a graphic equivalent of fiction. Yesterday I looked through a book of her work, *Dawns and Dusks,* in which she talks to Diana MacKown about what it is she does. Like the fiction writer who is humanity's magpie, she uses materials she scavenges for her sculpture: 'You're taking a discarded, beat-up piece that was no use to anyone and you place it in a position where it goes to beautiful places: museums, libraries, universities, big private houses.'

Nevelson sees this as a process of bringing these found objects to life, giving to them a new and vitalizing order. So, it seems to me in fiction, writers 'find' what they need in the junk piles of their minds, where everything they know is stored. What results is a conglomeration not unlike Nevelson's walls and panels. Like Nevelson, the writer considers the result better than the real world: 'The essence of living,' she says, 'is in doing, and in doing, I have made my world, and it's a much better world than I ever saw outside.'

Nevelson and I share an affection for Yucatán. It was, she writes, 'a world of forms that at once I felt was mine.' I read this to Sybil, who says that, to the contrary, she has always preferred European architecture precisely because it was composed of rounded forms. . . . Nevelson compares the United States to the Mayan world and decides that 'truly we are the primitive people' and they are the sophisticates. She comes out of St. Patrick's Cathedral in New York, looks into the windows of Saks Fifth Avenue, and thinks: 'How barbaric we are.' No one meditates on the land around this sacred church (as the Mayans did at the pyramids). There is no possibility of a 'larger spiritual experience' on Fifth Avenue and 49th street.

I stop reading, call my travel agent, and make reservations for the end of March for a visit, yet one more, to the great deserted cities of Yucatán. One more time I will stand at the bottom of El Castillo and think about the sacred moments of worship a thousand years ago.

✍

Jane telephones to report that she is doing very well at home. The pain is diminishing with the swelling. She is able to eat. Her good friend Blaine Trump has sent her a hatbox full of fine turbans to wear over her shaved head.

✍

So much for literary fame: Sybil tells me the story of a waitress in a Chesapeake Bay restaurant who whispers to a customer, and then points: 'We have a very famous man eating here tonight.' The customer looks. James Michener is having dinner at a nearby table. 'Frank Perdue!' says the waitress.

Sybil has another good story today. This one comes from a bookstore-owner friend she met on Seventh Street recently. A struggling bookseller wins the million dollar lottery.

'Will you give up your store now?' he is asked.

'Oh, no. I'll go on with it until I run out of money.'

✍

I am trying hard to work regularly on this notebook, on reviews, and on the untitled novel (like a week-old baby for whom the parents cannot agree on a name). It is comfortable, warm, convenient in this narrow study where I work. But I cannot recover from the feeling that I am in exile. I spend too much time looking up at the enlarged photograph of the Cove and wondering how long it will be until my visa arrives. In my regrettable state of suspended animation I keep trying to remind myself of Lambert Strether's dictum in *The Ambassadors:* 'Live all you can, it's a mistake not to. The right time is *any* time that one is still lucky to have.'

February

*I have nowhere
to go and

nowhere to go

when I get
back from there.*

—*A. R. Ammons*

*L*etters forwarded to me here: one from a former student in the days I taught high school. She is now a physician, a psychiatrist, I think, and she sends me her mother's words on the subject of aging: After fifty years in existence things become antiques. They have moved up from being discardables to collectibles.

Another, from Doreen Kelly, a former Saint Rose student, who reminds me that I provided a bit of spice to her English class. She recalls that I once explained the plethora of wire coat hangers by suggesting that they copulated and reproduced on the floor of closets. Odd what students remember. I cannot even remember thinking this, let alone saying it in the early sixties to a class of proper Catholic girls. Well, perhaps they were not as proper as I thought they were at the time.

⌇

If ever I have cause to create a character who is a fifteen-year-old boy, I will be able to use a valuable piece of background detail just given me. An acquaintance, Nancy Wittig, who is an

Episcopal priest in Philadelphia, had dinner with us this week at
Saigon Gourmet. She is on sabbatical and working, reading, and
writing at the College of Preachers on the Cathedral hill. She
told us that her son and his teenage friends leave pennies all over
the floor of his room, never bothering to pick them up because
they regard them as utterly useless to them in today's economy.
My grandmother would have been shocked. Regularly she
lectured to me about her first rule of thrift: 'Save your pennies
and the dollars will take care of themselves.'

သ

I have been thinking of my grandmother today. Sarah was a
kindly, gentle, parsimonious lady who lived to be ninety-three.
She was one of six sisters, and had a brother who was the
seventh child. Her mother, Rosa, a strong-minded emigré from
Germany, was left widowed in her thirties. She took over her
dead husband's secondhand furniture store on the Bowery and
raised her seven children on its profits, demanding that they, in
turn, leave school to work in the store until they married. She
was a moderately religious woman. When her husband died she
assumed his place on the building committee of Rodelph
Sholem, at that time a tiny progressive congregation on the
Lower East Side of New York.

I still can see my grandmother's sly little look of triumph
when she told me the story of her mother's conduct of the
family. The rule about marriage was inviolable: the girls had to
marry *in order,* that is, no one could become affianced until the
older sister had married. My good-looking grandmother was
third in line, and she told me, with some sly pleasure, I thought:

'My two older sisters were . . . not good-looking.'

'So, what did you do?'

'Well, Carrie [her closest younger sister] and I had beaux.
Max wanted to marry Carrie, and Moe wanted to marry me.

We told them Mama's law. They could marry us if they found husbands for our older sisters. So they did. They brought around two . . . not very handsome men whenever they came calling on us, and after a while it was all fixed. Emma and Lena got married, and right after that we did.'

Sarah's life was made 'comfortable,' as she always put it, by Carrie's marriage to Marcus (Max) Loew, the fur peddler turned movie mogul who borrowed money from his brothers-in-law to help finance his early nickelodeon adventure, and repaid them all handsomely with stock in his companies, Loews, Inc., and Metro-Goldwyn-Mayer. When Moe died Sarah was left with money to invest. The lawyer for M-G-M offered to handle this for her.

'Irving' (I don't think I ever knew his last name) did very well for her, finding stocks and bonds in addition to the ones she already owned that made her very satisfactory profits. But my grandmother was either extremely lucky or a genius. Once, she called Irving to tell him she wanted him to buy a new stock that had just come on the market.

'What stock is that?' he asked.

'Well, I can't pronounce it but it's spelled X-E-R-O-X.'

'What kind of stock is that? I haven't heard of it.'

'Well, I don't know. I read about it. It's twenty-five cents a share, I think. Just buy it.'

She bought a goodly amount of the unknown stock, and continued to buy after it (and she) profited. When she died, because of that stroke of genius, other astute purchases, and her generous will, I was able to help my husband send our daughters to private schools, a good university, and Seven Sister colleges.

She believed firmly that 'charity begins at home.' I never knew her to contribute to any charity or even to the uptown avatar of the temple her mother had helped to found. She was very free with money to my sister and me, but she refused to attend the high-holiday services at the temple when she was told that there was now a pew fee to pay. I can see her clearly: seated at the window of her bedroom, dressed in her services-going best black dress, reading the Union Prayer Book all morning on Yom Kippur.

Her frugal ways increased as she entered her nineties. Despite Irving's assurances to the contrary, she believed her money would not last her lifetime. So she imposed stringent rules upon her seventy-two-year-old housekeeper. When Grace (I think her name was) wanted to buy lemons by the bag for their tea, so that she would not have to take the long walk to the greengrocer's on Broadway so often, my grandmother objected:

'Buy two lemons,' she said. 'That will be enough for a while. I don't want them left over when I die.'

I have known people to use a teabag twice. My grandmother's custom was to use one three times before she discarded it, saving it between times in a saucer on the stove.

Except on the high holidays, my grandmother wore 'house dresses,' made, at that time, of a thin, inexpensive flowered material and varying only in pattern and the length of the sleeves. These suited her well, because in the last years she rarely left her overheated apartment. Grace secured them from a maids' outfitting store, but only on days when they were on sale. Then they cost three dollars, or two for five dollars; I never knew my grandmother to allow Grace to purchase more than one at a time. I believe she hoped to arrange it so that not one would be 'left over' after she died.

Her death was peaceful and very fast. I had come down from Millwood, a suburb of New York, where we lived at the time, for my usual Wednesday visit, to discover that she had fallen the night before in her bathroom and hit her head. When I arrived she was barely conscious. Grace hovered about in a state of confusion about what to do, and my father, who never could face unpleasantness of any sort, let alone dying and death, had taken to his room and shut the door.

My grandmother had soiled the bed and herself, but Grace and I were not strong enough to move her. I called the doctor to come at once, and the Yale Registry to send a trained nurse. She arrived before the doctor and did all the proper things to make Sarah 'presentable' to the doctor, as she said. I sat on the bed, held my grandmother's hand, and felt the moment when she loosened her grasp, and died.

The doctor examined her and then wrote a certificate of death, called the funeral home, offered me his condolences (my father still refused to come out of his room), and left.

After Riverside Chapel, the funeral parlor nearby on Amsterdam Avenue, had taken her body away, an attendant carrying her black dress and coat, stockings, shoes, and a round caracul cloche hat which she had said she wished to wear in her coffin, the nurse and I went into the kitchen to have a cup of tea with Grace. (I invited my father but he was still unwilling to appear.) The refrigerator was almost empty. Grace apologized. She cut the remaining half a lemon in three slices, made strong tea, and then placed the tea bags in the saucer on the stove.

It was two o'clock. While we drank our tea, the nurse explained that she had to charge me for the entire day, although she had been here only five hours:

'The rule of the Registry,' she said.

I said: 'Of course. I understand. Only fair.'

Then, writing the check, I smiled to myself and thought: If my grandmother had known that I would have to pay for the whole day, she would surely have held off dying until the eighth hour.

A few weeks later, when I came down to the city to help my father dismantle the apartment, I found that he had invited a secondhand furniture man in before me. The man had bought much of my grandmother's well-kept old furniture at a dealer's customary low prices. No matter. The linen closet was intact, the neat stacks of sheets, cases, towels, and facecloths held in place by strips of satin. The sheets were from my grandmother's trousseau, I believe, made of cotton so thin they were now almost transparent. Most of them were patched with her small, neat stitches in many places and, I noticed with pleasure, many of the patches had been patched.

As a memento of my beloved Sarah, I took one of these home and kept it at the bottom of my uneven and shaggy stack of poorly folded sheets. I don't seem to have it anymore. I don't know what happened to it. My grandmother would be shocked.

༄

I miss the Cove badly. Early mornings in the apartment I find myself returning to it. I am back reading at the kitchen table in Sargentville. The sun rises, coloring the windows and then the pages of the Book of Common Prayer. I drink coffee and, feeling a welcome jolt of energy, take out my notebook and put down some of what I sometimes refer to, with intentional irony, as immortal prose.

Later this morning I make a third attempt to read Harold Brodkey's *The Runaway Soul.* Of its more than eight hundred pages I have progressed to page 223. Twice I had to start over, feeling like Sisyphus pushing his stone almost to the top of the hill, only to have it roll back against him time after time.

By noon, the sun having risen over Hines Junior High and settled on the roof of the parking garage only a few yards from our living-room window, I know I will never finish the novel. In recent years I have lost my ability to enjoy long, difficult fiction as a scholarly reader would, relishing its problems and complexities, collecting images and seeing their significance, analyzing metaphors and making consistent sense of them, searching the underbrush of the writer's ambiguous language for hidden clues to meaning. This is the job of literary criticism, often a satisfying game, in which the critic loses herself in pursuit of an original 'insight.' I read *Finnegans Wake* in this way, and Eco's *The Name of the Rose* and Pynchon's *V* and Faulkner's *The Sound and the Fury.*

But Brodkey: while I have an idea that there may be more to the total design of his book than I will ever persevere to discover, I am going to abandon the old pleasure of making the summit and settle for an easy descent to base camp. This morning, reading Morning Prayer and Mary's prayer, the Magnificat, I was stopped at the line 'He hath scattered the proud in the imagination of their hearts.' I have not a clue to the meaning of this lovely-sounding sentence, but I twist it to explain my attitude toward *The Runaway Soul:* the prideful critic stopped in her tracks by a failure of affection for the writer and his book.

∽

Here in the apartment there are times when my somewhat-but-not-entirely-diminished *Weltschmertz* and Sybil's low spirits occur at the same time. My despair builds on hers. We enter a period of dark distance from each other, filled with silence. It is impossible to know how it starts or who instigated it, but there it is, sitting like a great mountain of anthracite between us.

This must happen to many couples who live together a long time, a natural, downward progress of early vital cheerfulness. We rarely grow used to each other's bleakness, only to our own. Custom erodes the sunny edges of our patience with each other. There is no longer anything unexpected to be expected, not even bad moods.

∽

The sight of the word 'reception' on an invitation in the city of
Washington sends me to the trash basket. Today there is one
from the Canadian Embassy to meet the eminent novelist
Robertson Davies. My response is very much like my young
daughter Barbie's when her kindergarten teacher, Miss Bechman
(strange how we never forget the names of kindly teachers, even
forty years later), wrote on her report card: 'Barbie is a bright
little girl, but every time I ask the class to come to the circle she
walks in the opposite direction.'

There is one characteristic of receptions, meetings, gatherings
of any size for which I have acquired a profound distaste.
Arriving at the door, you are asked your name and then given a
name tag. The worst kind reads: 'HELLO My Name Is
————' Others are printed with your name in large block
letters, some are handwritten, some are intended to be pinned to
your blouse or, occasionally, hung around your neck.
Sometimes you are asked to write in your own name.

Whatever the location or the method, these are impertinent
impositions, suggesting that you wish to have your name
attached publicly to your person, to be read by those few who
care and many more who do not. It is really a private matter,
one's name, especially if, in a small way, it has already become
somewhat public.

(I recall Auden's lines: 'Private faces in public places / Are
wiser and kinder than public faces in private places.')

What happens is this: A person approaches, stops, looks hard
at the tag on your breast before looking at your face. You can
see him wrestling with himself, trying to determine whether or
not to bother to speak to you. Finally he does, or turns away
and does not. You might have been a signpost or a door, the
name is all, the person nothing . . . or, as the case may be,
everything.

Is it ego that keeps me from wearing my name tag? Am I

saying, by refusing to put it on, if you don't know who I am, too bad? I am not going to bother informing you by means of a tag. And if, without the ugly little cardboard designation, you do know me, is it a victory over obscurity? If I attend another gathering where this odious requirement is in use, I might be tempted to write HETTY GREEN or EMMA GOLDMAN or LEONA HELMSLEY or MOLLY IVINS in large block letters, and then wait to see if someone approaches, looks, lights up with pleasure, and then talks to me for the duration of the meeting.

I decide to decline the invitation to the Canadian Embassy.

∽

In September of 1912, Houghton Mifflin published *Autobiography of an Elderly Woman,* anonymously. Sybil rescued an old copy from a barn full of books in Southwest Harbor, thinking it might be interesting to me.

It was. It is a very well written account of the life of a seventy-five-year-old widow who lives with one of her daughters and reflects upon the indignities and well-meant concerns inflicted upon an aging woman. I was entirely convinced by the old lady's voice, wry, ironic, self-deprecating, clear-eyed. But today I visited the Library of Congress, where I discovered once again how deceptive the most persuasive autobiography can be.

Autobiography of an Elderly Woman is a novel, and, what is more, it was written by thirty-two-year-old Mary Heaton Vorse, who, I surmise, did not put her name on the book because by then she was well known as a young journalist. It would seem that she wanted it to be accepted as a fictional autobiography. The narrator whose convincing voice I so much admired was the age of Vorse's mother.

What is astonishing is the contemporary sound of this old lady's observations, so close to my experience that I feel the urge to see if I can interest someone in reprinting the book. I call Bill Henderson of Pushcart Press and leave a message on his answering machine, suggesting I send him the book for his opinion.

∽

Sybil is working late. It is my turn to cook. I have never been able to overcome a dislike of the kitchen, despite my recognition of the fact that my feeling runs counter to the expectations for my sex. Looking back, and in the light of avid reading of such entertainments as M.F.K. Fisher's *The Art of Eating,* Margaret Visser's *Much Depends on Dinner,* and *The Alice B. Toklas Cookbook,* I realize what a poor cook I've always been. This opinion is amply supported by my grown children. Now, even hunger no longer propels me into the kitchen, a room I regard as useful for storage of the advanced equipment I rarely use, and the regular boiling of water for coffee.

Sadly, after twenty years of living with me, Sybil, once a good and interested cook, has arrived at the same stage of disinclination. Often, six o'clock in the evening having arrived, we come into the living room from our separate occupations, both tired, both silently determined to wait for dinner to be cooked by the other, both hungry but not stirred to do anything at all about it.

I suggest to Sybil we adopt a schedule of some sort, two days on mess detail (to use my old naval jargon), two days off, but Sybil says no, she is opposed to a rigid schedule.

Tonight this happens: No one moves from her chair. Then I put on a tape. Then we listen to the national news on the television. Finally, with the same indolent intent, we drift into the kitchen. In the refrigerator I find three small containers of leftover vegetables and two somewhat desiccated red potatoes. She concocts a bowl of cold cereal and milk, strawberries and a banana. We bring these dishes to the dining-room table (a euphemism for the small oval structure in the living room) and eat, listening contentedly to Joan Sutherland's extraordinary coloratura arias.

No one has won this unspoken contest of wills; no one has lost. I suppose this may be the ideal way to settle domestic impasses that seem to arise more and more frequently after the first five years of selflessness and generosity are over.

∽

Yiddish proverb: 'Make sure to send a lazy man for the Angel of Death.'

∽

Observation in the club car of the Metroliner from Washington to New York: I sit down beside a businessman reading the *Wall Street Journal* and drinking coffee. It is clearly too hot; he blows on it and I think: I have not seen anyone blowing on a hot drink to cool it for many years.

∽

In New York I see an enormous approximation of an orange housing an orange-juice stand. Somewhere I read that this is called *architecture parlante,* talking architecture, meaning a building that creates an image suggesting its function. In Maine I've seen tepees in which Indian moccasins are sold, although, I suppose, to properly conform to the definition, only tepees should be on sale there. I recall that Lewis Carroll wrote a poem about a mouse and shaped the words on the page to approximate a tail.

All this leads me to wonder, foolishly, about the possibility (for the aliterate who need a road sign with a hand on it to signify STOP) of publishing a novel in the shape of its theme:

The Old Man and the Sea as a marlin; *As I Lay Dying* as a coffin;
The Great Gatsby as a cocktail shaker (do people still own or use
silver cocktail shakers?), and so forth. Perhaps *Mr. Sammler's
Planet* in the shape of a fedora? An absurd idea, yet it might be
as interesting to depart from the dull, inevitable shape of the
book as it is to sell eggs from a counter lodged in the adobe side
of a giant chicken.

∽

Tools of the artist's trade are as personal as toothbrushes, as pens
and pencils are to writers. In Rosamond Bernier's memoir of her
friendships with Matisse, Picasso, and Miró, which I am reading
on the train coming back from New York, she says that Miró
liked to use 'old brushes, uneven, flattened out.' Such imperfect
instruments, he found, produced 'accidents' on his canvases. 'An
old brush has vitality . . . had lived . . . has had a life of its own.'

The black street artist Bill Traynor preferred to paint or
draw on dirty 'street cardboard,' even though his admirers gave
him clean white artists' boards. He liked to draw with stumps of
pencils. . . . It may well be true that the tool, the means, affects
the very nature of the product, the artistic end. In the case of
prose, advanced technology, like the personal computer, may
remove the character, the idiosyncrasy, of word choice and
sentences that flow out of pencils, sharpened or stubby, the shape
of a paragraph that once emanated from the frequent dippings
and scratchy sound of a quill pen.

In the same way, I worry that the presence of thesauruses on
most word-processing computer programs will begin to limit
the vocabulary of future literature. Instant technology, desktop
publishing, has now made it possible to produce a book as first
draft in place of a handwritten manuscript, which displayed all
the paths not taken, the rejected clauses, the scratched-out word.

Last spring Annie Dillard sent me a first draft of the book

she was working on, a 339-page novel, *The Living*. It had been *printed* and bound in full cloth. The accompanying letter assured me that she wanted to hear 'how best to shore up its faults,' the faults that 'a real grouch' might find. I took that to mean me, having so often had that appellation bestowed upon me. She went on to say that although she had put it into this format to spare me (and 'one other friend') the inconvenience of 'a sliding mound of papers,' 'I won't hesitate to take the whole thing apart and rewrite it, though—I plan to.'

I spent some time going through the first hundred pages, line by line, taking notes as I proceeded. Then Annie called and told me to forget the first seventy-five pages because she had already put them into another form. This stopped me in my already well-worn tracks, and I put The Book aside to work on my own recalcitrant novel. In August, *Harper's* arrived, and lo! there is a story by Annie Dillard, called 'A Trip to the Mountains,' the beginning of her new novel, *The Living*. Except for a number of small, verbal changes and some sentences either inserted or deleted, it is just as it was in my almost unique copy of The Book. In the first sentence there *is* an important change: 1873 has been set back to 1872.

I tore up my notes, stowed The Book on an out-of-the-way shelf in my study, together with the copy of the magazine, and tried to decide why Annie had sent it to me in the first place. True, when we met at a Literary Lions gathering in New York, and she told me she was working very hard on a new form, fiction, I offered to read it as she went along, if she wanted me to. But she did not wait for the comments she solicited, did not rewrite, in any real sense, and published the start of the book before I could comment, indeed when I had been warned off commenting until a new version arrived.

My theories about technology's effect on the manuscript may explain what went on. The apparent perfection of the

printed-and-bound first draft may be convincing evidence to the
writer of the perfection of the rough copy. Even a typescript
looks more finished than a handwritten page. A printout is even
better-looking. And a book . . . nothing more appears to need
doing. It is at the same time the first draft and the finished copy.

Did she print the two copies (was it truly only two copies?)
because she could not bear the delay between the first and the
second draft? Who knows? Perhaps even she doesn't. Goethe
once said: 'Know thyself? If I knew myself, I'd run away.'

ᔕ

With the arrival of one tardy review of *End Zone,* sent to me
by a friend, the critical views of the book have ceased. Its long
birthing is over. If it survives for any length of time out there in
the world in its maturity, it will be on its own. In some
notebook, ah, here it is, I have written down a sentence by
Georg Christoph Lichtenberg: 'I regard reviews as a kind of
infant's disease to which newborn books are subjected.'

ᔕ

Why is it that I feel very old when I am living on the Hill in
Washington? People here walk briskly. I lag. They chatter to
each other in high-pitched, self-assured voices in Provisions, the
coffee shop, their shining brown hair and perfect white teeth
lighting up the underground cave where the little tables and
chairs are set. Their high heels, their starched white shirts, their
lustrous shoes, their leather briefcases stowed away under their
chairs: they are all Congressional aides, or Library of Congress
trainees or Folger scholars or professors or White House
assistants or real estate agents or lobbyists. They shop at the
Eastern Market, across from our apartment house. They are
oblivious to the high price of asparagus or artichokes or
raspberries. They buy large bunches of flowers from the vendors

outside. They hold the leash of their well-groomed dogs with one hand, a French bread, newly ground coffee, and roses in the other. They greet each other on the street with happy little cries of recognition and pleasure.

They all seem acquainted, affectionate, part of a coterie alien to me in age and occupation. They live on a heady plain or better, on an upward slope of advancement and success, surrounded by public admiration of their status. Their self-esteem never seems to flag; their ambitions appear to be boundless.

The sight of all these happy settlers makes me homesick for Maine, where others of my generation have come to live, as have I, after the gritty, brash years of striving and pushing ahead and achievement are over. Down East on our peninsula, which I miss so badly, many of us have settled, in the real sense, for being old. Out of the race. Dimmer of wit. Shaky of foot. Over-age in grade. . . . I remember that in the Middle Ages extreme nostalgia and homesickness were treated as diseases. Clearly I am in need of a doctor.

ᔕᕝ

While I was in New York a few weeks ago I went to a publication party for Joe Caldwell's new novel, *The Uncle from Rome,* held at the beautiful East Side building that the American Academy in Rome owns. It was crowded with his friends, noisy with all the polite voices of his admirers. New York, like Washington, has its exclusive groups, literary clans, publishing cadres, arrivistes and clingers-on. Nothing makes me realize how passé, how far out and away I am in my present existence as much as attendance at one of these roundups, where the crowd (herd? no) all know each other and rejoice in their familiarity.

Of course, my ego is not beyond resurrection. Susan, a librarian at the University of Delaware and caretaker of Yaddo's books every August, shows me a rare-book catalogue in which my first novel is listed for $175, the second for $275. I have a short rush of pride before it is washed away by the usual river of anonymity. I face it: Those books, like me, are old hat; they disappeared almost thirty years ago after a single printing each. Their publisher, Doubleday, in its economic wisdom, trashed the remainders of tiny printings in its Garden City warehouse, thus accounting for their present scarcity.

∽

Bill Henderson calls to say he has received *Autobiography of an Elderly Woman,* admires it, and wants to republish it. I am delighted. I agree to write an afterword for it. I come away from the telephone feeling the elation of the owner of a stray mutt who will be groomed in order to be shown at the Westminster Dog Show.

∽

Last night we had dinner with our friend and neighbor Luree Miller, a writer on travel, travelers, and women explorers. We talked at length about community matters, and about the Bench.

At the other end of the Eastern Market is a small stone-and-grass area called Turtle Park. It houses a stone turtle on which two- and three-year-olds love to climb, and seats for adults who watch over their endeavors. At the side is a lovely wooden bench given to the park by Luree. Mounted on the bench is a small gold plaque, a testimonial to her husband, Bill Miller, who was born in Alaska, was a dedicated world traveler, served in the State Department, and died in his early sixties of cancer. Theirs was one of those marriages of which it is said, curiously, that they were made in heaven, which I suppose means that it was that rarity, a happy alliance formed on earth. Knowing the Millers made me renege a little on my cynical belief that a happy marriage is one about which one knows very little.

Four years ago, the bench was stolen by some unneighborly yuppies, who wanted it to furnish their living room in a unique way, I suspect. Led by Gary Hortch, the young man who owns Hayden's, the nearby liquor store (and who voluntarily keeps up the little park), people in the community searched for the bench and finally shamed the anonymous couple into returning it to an alley where it was found. It was promptly restored to its place in the park, this time chained to the ground.

Some late mornings I take my scone from the bakery and my cup of coffee from Bread and Chocolate and sit on the bench, thinking of the good marriage and the good life that this fine, useful seat signifies, and watching the children, oblivious to everything but the mountainous hump on the turtle's back, make their Everest climbs.

∾

We are packing our books in the apartment, slowly, getting ready to ship them to Sargentville should we be fortunate enough to sublet the apartment for most of the coming year. Out of one book I decide to keep falls a New Year's card sent to me a long time ago from New Directions and Anne and James Laughlin. It contains some lines by William Carlos Williams in a poem called 'January Morning,' and reminds me of the view from Jane's hospital room, looking down the Hudson from close to the George Washington Bridge, and across to the Palisades: 'Who knows the Palisades as I do / knows the river breaks east from them / above the city—but they continue south / —under the sky—to bear a crest of / little peering houses that brighten / with dawn behind the moody / water-loving giants of Manhattan.'

The peering little houses have long since given way to towering condominium buildings and other unsightly

developments. Williams would not recognize the Palisades of
his time and my childhood.

∽

A letter today from a friend on the West Coast who inquires if
(unexpectedly) enough good time has passed so that I no longer
am ridden by despair at having grown old. Someone else has
sent me a taping of John Leonard's review in which he says he
would like to shake me when he hears (reads) my complaints
about entering the end zone. Three elderly ladies in the last
month write to tell me I am wrong: their seventies (one is
eighty-four) are the best time of their life; one quotes the old
Robert Browning saw: 'Grow old along with me / The best is
yet to be.'

Today, seated at the counter at Bread and Chocolate for
late-afternoon coffee (theirs is the best on the Hill, in my view),
I try to dig deep into the aging shell of myself to find an answer.
Have I come to terms with old age? Does the fact that I have
survived for five years since first I began to record my anger at
aging reassure me that it is all not as bad as then I thought? Did I
exaggerate my melancholy? Was I unduly pessimistic?

No. Oddly, there are no changes in me, except perhaps for
one: In place of my fury of rebellion I have grown more patient
with what is. Privately, I still war against my elderly condition
of weakness, frailty, powerlessness, but now I accept its
inevitability. Publicly, I am quieter about everything. I've
abandoned the barricades for the veranda, the foxhole for the
hammock.

It is all a matter of disposition, perhaps even of character. I
am not happier with what I have than I was but more grateful
for what I have left. I continue to mourn my lost youth and my
active mature years with all their excitement, energy, and ability
to anticipate the future. I miss the pleasures I once felt at waking

to an unlimited day and the old contentment of going gentle
into a good, long, secure night.

∽

Dinner tonight with Rod MacLeish, who has left his commentary
job at National Public Radio and gone on to a better berth at
the Christian Science Monitor cable channel. Rod is a writer of
fiction, the only one I know who enjoys telling, in detail, the
plot of the new novel he is in the process of writing. I am
always surprised at his daring, I who am afraid to breathe a
word about anything I am doing for fear it will all be jinxed, or
that I will lose it in talk and have nothing left for the pen.

Rod is in good spirits tonight. His plot summation is
interspersed with assurances that the new book is hilarious. 'I am
really a humorist,' he tells us, although, to be honest, I have not
been able to spot any humor in his abstract.

His daughter Cynthia now lives in Alaska, where she has
married an Aleut, and is pregnant with their child. She loves her
life there and expects to settle permanently. She listens patiently
to my hymn of praise to life in Sargentville and then tells a
story about a Texan who brags to a Maine farmer: 'My spread
down there, well, it takes me a day to drive from one end of it
to the other.'

The Maine farmer replies: 'Ayeer, I had a truck like that
once.'

I haven't heard this before. I notice that as soon as you tell
someone you live in Maine, you are told a story of this sort. I
can laugh easily at her story, more easily than I could at her
father's novel.

∽

This week the fish stall in the Eastern Market across the street
was robbed, at two o'clock in the afternoon. Two teenagers

entered through the back door and coolly garnered five
thousand dollars, we're told. Reporters are more horrified at the
sum of money the little stall had in it than at the audacity of the
well-informed youngsters who knew exactly when to 'pull off'
the holdup and how much money there would be there at that
time. The two boys were, of course, both armed. I have heard it
said that few black youths over the age of twelve now appear
on the streets of D.C., or in school, without a gun. I hope this is
an exaggeration.

Three weeks ago, we are told by the owner of Clothes
Encounters, a used-apparel shop two blocks from our apartment
on Seventh Street, that a lady was robbed by a chap who got
out of a car, took her handbag, got back on the passenger side of
the car, and was driven away. . . . I am quite ready to leave this
city, and it is only February.

♫

Today I spent the morning at a local public radio station on the
campus of American University, doing an interview with Diane
Rehm. She is an intelligent woman who actually reads the
books she talks about, and then asks incisive and original
questions. It took an hour, she asked about my life, career, and
End Zone. Then she told me she approved of my contrary
opinions on photography (I dislike it because I believe most
amateurs use it in place of committing persons and places to
memory; the view goes from lens to film without passing
through the brain of the picture-taker). On the day of her
wedding, she said, the hired photographer failed to appear. She
was distraught at the time, but now she celebrates his absence,
for she is left with her choice memories rather than a set of
posed and artificial pictures.

♫

Late yesterday afternoon: Confused by the number of people walking, rushing, crossing, standing, all on our corner of Seventh Street, I froze where I stood, wondering, for the moment, which way to go. This happens to me often in crowds, as though every possible path were closed to me by too many people already occupying them.

Then Irving, the bake shop owner, came out of the Eastern Market carrying a large bag. I watched him as he crossed to the schoolyard, opened his sack, and threw out handfuls of crusts. Suddenly, and in great numbers, a flock of sea gulls arrived to claim the bread. I decided they must be accustomed to his being there every day, so they leave the Potomac River and come inland (like the Moody Beach gulls who used to eat their dinner at McDonald's on Route 1) to feast on the basketball court of Hine Junior High School.

Political affairs in Washington, D.C., seem more heated, more immediate, more urgent, than when we are in Maine, as if important things were happening down the street, across the park, in the buildings we see from our windows. Even if the candidates now vying for public office are politicking in New Hampshire or Texas, it appears to us nonrepresented residents in the capital that they are in our front yard.

I am stunned at the amount of 'dirt' about the private lives, the sexual peccadilloes and twenty-years-ago drug parties, that is the conversational nourishment of every gathering and meal in D.C. Sybil suggests we think about writing an op-ed piece for the *Post* about the curious fact that the really good senators and governors, those who accomplish a great deal in their official positions, are often the ones whose private lives bear the least scrutiny: Edward Kennedy, Governor Bill Clinton, Franklin Delano Roosevelt.

⟡

February 20: I am struck by a terrible blow of homesickness for
the Cove, for the house, for Sargentville, for Maine. Sybil tries
to counter it by challenging me to a game of gin rummy. I lose
badly. We go out to a late dinner with old friends Tori Hill and
Elizabeth Carl. We talk about the improvements to the Main
Reading Room at the Library of Congress, which Tori heads,
and life at the Episcopal church in which Elizabeth serves as
curate. Even their good talk and company, and excellent
Vietnamese food at the Queen Bee in Arlington, do not help.

⟡

I've been wondering about the origin of the clause 'applauding
with one hand.' The image is evocative—and mysterious. Does
it mean halfhearted approval? Or soundless praise? I seem to
recall that it is Quaker in origin. When I get home, I shall have
to ask Grace Perkinson, one of the few Quakers I know.

⟡

In the last month I have published two pieces on Willa Cather, a
long review in the *Chicago Tribune* of the three Library of
America volumes published in the last few years (including
almost all her work), and a longish review in the *Village Voice*
of Hermione Lee's excellent study of Cather's writing, now
available in paper. Soon I will be the only living critic of Cather
who has not produced a book of her own, only two
insignificant journal articles. . . . Hermione Lee writes to me
from England, urging me to write the book I have been
planning for so long. But I doubt it will ever come about. Too
many good studies have been published since I stopped working
on mine and turned to fiction and memoir. Another deplorable
result of entering the end zone of one's life is that projects that

once were vital and promising now seem too much, too late, too untoward, too unlikely.

∽

Story I will probably never write, but one that seemed possible at two o'clock this morning: Two poets, young men, live together. The more talented of the two dies at an early age, of AIDS, without publishing any of his work. The other, desperate for recognition, publishes his dead friend's poems under his own name. The book appears, highly praised, in the Yale Younger Poets series, and the survivor wins the Pulitzer Prize for poetry with this, his first book. But, with this volume, he uses up all his friend's work. Try as he might, in the next two years, he finds he cannot write poetry as good. Cold-bloodedly, not in despair, but determined to ensure his own immortality, and knowing the renown guaranteed to poets who die young by their own hand, he takes his life.

∽

I need to prepare a talk for the Women's National Democratic Club, to deliver on Tuesday of this week. It has to be something I've never said before because Sybil is planning to attend and she has, perforce, heard all the other speeches I have given. In this regard, she is a good influence; for fear of boring her, I am impelled to change the contents every time.

Yesterday I saw something in the book news of the *New York Times* that interested me, that might work if I used it to introduce what I have been thinking about for some time: the lack of a firm distinction between fiction and nonfiction. For me, fiction always has a strong component of fact, and fact, used successfully in fiction, extends and legitimizes the imaginary.

The *Times* reports a unique phenomenon. In one week, a book has moved from the nonfiction to the fiction best-seller list. How can this be? Well, it seems that a university press had reprinted what it thought was a memoir of the childhood of an orphaned American Indian named Forest Carter. A first (and only) book, it did very well, and became a best-seller. But it turns out that Forest Carter is not the autobiographical author but instead an American white supremacist named Asa Carter, and *not* an orphan, who died in 1979. The title on the reprint, *The Education of Little Tree,* was followed by the words 'a true story.' The cover will be remade and those words removed.

Meanwhile the *Times* has accommodatingly switched the book from its best-seller nonfiction list.

March

*I like trees because they seem more
resigned to the way they have to live
than other things do.*
　　　　　　　—Willa Cather

A chap in Iowa City, Paul Mandelbaum, has a curious project in hand. He is collecting juvenilia from contemporary writers. In fact, he wants the first thing they have ever written, if they have a copy of it. He asks me to contribute. I think back to my terrible first story which I entered in a contest held every year (back in the early 1930s, that is) for New York City public high school seniors.

Why did I write it? I remember that I needed some concrete evidence of my suitability to enter college, having been turned down by all the New York City colleges because I had failed the Civics Regents examination, the English 4 Regents, and one other whose subject I forget. So I thought if I could win the contest, I could go back to the rejecters, tell them about the award, and ask for some reconsideration. Maybe.

I should make a full public confession. I failed so many Regents exams because Civics, English, and the other class I can't remember all met in the afternoon. Too often I was no longer in school by then, having signed myself out of the station at noon, at a door for which I was a warden. In my final high school years I was enamored of the theater, regularly read *Variety,* the so-called Bible of the legitimate stage, learned where shows were rehearsing, and slipped into the side doors of those theaters after I had sprung myself from school, 'played hooky' as we used to say.

I failed the tests because I hadn't read the books they were based on—simple as that. They were part of statewide assignments. I recall trying to read *The Mill on the Floss* on my own without success but having no trouble at all with *Dr. Martino and Other Stories* by William Faulkner that an aunt gave me, a first edition because it had just been published. I still have that copy.

Writing a short story involved no assignments and no attendance. So I was able to do that. To my amazement, I won the contest. Think how bad the other stories must have been when you read what I can remember of the plot of mine. An old man is tired of life. I think I sketched in his life history but I no longer remember it. He has settled his affairs, plowed under his vegetable and flower garden, locked the door to his cottage, and walked to a wharf where he intends to end it all (certainly I must have used that fine old cliché). Seated there he finds a young child, her feet dangling toward the water. He sits beside her and tries to talk to her but she does not respond, indeed, does not appear to be listening. Then she signs to him and he realizes she is 'deaf and dumb.' I *do* remember using that now-outmoded phrase, which I knew because I had a second cousin in that condition. He was a linotyper for the *Herald Tribune.*

Wait. There is still more of this stuff. She takes his hand, they leave the wharf, she leads him on a path toward her house. On the way, she picks a wild daisy and gives it to him. The old man goes home, unlocks his door, puts the daisy in a glass of water, and then gets out a tiller to prepare his flower garden.

Terrible. Soupy. Boring. I don't know if it was well

written—I cannot think so. Even though I promised Mr.
Mandelbaum I would look for the manuscript, I cannot bring
myself to. I cannot believe that publishing something as bad as
this has any value at all, unless it would prove to a young,
would-be writer that a mediocre start might result in a halfway
decent writer. . . . I send my regrets to Paul Mandelbaum.

~

Picasso: 'To copy others is necessary, but to copy oneself is
pathetic.'

~

Yesterday I encountered an acquaintance in the bank in
Washington:

'You look well,' he said to me.

I replied: 'So do you.' What else does one say to a bald old
man full of wrinkles but very sun-tanned.

'I've been in Florida.' Then he laughed. 'At my age—I'm
almost eighty—you no longer go there to find the Fountain of
Youth.'

I tell him about a Rumanian gerontologist I read about, Ana
Aslam, whose obituary I had just read. She died in Budapest at
the age of ninety, and was the head of an institute that offered a
treatment called Gerovitae. There, injections were given of a
substance she invented, to such notables as Charles de Gaulle,
Nikita Khrushchev, Indira Gandhi, Marshal Tito, Konrad
Adenauer, and the film stars Lillian Gish and Marlene Dietrich.
Aslam must also have given it to herself, for it was reported that
at her death she looked thirty years younger.

When the drug was analyzed in this country it was shown to
be compounded of procaine, an antidepressant, and a painkiller,
nothing more. Its recipients may have felt very good, cheerful,
even ebullient, but were not necessarily rendered any younger.

True, Adenauer died at ninety-one, Tito at eighty-nine,
de Gaulle at eighty. Gandhi was assassinated, so we do not know
how effective the treatment might have been for her. 'You're as
young as you feel' might have been the operative cliché for
Aslam's Institute.

I think Lillian Gish, now in her nineties, is still alive. I know
Marlene Dietrich, now ninety, lives in seclusion. Since she broke
one of her fabled legs falling from the stage into the orchestra
pit, she has become hermitic. She does not wish to have her old
age witnessed by a public that will, in this way, forever
remember her as an extraordinarily beautiful young woman.

I wonder: If one prolongs one's youthful good looks beyond
a reasonable age, does one have time to grow slowly accustomed
to having lost them?

꙳

Dwarf-tossing, a heartless game played in bars in the South, in
which midgets are thrown high in the air and caught as one
would a ball, is now paralleled by another inhuman
phenomenon called 'Granny-dumping.' Its causes are senility,
extreme old age, desperately poor physical condition, and the
exigencies of a bad economy. This week in San Francisco some
person brought an elderly woman in a wheelchair to the
entrance of a hospital emergency room and left her there.
Pinned to her housecoat was a note: 'Please take care of her.' In
one county of California, physicians report eight such
abandonments a week. They occur most frequently in states
with large retirement communities: Florida, Texas, and
California.

Every day reading the news reminds me of what I often try
to forget, the terrible indignity to which old age is subjected.
Once it was almost irrelevant to me, a distant and unimaginable
state of being. Now it is the final condition in which some of us

are destined to live. Such stories, to which in my youth I might
have been indifferent, now seem pertinent to the general
predicaments of an aging society.

〰

My sister's affliction, agoraphobia, is the subject of an article on
the medical page of the *Times*. A psychiatrist, Arthur B. Hardy,
has given the disease a new, euphemistic name. He calls it
Territorial Apprehension. Such retitling is rife in this age of too
much talk and a reluctance to call things by their harshly
indicative names.

〰

At the flea market last Sunday I acquired a wonderful, doubly
useful instrument, a cane with a steel point at its end and a
three-sided leather collapsible seat attached to the shaft. Near the
top it has a gold band on which is engraved 'Heidelberg.' I
intend it to use it to keep me from slipping on the ice next
winter when I begin my permanent, year-round residency in
Sargentville, and to sit on when I grow too weary to walk any
further.

〰

Useful new (for me) word: 'vealy'—meaning immature, as in
the condition of veal in comparison to beef (mature).

〰

Maya, my small (vealy?), solemn, beautiful granddaughter came
to visit yesterday and stayed to lunch. She was accompanied by
her mother, of course, and her omnipresent soiled white blanket.
She keeps it in her sight and resorts to it whenever she feels the
need for comfort.

Strangely enough, I remember my own baby blanket. It is

my earliest memory, so I must have been about four. I don't
remember its color (by that time it may have lost whatever
color it once had) but I do know it had a tattered white satin
binding and a memorable odor, a sweet, sweaty smell that, I
now theorize, must have reminded me of my mother's breasts,
milky, ample flesh, damp and hot with the temperature of her
body.

I am touched by the sight of Maya and her comforter. There
is a continuity between generations, so strong that something
like the memory and possession of such objects may hold
together whole generations of grandmothers, mothers, and
granddaughters and grandsons. Early today, during Morning
Prayer, I recite to myself a short intercessionary prayer, called a
suffrage, for Maya, that she grow to be as intelligent as she
now is beautiful, and that I be around, at least at the start, to
witness it.

ᔕ

At the meat counter in the Eastern Market, I hear a well-dressed
young woman tell a well-dressed young man (who smelled
pleasantly of after-shave lotion) about a new restaurant at which
she had dined the night before. 'The waiters danced attendance
upon us,' she reported, a phrase I have not heard since I was a
girl. It does conjure up a lovely, airy vision of the twenties, a
sentence Scott Fitzgerald might have used it to describe Tom
Buchanan's behavior when he was wooing Daisy.

ᔕ

A large gathering of sea gulls lights, for a moment, in the tall
grasses growing on the roof of the garage outside the
living-room window. Once again I am reminded of how little I
know about their habits and their lives. E. B. White knew about
geese. He had raised a few, and then gave them up. In *The Points*

of My Compass he writes: 'I have always envied a goose its look of deep, superior wisdom. I miss the cordiality of geese.'

An acquaintance, a woman named Bunnie, came into the bookstore in Maine last fall. She happens to raise goats near Lubec in Maine, but she too is fond of geese and assured us that they are not silly or foolish.

'Indeed the goose is a most intelligent fowl,' she assured us. Oh well, gone is another useful simile.

Wednesday. Noon Mass at St. James. A treat for someone like me who rarely can find a weekday Mass in Maine. I walk the few blocks to the church, passing a number of older persons who say hi or good morning and smile the wide, white grin that belongs only to black faces.

Sybil and I agree that one virtue of living in this city (one of the few) is that the population is not homogenized. In Maine we miss seeing and talking to black friends and acquaintances— David Tilghman, Reggie Wilson, Jerome the detective, Mary at the Market Lunch, Melvin at the Market chicken counter, Debbie our radio-broadcasting friend, the poet Ethelbert—all the welcome faces of color that enliven the whiteness of the Hill's citizenry and allow us to have a glimpse into their rich culture.

At St. James there is no one but me and the elderly, rotund retired priest, Father Aldrich. No one arrives to serve him, so I move to the front pew to say the responses. I love this old fellow. Goodness shines from his faded blue eyes; his hands and head shake with what seems to be a genuine passion for what he is saying, for the holy act he is performing. Mass takes a little more than half an hour, but it is somehow a pure time—the cold, empty church, the totally absorbed celebrant, the quiet and dusty air of prayer, time before and after the Mass to myself.

He says: 'The Lord be with you.' And I respond: 'And with thy spirit.' And somehow, in this simple exchange, we reach a kind of communion unlike any other. Call it spiritual. Call it human.

∽

Tonight we experience another advantage to living here: hearing wonderful chamber music free under the auspices of the Library of Congress. Because of continuing repairs to the Coolidge Auditorium in the library's main building, the concerts have been moved to the National Academy of Sciences. The acoustics are very good, the program excellent, although I have trouble understanding the difficult Elliott Carter piece. The new second violinist is as expert as his fellows.

Afterwards we are hungry and drive around downtown looking for a place to have a sandwich. Nothing is open. But one of the streets is full of miniskirted ladies of the night. The recession must have affected their trade. After a while two of them hail a cab and are driven away. Others are still there when we leave, waiting for customers.

∽

After Joe Caldwell's reading from his new novel, *The Uncle from Rome,* at Lambda Rising bookstore, we have dinner with him, and two of his admirers, our friends Jeff Campbell and Gene Berry (who writes fine letters to literary people, so intriguing that they willingly sign the books he then sends them). During a good Vietnamese dinner, Joe tells two good stories:

An admirer rushes up to Franz Kafka (or substitute the name of any great writer little read in his time) and says:

'I am honored to meet you. I have bought all your books.'

Kafka replies: 'Oh, you're the one.'

I tell the gathering the story about surgeon/writer Richard Selzer in this book, and Joe says he knows another one. Seems that Richard, in his cups one evening at Yaddo, promised the diners at the table a free appendectomy should they require it. Someone said he would take him up on it—he'd been having a bit of trouble in that region recently.

'Would you really do it for free?' he asked Dr. Selzer.

'Oh yes,' he said. 'But you'll have to promise to hold very still.'

༄

My bathroom at the apartment has two mirrors—two too many, as I see it—in which I can observe my failing face. I do not look too often but still, the memory of what I now look like follows me out of the bathroom and remains with me without the evidence of further glances in the mirror.

Later this evening I pick up a copy of *TV Guide* and discover how many famous people ('almost all the people on stage, screen, and TV,' the magazine says) have plastic surgery on their faces, necks, and breasts. Cybill Shepherd says: 'I'm aging. I look in the mirror and I see how my face has changed. I see the wrinkles. I know what I used to look like and what I look like now.' She is forty-two. She believes her career depends on plastic surgery.

Joan Rivers, a TV comic, says every woman on TV who is over twenty-five has had something or other done to her: 'A little cheekbone implantation or tummy tuck, a butt tuck, or liposuction around the chin.' She is fifty-eight, has had her face lifted, her nose thinned, and her thighs 'vacuumed.'

When these women, and all the others who have had plastic surgery, look in the mirror after the additions and subtractions have been done, what do they see? The new, artificial, bland, almost blank skin, the plastic, unaccustomed shapes and surfaces. Do they wonder: Where am I?

In a novel, *The Missing Person,* I thought about these matters, about a star of 'the silver screen,' as they used to call it, who is destroyed by the realization that there is nothing to her but her shadow-thin, celluloid image that moviegoers adore, no *person* there who is loved and loves. This novel takes place in the last year of silence and the first years of sound in motion pictures, when the star who could not sing was 'dubbed' (an 'absence' of voice) and often had a substitute in her place on the set called a stand-in.

Now the image itself is modified. The changed woman may well ask of her own changed face: 'Who is it?' For inner identity and outer visage is all we have. We are not a name, given, first, and then often changed in marriage, not a photograph, which belongs not to us but to the eye of the taker, not our reputation, which is always subject to alteration without notice. We are the person that is our bodies and the entity we call our souls (name it psyche or whatever else you wish). These are both affected by the forces of aging and time, but they are all we have of ourselves.

⌒

Our former customer and friend Reggie Wilson has his sixtieth birthday on the same day his new book appears. This is Black History Month as well, so there is a party for it, and for him, at the Southwest Public Library. His wife, Arlene, calls to invite us.

The Wilsons' is one of those biracial marriages that prove how mistaken is society's distaste for miscegenation. These two are talented, energetic, attractive people. Looking at them one could not possibly guess their ages; somehow this very good alliance has kept them both youthful-looking and productive. The audience for the program of recitations from black writers and songs is a mixture of races, with blacks in the great majority. Such a condition is healthy, because it makes me realize once again what it feels like to be part of a minority. Together, we sing a song written by James Weldon Johnson with music by his wife, J. Rosamond Johnson: 'Lift Ev'ry Voice,' which Sybil has been told is now sung at many black gatherings in the area, even perhaps around the nation.

Afterwards we eat well from a buffet table. There is no spread of food in the capital as good as one in which the cooking is done by the black community. Ridgewell's, the caterer of choice for glitzy events here, may be fancier, but it is not better.

~

My daughter Elizabeth Cale sends me an expert piece of needlepoint to match the one I already have framed on the wall of my study in Maine. It records my 'later books.' She is very skilled at this intricate work, doing it as the spirit moves her, that is, without a plan. She proceeds freehandedly to design and then embellish the canvas.

In this sense, her needlepoints are representative of her way of life. Unlike the rest of the family, she lives without a set pattern. She moves wherever her fancy takes her, frequently, has never married, has no dependents except for her eleven-year-old Toyota, which has been driven almost one hundred thousand miles, and for which she has a maternal affection.

Elizabeth's memory is perfect; she recalls everything about her more than forty years of life. Her personality is warm and childlike. Sports are her consuming interest and she knows more about baseball (the Yankees have been her team since she was a small girl) and football (the New York Giants) than most men I

have met. She swims laps, jogs, cross-country-skies, and looks
ten years younger than she is. When an enthusiasm takes hold of
her, even briefly, she immerses herself in it, becomes an
authority, and never entirely abandons it, because her memory
will not let anything go. Rock and roll, contemporary
American art, hockey, the Civil War—she knows a great deal
about all these subjects.

Once she told me that she remembers the exact moment
when she became enamored of baseball. She was eleven, and
riding in the back of our old Ford station wagon. I was listening
to the seventh game of the 1960 World Series on the car radio.
The Yankees, lordly champions for many years, and the
underdog Pittsburgh Pirates were playing. It was the ninth
inning, the score was tied, no one on base, two men out. Bill
Mazeroski was at bat with three balls and two strikes against
him. Ralph Terry pitched to him (she says she doesn't remember
what kind of a pitch it was), Mazeroski hit a home run, and the
game, and the series, were over. The underrated Pirates had
won.

Elizabeth asked me what it was all about. Too impatient to
review the rules and the progress of that game (now, she says,
regarded as one of the greatest of all baseball games), I said:

'You can read about it in the *New York Times* tomorrow.'

She says she did, and from then on became addicted to
baseball, and has never been cured. She is impatient for opening
day, and thinks of the end of the season as the beginning of a
long drought, although she switches to football and the Giants
for the interim.

She finds genuine irony in this story, because it seems that I,
an indifferent and occasional sports fan (I think in those days I
listened only to the final games of the World Series, for the
drama involved, and could not remember from year to year

who had won), should be inadvertently responsible for her great passion.

⟡

Every now and then one meets someone who is a remainder (as we say in the book trade) from the sixties, a mature person who still carries with him a young aura of those idealistic years. John Kidner, our many-time mover, is such a man. In profile he is the image of Doonesbury, the cartoon character who is another sixties survivor. John has tried hard to become like the rest of us, but somehow his life is still determined by free-spirited accidents and the unworldly economics of his youth.

Three years ago, in April, he brought our belongings from Washington to Maine in an old Mercedes truck that drove blindly into our driveway and promptly sank axle-deep into mud—it was that season. A year later he overloaded thousands of books from our Washington bookstore into another Mercedes van, which proceeded to blow two tires, serially, on its way up, a situation that could not be easily or quickly remedied because Maine is profoundly indifferent to tires that fit a Mercedes. Finally the battered vehicle limped into the driveway of the bookstore at six miles an hour, having been sighted all the way from Blue Hill by our acquaintances and prospective customers.

Tonight we talk to John again, wondering if he still has the courage to take much of the contents of this apartment to Maine. Because he is a trustworthy and charming fellow, we have faith in him, remembering that he used to refer to his company as the Manly Movers, a name as indicative of him and his help as, I assume, was the name of the company of women movers in New York City who called themselves the Mother Truckers.

He assures us he now has new American-made vans, that he
no longer uses the alliterative appellation, and that he figures his
estimates on a computer.

We sit in our half-packed-up living room and talk of our
lives and fortunes. He tells us about his father, who was a
military man, which accounts for John's conscientious objections
to Vietnam, he believes. He has survived all his old anger and
now has a good relationship with him. But John's marriage has
collapsed, a state he attributes to his time-consuming efforts for
the moving business. He is a gentle, warm-hearted man who
reminds me of Elizabeth Cale: they both left the mainstream of
society in their youth and, to an extent, are still living in the
meanders.

∽

From home (that is, Maine) comes word that a sixty-one-year-
old woman who now lives near Portland has decided to try to
reverse the poor economy in the state. She has opened a bank,
after two of the state's major banks failed. Elizabeth Noyce's
ex-husband, Robert, was the co-inventor of the integrated
circuit chip, the basis of the modern computer. She has a fortune
of more than one hundred million dollars, and what she calls, in
a newspaper interview, 'disposable income.' Her needs, she says,
are modest. 'I don't like a lot of frills. I don't like to travel. I'd
much rather be home raking the leaves and sawing off extra
branches from spruce trees.'

Mrs. Noyce, a native of Massachusetts, has given the state
millions of dollars before—to hospitals, museums, and other
nonprofit organizations, more money than any other individual
in Maine's history. But now she is worried about the depressed
economy, so the new bank, which is doing very well at the
moment, is intended to demonstrate her confidence in the state's
future.

I find this wonderfully heartening. I wonder if it is the result of a new warming of her heart as she settled permanently into the little fishing village of Bremen, which has less than seven hundred inhabitants and sits quietly on Muscongus Bay, or whether she has always been a generous woman. I see her there, piling her leaves into the compost heap, clearing the brush, walking to the small village store to pick up the local paper and her groceries, determined that henceforth she will be unburdened by great wealth, indeed by everything but the milk, bread, and tea in the paper sack she is carrying.

I get lost in another fantasy: Settled permanently into the little village of Sargentville, which sits quietly on Billings Cove and Eggemoggin Reach, inhabited by less than three hundred persons, I put into the local bank whatever excess income I have, much as Katherine Schaff did in New Jersey. When I die, it is discovered that my entire fortune (?) has been left to purchase all the now-available land on the Reach to be used for low-income housing, built by Habitat for Humanity, one house to an acre, the shore of said property to be, not private, but made available to every hiker, sailor, clammer, fisherman, and swimmer who wishes to use it. Up to the high-water mark.

✑

March 6, Michelangelo's birthday, 517 years ago. This year, this Friday, the day will be remembered because of a dire technological threat. It is feared that a virus, maliciously programmed into recent software, will wipe out the contents of the hard disks of thousands of computers all over the world.

Like every one else, I worry. I ask computer-wise persons I know what I should do. Change the date on your disk. Leave the computer on all day. No, unplug everything. Don't turn it on. In the end I decide to stay far away from the machine (am I afraid it is contagious?), and write by pen on white lined paper on my clipboard, feeling that any sort of contact with the PC, even with it turned off, would activate the evil invader. Of course, nothing very much happened to anyone. For the most part, it was a false alarm. The effective little monsters went on operating as efficiently as ever.

Secretly, I fantasized about the prospect of wipeout. To have all that stored data destroyed on a predicted day, at a single stroke, appealed to my sense of the fitness of things. Any breakdown of my IBM clone (after, of course, I have it all backed up and printed out), any failure of this incomprehensible contraption, in contrast to the old reliability of the manual typewriter, or the #2 lead pencil, or the Sheaffer fountain pen, pleases me.

I liked to imagine that my computer, and millions of others, had contracted a fatal illness, a deadly virus for which there was no cure. If the virus was catching, it might have infected elaborately programmed toaster ovens, keyboard touch telephones and their answering machines, five-disk CD players, and preset VCRs, all of which I have still to master.

With impunity, should all this happen, I will go back happily to making toast in the oven, getting my party on the telephone by jiggling the handle and summoning up a human voice, playing my old, still serviceable 78-rpm records with a reed needle on a wind-up Victrola, and, with a flourish, writing with a quill pen.

ᗢ

'Toute heure blesse l'homme, la domain letal.' 'Every hour wounds a man; the last one kills.' I try to find the source of this aphorism, without success.

ᗢ

Sybil has returned from 'doing' a New York book fair. She
wanted to stay within a short distance of the Greenwich Village
school where the fair is held, so she took Helen Yglesias's advice
and reserved a room at the Markle Residence on West 13th
Street.

It turned out to be a wonderful choice, reminiscent of those
old-time residences that used to be common in the city, a place
for single young women or older women to reside, protected
from the lascivious approaches of urban gentlemen. This one is
for senior citizens, young businesswomen, and graduate and
undergraduate students. It is possible to live here permanently,
with two meals a day, for a very moderate sum, or, on occasion,
to have a room with meals as a transient. No drugs or alcohol
are permitted, on pain of eviction, and no gentlemen visitors are
allowed in the rooms.

Sybil returned from her two-night stay somewhat chastened.

It seems to have happened the first morning when she came
down to a sumptuous breakfast feast. 'Everything you can think
of that might be offered at that meal,' she said. She filled her
plate, took her tray to a table in the corner of the room, and
settled down with the fresh *New York Times* she had gone out
of the residence to buy. She said she felt in a fine mood,
privileged to be able to read the paper the morning it was
published instead of having the usual Sargentville delay.

Still gloating about her triumph over distance and late
delivery, she was tapped on the shoulder. A waitress said: 'I'm
sorry, but newspaper reading at breakfast is not permitted.'
Without asking the reason, Sybil hastily, guiltily, stowed the
offending paper under her chair and continued to eat her
enormous, solitary breakfast.

We thought about this stern injunction and decided it must
have had to do with the threat of newsprint to the white

tablecloth. But this did not seem to console her. She said she felt
like a freshman early in her first semester at college.

'I flunked breakfast,' she said.

∽

Baby Doe Tabor: Sandy Kirschenbaum, my friend who founded
and edited *Fine Print* (now, sadly, no longer being published), is
in Leadville, Colorado, for a conference. She sends me a
postcard about the legendary lady, the same one who is the
heroine of the opera *The Legend of Baby Doe.* There is a pouting,
golden-curly-haired picture of her, clearly a most beautiful
woman, who closely resembles the singer Madonna.

The story on the face of the card is this:

Baby Doe had married and divorced many times by the time
she was twenty-five. She met a Colorado silver baron named
Horace Tabor, twenty-four years her senior. He divorced his
wife and married Baby Doe, who was considered a
'gold-digger,' creating a great scandal in Leadville and
Washington, D.C., where they lived. Scorned by society, they
nonetheless lived an extravagant and happy life with each other,
until Horace's fortunes were wiped out in the Silver Panic of
1893.

To everyone's amazement, Baby Doe stood by her ruined
husband and sold her lavish jewels to pay his debts. They had
two daughters. Six years later he died, and it was said that all he
had to leave her was the worthless Matchless mine in Leadville.
Legend has it that on his deathbed he made her promise to hold
on to it at all costs. Fact was, *True Confessions* magazine
fabricated that detail.

But fact again: After his death, Baby Doe went to live in the
manager's shack at the mine, and stayed there for thirty-five
years, living in rags as a recluse. The children grew up and ran
away as soon as they could. One of them was scalded to death in

the red-light district of Chicago at the age of thirty-five. Baby
Doe stayed at the mine until her death in 1935.

She had become a poverty-stricken 'hag,' the story goes.
Hers is a classic tale of rags to riches to rags, from poverty to
great heights and then into the lowest depths, a role Lillian Gish
(I remember *Greed* in the silent days) might have played. Sandy
thinks it would make a wonderful movie. We ought to write
the script and persuade Madonna to play Baby Doe.

~

Mexico, for two weeks: Last year I did not visit the Yucatán
ruins and the Kailuum campgrounds because Sybil was
unwilling to make the trip, and I was unwilling to make the trip
without her. This year, once again, she hesitates to go. Her
reasons are various. Primarily, she distrusts the food, having
once been ill there, and later having witnessed the long and
miserable case of hepatitis that our friend Tori Hill brought
back from the campground.

Ted Nowick, Bob Taylor, and I meet in Washington. Sybil
drives us to Dulles Airport, says goodbye with no regret,
clearly, and heads back to her beloved city. The plane is full of
snowbirds, as they are termed with some derision in central
Maine, where leaving the state for the South even for a short
time in the winter is regarded as an act of moral weakness.

Three hours later we are in the shiny, refurbished,
much-expanded Cancún airport. We obtain our rented car and
head inland toward Chichén Itzá, determined to avoid at all
costs the ugly and crowded Miami-on-the-Caribbean that
Cancún has become. It is pleasant to step out of the Hertz office
into the warm, dry, summer air of peninsular Mexico, after the
raw winter air we have left behind. It is the 19th of March.

We plan to spend the night in the little city of Valladolid,
close to Chichén. One of the few hotels in this bustling town

has two rooms reserved for us, but when we arrive only one is 'ready,' so we three camp in it, tired from the long day of flying and driving. I am undone by the usual hassles of travel: early rising, rush for the plane, inedible food, and arrival at a place unprepared to receive us. It is a two-hundred-year-old hotel, or at least it is that old in parts. The newer additions have unartfully been made to resemble the old arches and stones. In Mexico I have learned a lesson that one should not ever look closely at what pretends to be original. ('Authentic reproduction'?)

In the early evening we walk about the town plaza to find the restaurant recommended to us as the best. Ted spots a dark, dirt-floored shop inhabited by a sandal-maker. His products have an elaborate name—*alpargatas en campañas*—and he says he can have them, made to order for Ted's special needs, by tomorrow. They are interesting sandals: the straps are of very heavy leather and the soles are thick and unbending, made of pieces of rubber car tire. I wonder if they will be comfortable.

We are all very hungry, but it is so early that we are the only customers at the restaurant. It cannot be said that we are dining in solitary splendor, because we elect to sit at the front of the place, which is open to the busiest street in Valladolid. There is no emission control in Mexico, and most of the vehicles on the streets are old. We are at the mercy of the loud noises of very decrepit cars and their exhaust. But the food is good.

It is still early, so we sit in the plaza to watch the evening social life. Near us is a gathering of high school boys in their brown uniforms, their books in bags on their backs, acting foolishly for the high school girls clustered across the path. The boys laugh among themselves, their eyes always on the girls. Old men in spanking-clean, long white shirts—called *guayaberas*—and heavy black serge trousers (despite the heat) form small circles farther down the walk, their dark, expressive faces turned to each other in the privacy of their talk, nodding and smiling to each other. Ladies in their *huipils,* white embroidered dresses with wide bands of petticoat showing beneath, pull along little children in plastic sandals, talking as they walk. The square is a hive of conversation. Groups move about but never seem to intercept each other. Ted, Bob, and I are the only ones sitting still, watching, learning. . . .

Next morning I wake at six and go out to explore the early-day life of the plaza. I sit in an open-air restaurant, drink *café con leche,* and eat a sweet roll. I watch men at the tables around me eat huge breakfasts and, when pickup trucks stop in front, pile into the open flat beds at the back, ten workers to a truck, more than appears safe to me.

A stream of tricycles with oversized wheels come by, pedaled by young men, their wives riding in little rear cars, their children astride the single front wheel. The fathers' white shirts and the mothers' white dresses gleam in the sunlight. Little kindergarten-aged *niños* walk through the café, now carrying their book bags, their straight black hair cut squarely around their broad little heads. The girls come a little later, holding hands, their long black hair and coal-black eyes shining.

My breakfast over, I go back to the hotel to pack for the short trip to Chichén Itzá.

But it turns out to take most of the day, because we elect to make two good detours. Bob sees a photograph in a *National Geographic* of the beautiful, vast Dzitnup cenote (well). Cenotes and underground springs that feed wells have for centuries been essential to Mayan life, since there are no surface waters. We pay our pesos and make the long climb down the winding, steep, damp stone steps, I clinging both to the rope provided and Ted's arm. We are in the Mayan version of a Gothic cathedral, at the bottom of which are the pure blue-green waters of the well. Stalactites of tree roots hang from the ceiling, almost reaching

the water, and slim black fish swim near the edge of the water.
The silence is absolute, broken only by the tiny flicker of their
tails. We are alone, fortunately, for half an hour. The old
mysteries, the worshipful spirit of long-gone Mayans who threw
jade objects (and, it is claimed, human sacrifices) into these
waters to propitiate the rain god Chac-mool, seem to be with us.

We climb back up the hazardous way. In the parking lot
there is another car, full of Americans carrying bathing suits.
They have come to swim in the holy waters. I feel resentful at
their lack of reverence and, at the same time, regretful that I did
not know this was permitted.

Then, on the map, we see a black triangle signifying a ruin
on the way to Chichén. We cannot find the road to it, so we
stop in a small village to ask a workman if he knows where
Balankanche is. He grins, the wide, gracious Mayan smile, and
says yes, he will lead us there. How far? Oh, not far, about half
a kilometer. Okay, we'll go. He is joined by a friend who has
been working on a building with him.

We start out on a broad plain made of red dirt with
outcroppings of limestone. It narrows to a footpath and then
disappears into a tangle of unmarked underbrush and thorned
brambles. We climb steadily. I hold Ted's arm, stopping often to
catch my breath. After more than an hour of hard climbing, we
arrive at what appears to be the top of the hill, although it is so
overgrown that I cannot be sure. Here and there in the brush we
see small grey stones; nowhere is there evidence of a structure.

Sí, Pedro says, there was more here before, but gringos came
in a big car and took away some carved stones to give to the
museo. They said they would return to start uncovering the
mound, but never did. I wonder: Did the historic stones, loaded
into the trunk of the gringo's Lincoln Continental, end up in an
antique shop in Manhattan? Who knows?

We climb back down, rather more easily. Bob claims he was able to sense a structure up there, but I am less sure. Pedro tells us the story of a man who built a cabin at the top and then was driven off the mountain by the sound of a woman crying every night. I am driven off by bad scratches from the rough foliage, a myriad of mosquitoes, and thirst. We pass Pedro's house, a Mayan *choza*, the one-room structure made of slender wooden poles holding aloft a thatched roof. Inside we can see hammocks, some stools, a table. His wife is at the doorless entry, and two stalwart boys. They wave to us. We go on to Pedro's store, which he opens for us, and where, from his freezer, we buy Coca-Colas. I am so parched I hardly stop to breathe as I drink.

On the drive to Chichén, Ted devises a scenario: The two gentle Mayans observe our eagerness to find ruins and note our generosity at the end of the trek. Their wives are equally observant. They say to their husbands: See how these strange gringos come here, and pay, to see these, ah, holy places, these stones and jungle. We should build a road, clear the hill, put up some stones, one upon another, charge three thousand pesos for entrance, sell food and drink at the exit, straw hats and replicas of the Chac at the entrance. . . . We return a few years from now, and are struck with terrible guilt for having ruined yet another 'undeveloped' site.

On the other hand, I confess to having written a different scenario as we climbed the hill: The Mayans are weary of Americans interrupting the serenity of Balankanche. They will lead us farther and farther into the deep brush, separate us, and then strike us down. In this way, they will gain far more cash than the pittance we have agreed to pay them for conducting us to the ruin, in addition to suitcases crammed with useful objects and clothes, watches, rings, jewelry, and all the parts and tires of our rented car. They will drag our carcasses and the stripped-

down body of the car into the far reaches of the dense scrub and
thicket where no one has been for centuries, and no one will
ever go again.

No one knows we have made this detour, far from the direct
road between Valladolid and Chichén Itzá. So this foolish,
romantic jaunt into the wilds of Yucatán will end in the
unsolved mystery of our disappearance.

Then I realize I have been populating gentle Balankanche
with the thugs and street muggers of the city I have left behind.

∽

The ruins: After many visits over a period of fifty-five years
these places have become both more familiar and more distant to
me. When I am permitted to be alone with a building—a rare
opportunity—I feel what Rose Macaulay called the 'pleasure of
ruins.' I sense their mystery, I realize more strongly than I am
able to bear my own mortality, surely the emotion to which
one's presence at the ruin of a thousand-year-old civilization
must most often lead.

Macaulay, in *Pleasure of Ruins,* writes: '. . . ruin is part of
general *Weltschmerz, Sehnsucht,* malaise, nostalgia, *Angst,*
frustration, sickness, passion of the human soul; it is the eternal
symbol.' Ancient Mayan cities, deserted for reasons no one seems
to understand, strike terror into me, push me down to the knees
of my habitual despair, make me long for death and then for
further life, as these places disappeared and then were restored. I
worship my God there, and theirs. The magnificence of these
places seems greater because it is only partial ('This broken
beauty is all we have of that ancient magnificence'), my
despondency greater. Macaulay says we take a morbid pleasure
in decay, and surely this is what I do, because it seems to match
my innate pessimism.

But there is another thing. The Mexican ruins are now

blackened by acid rain and pollution emanating from tourist buses and cars. Sculptures on the columns at the Temple of the Jaguars in Chichén Itzá are so dark that the *tigres* and feathered serpents are almost invisible. What is being rapidly obliterated, on the one hand, is being fraudulently restored on the other. At three smaller sites, Labná, Sayil, and Kabáh, you can watch restoration being accomplished from trucks that bring foreign stones to the sites. They are hoisted up over broad strips of concrete, in such a way that the newly erected places are yellow and machine-cut, and bear little resemblance to the original stone structure.

These places now suffer from inaccuracy and haste, aimed at quickly pleasing the hordes of tourists who arrive late in the morning and stay until the buses honk for them in early afternoon. The ruins seem to be sinking into modernity, to be backdrops for the many shops that have sprung up at their entrance. Years ago I walked in through narrow footpaths; now there are grandiose entrances and boutiques to the major sites.

ᕫ

At the edge of the hacienda where we are staying there is an orange tree. We ask an attendant when the oranges come out. He replies: 'Whenever they want to.'

ᕫ

Last year, when we passed a little shop in Playa del Carmen without entering, the shop keeper called out to us: 'Come on in and let me rip you off.'

ᕫ

After a siesta and a swim in the late afternoon, we go back to the great pyramid at Chichén to find that it has been taken over by climbers. Today, in these places, appreciation of archaeological splendors is shown athletically. Mystery has given way to sport. From afar the temple resembles an ant hill; close up it is a slanted column of human bodies which move up fast and then come down more cautiously, many of them clinging to the iron chain that goes from top to bottom, screaming, calling, laughing as they come. The holy air of the place has been supplanted by the overheated, noisy atmosphere of a gymnasium or a boxing arena.

I retreat from this display of muscular prowess, walk the hot path to where we are staying, and stand in the shade of a banyan tree, whose surface roots are more widespread and convoluted than its branches. It is one of those spectacles of the natural world that reverses the expected. The roots, like the adventitious roots of the mangrove tree, refuse to be buried. They roll about on the ground like ocean waves and display themselves as if in competition with their leafy crowns. The rebellious roots of the banyan tree are refreshing.

One magical evening Ted finds a secret footpath into the site grounds. The moon is covered, the second light show, that terrible evening violation of the grey stones that is put on for the tourists, has not yet begun. We sit on a wall in the shadow of El Caracol (the shell-shaped observatory), sensing the presence of long-dead spirits. We say nothing to each other for almost an hour. Then the moon is suddenly uncovered; we walk in silence and without our flashlights into the empty chambers at the foot of El Caracol and then turn back. My heart beats fast, from the pressure of awe and from the more immediate fear that we will be caught by the Mexican guards and put in prison for illegally invading the site.

〜

I feel the urge to write a travel piece full of advice to someone planning to visit Maya. I probably will never do it, but if I did, it would go like this:

1. Leave your camera at home. Use your eyes, and work at committing to memory what you see. The sun is usually in the wrong place for picture-taking, film is exorbitantly expensive here, it is too hot to carry heavy equipment. Most of all, the optic nerve, retina, cornea, and crystalline lens are more reliable that the Kodak and its complex successors.

2. Leave your camcorder at home. Standing still for a long time, in one place, and fixing your attention on one object at a time will serve you better than moving pictures of your fellow travelers and crowds walking in front of the camera.

3. Politely refuse the services of guides. Their knowledge of languages (English, French, German, even Spanish) is often rudimentary, and their acquaintance with history, archaeology, and the Mayan sciences such as astronomy and mathematics is not only slight, but replete with error.

4. Do not purchase guidebooks sold at the sites. Look up a good bibliography before you leave home, and study authoritative books like John Stephens's account (1842) of his travels, the first and still most vivid such work, and writers like Michael Coe and Eric Thompson,

5. Be prepared to spend time examining the carvings on the stelae and the glyphs, by studying first their meanings, in a book like the recent *The Blood of Kings*. It will teach you how to read the codices and what the carvings mean. The book is too heavy to carry. Learn as much as you can from it at home. Take notes.

6. Rent a car if you can. Arrive at the ruins a few minutes before they open and have a few blessedly quiet hours to explore before the buses and cars come. It is the only undisturbed time you will have to try to get a feeling for the

past. On the other hand, visiting ruins is, as Henry James has said, 'a heartless pastime, and the pleasure . . . shows a note of perversity.' Enjoy your own private perversities.

7. Get there soon, before it all disappears under the weight of pollution, crowds, noise, and guesswork reconstruction, and before the spirits of its Mayan builders and worshipers vanish into the jungle.

↫

I have a feeling this may be my terminal visit. It is very likely I will not go back to Mexico. I cannot see the Museo Arqueológico in Mexico City again because that city is too high and too polluted for me. I regret this. It would be good to have a last look at Palenque, and to go to Copán and Tikal, but perhaps ending it here is as well. Eventually one needs to let go of one's passions and assign them to the realm of memory. I have grown too demanding of these ruins, too impatient with the behavior of everyone but myself and my traveling companions.

I feel very much like the little boy I saw the last afternoon at El Castillo. He stood at the bottom, grabbed the chain, that runs from top to bottom of the pyramid, and began to wave it vigorously. People climbing down who felt their hold threatened screamed. He had to be dragged away by his mother. I want to shake everyone off the buildings, sweep clean the great plains between them of touring groups and guides, and pass a law forbidding conversation within the confines of the ancient cities. Short of all that being made into law, I'll stay at home.

↫

At month's end, in Washington, I browse through my shelves and find Willa Cather's copy of George Santayana's *Obiter Scripta.* Out of it falls a note in her handwriting containing two quotations she took from Santayana's essay 'Turn of Thought':

'To turn events into ideas is the function of literature.' And: 'Literary art demands a subject matter other than the literary impulse.'

On the back of the book jacket is an advertisement for Santayana's *The Last Puritan,* with its subtitle, 'A memoir in the form of a novel.' I hold to my theory that all memoirs, like this one, are in the form of a novel or fictional in impulse and concept, and surely in execution.

April

Life can only be understood backward.
—Kierkegaard

*A*pril 1 in Washington is cold, wintry, windy, not so much cruel as it it is disappointing. Mexico accustoms you to warmth, but spring has not come here yet. I require more layers of clothing to stay warm and need to bury my suntan under heavy sweaters. Still, there are virtues to city life. Today I went to the Seventh Street flea market and found a fine carved wooden plover. At the Mission Traders around the corner, a place that carries only imported objects from Central and South America, I bought a cloth macaw, mounted on strings. You pull one end and his great wings flap gently. I am planning to take both birds to Maine, and set them free, figuratively, into the circumambient air.

∽

In the pile of mail that came while I was away is a volume from Villard Books called *Sweet Revenge*. It is written by 'the celebrated socialite' Sugar Raubord and accompanied by elaborately printed publicity. The book is described as being about 'High Fashion. High Finance. Hot Sex.' It is, the publicist

assures me, the 'year's most tantalizing novel.' What *is*
tantalizing is that I cannot even guess what that implies.
Raubord, a 'real-life member of the upper-class elite,' 'takes us
into her world—a high society whirl of glamorous parties,
steaming affairs, high-stakes business deals, and secret intrigues!'
(The exclamation mark is the publicist's.)

The *heat* of those words! Whirl, glamorous, intrigue,
steaming! And written by a society lady whose first name is
Sugar! I find myself overusing the exclamation point as I write
this—punctuation I rarely resort to—in order to add fuel to the
warmth of the description. This is the secret of all romantic
writing: to use words that burn on the page, setting fire to the
susceptible reader's imagination.

∽

Mistaken definitions: I have always believed that 'pericope' was
a variation of the word for a sea instrument of some sort. I learn
today from a crossword definition, and then considerable
path-finding through the dictionary and at last into the *OED,*
that it is a section or extract from a book. The root is *ope,* the
Greek for a cutting.

Alewife: a North American fish. I knew that, in Chaucer, I
think, it designated a woman who ran a pub, but a fish? No one
is quite sure how the fish came to be so named, unless it
originated in this country with the French *allowes,* for shad. Fish
names tend to be descriptive: flounder, pike (for its pointed
head), swordfish (for its elongated upper jaw). But alewife: that
is a curious cognomen.

Another mistaken belief of mine. Consider the well-known
apology 'Forgive this too long letter. I had not time to write a
short one.' When I have quoted it I always wrongly ascribed it
to Mark Twain. *Sounds* like Twain. Then someone told me it
was written by Voltaire, someone else, Pascal. Turns out, I learn

today, to be by Madame de Staël, famous for her letters. . . . I
find those sentences useful whenever I indulge my prejudice of
preferring short works of fiction to tomes.

Looking up the origin and precise meaning of new words is
hazardous. When Alan Bisbort inherited my decrepit copies of
the eleventh edition of the *Encyclopaedia Britannica* he wrote to
me: 'The *EB* is a blessing—and a torment. Every time I pick
out a volume to look something up, I get sidetracked, endlessly,
along the way. Today, for example, I wanted to look up George
Gissing, but I ended by making unscheduled stops at Gipsy and
then Girdle before I remembered why I'd picked up the volume
in the first place.'

∽

The city is now in the grip of a beautiful spring. The dogwood
outside our apartment building is budding, all the fruit trees
show signs of flowers, and the cherry blossoms, we are told,
should be 'ready,' as they say, in a few days. In other years we
went to the Jefferson Memorial and breakfasted under the low,
fresh, dark-pink flowers, but this year, because we are so busy
preparing to sublet the apartment, we drive through the
tree-lined ways, thinking that all this unlimited beauty
disguises—for the moment—the social and economic injustices
of the capital.

∽

Sybil is delighted to have found a well-known writer who will
take our apartment for the eight months we plan to stay in
Maine. She is not ready to break her ties here, to become a
country person 'for good.' So she happily buys a secondhand rug
to replace our prized oriental one, three lamps to be left in place
of my grandmother's lamp-vases, a serviceable set of stainless-
steel cutlery, and some white porcelain plates to eke out our

very scanty supply. We retire the worn toaster-oven and replace it with a new toaster, stow away Sybil's good pewter, and inform our friendly mover, John Kidner, that we will be ready for his services in mid-May, to bring to Maine books, clothing, lamps, the good rug, and other things that will make more room for our tenant. Everything of mine, including my ailing, elderly PC, and all my books, pictures, and papers will go, a sign that I am indeed moving to Maine. Sybil will leave some of her clothes and various memorabilia, a sign that she is not.

∽

Yesterday we drove to Columbia to see my daughter Kate and her children. Hannah, the new baby born while I was in Mexico, is doing well and, like all infants, making the usual unreasonable demands upon her mother for comfort and nourishment at all hours of the night. During the day she sleeps contentedly. It appears she will be dark, unlike the blond and blue-eyed Maya, who is now a little over two. This is good. Hannah will be her own person rather than a clone of her sometimes too-much-admired, beautiful sibling.

Maya is taking the new arrival rather hard, with the usual moments of regression and audible objection. She showed me her baby doll, whose eyes she was wiping with her favorite blanket.

'She is crying,' she said.

'Why?'

'Because her mommy and daddy went away.'

Kate tells us that one day Maya was acting badly at dinner and was sent to her room to stay until she felt calmer. Nothing was heard from her for a long time. Kate went to look in on her and found her piling up her dresses and diapers in the middle of the floor.

'What are you doing, Maya?'
'I'm leaving,' she said.

∽

I express my contentment at leaving Washington, perhaps too
often and too openly for Sybil's taste. But as I do it, I think that
my pleasure is not entirely unalloyed. I shall miss the *Times* at
the door at five in the morning, the good afternoon coffee and
pastry at the corner, the Saturday-morning farmer's market
across the street and the flea market on Sunday, and the
unexpected, pleasant encounters with friends and acquaintances
as I walk the streets close to our apartment house, making me
think of E. B. White's 'the cordiality of geese,' for some reason.
I shall miss the wandering city gulls I see from the balcony on
the roof of the garage, the same roof that now is sprouting
daffodils, grasses, and small bushes. I shall miss the lovely
high-church, Anglo-Catholic liturgy of St. James Church, a
ten-minute walk from where I live.

Simone Weil once made a note to herself: 'As soon as one
has arrived at any position, try to find in what sense the contrary
is true.'

∽

While I pack I read Anatole Broyard's extraordinary book
about how he dealt with dying (his style was to make fun of it,
to disparage it). Titled *Intoxicated by My Illness,* it is a fiercely
literary and literate small book, detailing how he prepared to die
of cancer. Broyard was a well-known book critic and essayist
whose writing life was led mainly at the *New York Times.* I
knew him slightly and always felt a connection to him because
he appeared to share my preference for reading and reviewing
short books. Occasionally we talked on the telephone when, in

his last years, he would ask me to review a book. I remember once saying to him (of a short book by a black writer) that I would do my best. His charitable and comforting reply was: 'You usually do.'

In these essays Broyard is witty and astute:

'So much of a writer's life consists of assumed suffering, rhetorical suffering, that I felt something like relief, even elation, when the doctor told me I had cancer of the prostate.'

Because he was a writer he turned his terrifying experience into good prose: 'As I look back at how I used to be, it seems to me that an intellectual is a person who thinks that the classical clichés don't apply to him, that he is immune to homely truths. I know better now. I see everything with a summarizing eye. Nature is a terrific editor.'

Broyard rejects the polite treatment of him by his friends: 'all these witty men suddenly saying pious, inspirational things.' His view of himself is never pious, always sharp, funny, honest, and critical. He, the patient, examines his doctors, and finds them lacking in imagination, in the ability to converse, to listen. After all, 'the doctor is the patient's only familiar in a foreign country. . . . It may be necessary to give up some of his authority in exchange for his humanity.'

I admire Broyard's untamed courage, his ability to move into himself in a metaphoric, poetic way, to use language wildly in order to write paeans to the self he discovered at the center of his suffering. Introversion of this acute sort is often the result of being terminally ill. There is usually not another easy path into the core. (Good health encourages extroversion.) Broyard's gift was to make exuberant, intoxicated literature out of the fourteen months of his illness.

He thought 'books about illness are too eloquent . . . so pious that they sound as if they were written on tiptoe.' This is true of so many self-help books on aging, and of letters I receive from persons angry with me that I am not eloquent in my praise of its virtues. Growing old, facing old age, being old, are all, in Broyard's words, 'a matter of style.' Like him, I cannot write on tiptoe. My style, if indeed I have one, is to stand flatfooted, terrified, at the edge of the pit.

∽

After dinner at a nearby Chilean café, we take an unusual turn into East Capitol Street. Through the growing dark we come upon a wonderful procession. The traffic has been halted by motorcycle policemen so that elephants can make their way up the avenue, the little ones holding on to their mothers' tails with their extended little trunks, followed by four zebras, elaborately covered horses, and two majestic llamas. The circus has come to town, pulled in at Union Station, and these creatures, alien to the Hill, are making their way to the Armory, where they will perform tomorrow. There is something fine about their incongruous appearance on streets usually reserved for streams of indistinguishable cars and buses. I go home feeling extraordinarily good.

∽

Mid-April. The car is packed to overcapacity. We leave the garage at seven in the morning and make a block's detour to pick up a copy of the *Times* from the box at the corner near the Metro. At Pennsylvania and Seventh street, around our corner, the drugstore, the little Irish pub, the Egg Roll King take-out, and another new restaurant are all cordoned off with yellow police tape. In front of the restaurant there are an ambulance and four police cars. When Sybil gets out for the paper, she asks a bystander what is going on.

'Restaurant's been robbed. And there's a dead body in there.'

We drive on in silence, she thinking (as she later told me)

that it had been a mistake to make that detour, and I telling
myself: 'I will never live here again.' When we moved here,
almost twenty years ago, Washington was the most beautiful
capital in the free world. Now it is the sordid murder, crack,
and mugging capital of the country.

⟡

At one point on our drive, as we approach Great Neck on Long
Island, we become unsure of which road to take, and stop to ask
a pedestrian for directions. His instructions turn out to be
wrong. We ask two other persons. After the third counselor has
misled us, we stumble by accident upon the right road. I
speculate on why it is that most persons will not admit that they
do not know how to find the road you are searching for. Can it
be that they have lived here all their lives and are embarrassed to
say they do not know?

⟡

We stop in this suburb of New York City so that I can read to a
women's group. Charlotte Marker, a college classmate, has lived
in Great Neck for almost forty years. She went to medical
school at Bellevue, became a psychiatrist, and married Arthur
Zitrin, who is in the same profession. Their children, both
lawyers, are grown and 'away.' We rest at their house, have
dinner with them and the officials of Womanplace, and then,
after the reading, go back to their house.

Over coffee and late-night, notably good little cakes, we
rehearse our lives as we have lived them and as we live them
now, announce cautiously our political and social views (which,
fortunately, turn out to be compatible), and try to bridge the
gap of fifty years that separates us, what we were, what we have
become. I remember meeting Charlotte's brother when she lived
with her parents in Coney Island, where she was born. I ask

about him, and she tells me that while at law school he had an emergency operation and died under the anesthetic. Then a medical student, she was devastated, and still, after all this time, she seems affected by his death.

We leave very early the next morning, eager to be on our way to Maine. They are both up to give us coffee and bid us goodbye. The atmosphere is friendly and, I suspect, compounded of pleasure and relief. We all liked each other, but of course we had no way of knowing that we would. I, for one, felt no disappointment: Charlotte is as I remembered her, thoughtful, honest, unassuming, with nothing of the professional physician (lofty, pedantic, vain?) about her.

◡◠

The drive to Maine is quick. We hardly stop. We both are eager to be home again. We consider stopping at May Sarton's but decide it is a bad time; she will be resting. So we aim for Nickerson's Tavern, our favorite restaurant, an hour or so from Sargentville. For miles we do nothing but plan what it is we are to eat—the duck perhaps? the fresh fish of the day? We race against time (do they close at eight?) to get there, and we lose. We make it by seven-thirty. No cars in the darkened lot. It is closed. Glumly we push on to Bucksport, where we have a dull meal, made even less interesting by the weight of our disappointment.

◡◠

We have left spring behind. It is very cold and bare as we pull into our driveway and frigid in the house. Sybil brings in my computer for fear it will freeze in the car, remembering Ted Nowick's experience with his PC. Seems he kept it in his guest room, which is usually forty-five degrees, and couldn't get it to start in the morning because it had 'taken a cold,' as my grandmother would have said. He used a hair dryer to warm it up. The dryer melted it down. So I am as nervous about the state of health and comfort of mine as I would be about that of a child or a pet animal, especially since she (I believe it is female but I cannot be certain) is six years old, ancient for a PC. I feel I must take care of her in her last years.

℘

The first morning home: We walk our property, noting that everything is in early bud. Our boats are where we left them and seem in good shape, and the covered bushes and perennials seem to have 'wintered over' quite well. The sun comes out at noon, the air warms to almost fifty degrees, but it begins to darken early. We celebrate being home with a good, early dinner, reclaiming the kitchen and trying to remember where everything is stowed. Sybil opens the bookstore, which is even colder than the house but shows no signs of winter damage. Tracy has painted the floor, and everything is as Sybil left it. She sighs at the prospect of finding space for the cartons of books she bought in Washington. The store, which looked big enough when we first built it—someone suggested it would make a fine bowling alley, and someone else thought we should put a pool in its center—now is filled to capacity. Books, I've learned, reproduce themselves like wire hangers.

℘

We remembered to have the water turned on, and the furnace, but we never gave a thought to the telephone. So, for two days until Good Friday, we are without it. I find its silence very pleasant, having grown to dislike the instrument. Sybil cannot understand how this can be. When she is in a good mood she is moved to make long-distance calls.

I am not certain why I feel as I do. In its advertisements, the

phone company urges us all to 'stay in touch' with our friends
and relatives. I think it is the disparity between the concept of
talk and the idea of staying in touch that offends me. Except in
emergencies, I think letters are better agents for communication
than telephones.

One of my daughters once said she liked letters better than
calls. 'I like to be able to read them over.' Letters are history.
They are the savored and saved past, the instigators of memory.
Telephone calls are the ephemeral present and play a part only in
the immediate future.

∽

Today, the 18th of April, it is snowing. (Someone at the gas
station told me, when I wondered at it, that it could snow in
June in Maine.) We have had almost three inches. Yesterday's
warm landscape has turned quite beautiful, but icy and, along
the edge of the Cove, frozen. A useful indoor day: I hook up
my PC, put my files away, and restore my study to the state of
order it must be in for me to be able to work.

Odd. Some people enjoy writing in disorder, feeling
pleasure in bringing order out of it in the process. The obstacle
to progress in my writing is that I cannot get to it until
everything around me is in order—my desk, my study, the
kitchen, the rooms between. Sometimes I try to avoid this
foolish necessity by ignoring the confusion in the house and
going to the deck to work, only to find that the rock garden
needs weeding and the spaces around the bushes require some
mulching. I must do those things before I can sit down to the
pen and paper.

Absurd. We are creatures of irrevocable habits, I believe.
And if we were not, would we come apart, fall to pieces,
without the glue of custom? Are habits somehow the cement of
character? Somewhere I read that habits begin by being cobwebs

and end as cables. And then there is that old Latin proverb: *Plura faciunt homines e consuetudine quam e ratione*— Men do more things though habit than through reason.

∽

By three the snow begins to melt. Helen Yglesias, who now lives alone in her Brooklyn house and is at work on a new novel, is coming to dinner. So we begin our life as full-time, permanent residents of this place, with a friend, the cables of our lives firmly in place.

∽

Sybil went back to Washington this morning for her annual trek to the Vassar Book Sale, and to prepare the apartment for our tenant. Elizabeth has come from Lake Placid to spend her vacation with me. For the first three days of her stay, there is nothing but fog. She had expected time in the sun to renew her tan, so she is a bit disgruntled. I remind her that we live close to the sea, so fog is our natural and very constant element, and bright, clear sunny days a dispensation from it, an unexpected gift.

Crocuses follow the snow, brave little flowers that act to assure me that the winter is almost finished. But the house still seems cold to Elizabeth, who is crocheting an afghan for her sister Jane. She feels better when it is big enough to wrap around her legs as she works.

More fog, which I find I like because it keeps me inside working, without regret that I cannot be out clearing the flower garden of its protective covers. And the silence of fog is a boon. Perhaps dying is like this: walking, without stopping, into absolute, complete, silent fog toward an inscrutable clearing at the end.

⟲

We watch movies in the evenings on a tape that Bob Emerson sent. The first is a long and very slow story, *The Fabulous Baker Boys,* a movie set in the world of lounge music starring the Bridges brothers, sons of Lloyd Bridges, whom I remember from my moviegoing days. Neither of his sons resembles him. . . . The second is a terribly violent account of how dishonest policemen are detected by a special branch of the police department. The hero is a current movie favorite named Richard Gere who is handsome and attractive, and very clever in his undercover criminal activities. The good guy who brings him to justice is ordinary-looking, and a stiff actor. I found myself hoping Gere would not be caught by him. This is the power of the screen image, to be so biased toward the beautiful and the powerful that one is persuaded against one's better moral judgment to root for the villain.

Elizabeth celebrates the lifting of the fog and the warm days by working in the woods, clearing away dead trees and cutting down broken and obstructive ones. I work inside at my desk, watching the to-be-burned pile grow as she adds refuse to it. The pile has been there now for almost a year; we await the ideal time to burn, when there is no danger of fire spreading to the whole rough field and, for that matter, to the house.

The days now seem very long. Quiet and solitude are Procrustean beds that stretch time beyond the usual hours available to work, to think, to eat (these are better, of course, when there is someone else to cook), to look at the natural world coming slowly back to green, growing life, and the white of winter sinking away.

And safe. There is a natural safety in this place, after the threat of Washington, D.C., disturbed only by dire TV and

newspaper reports from the outside world. Yesterday there was
a terrible accident in Washington Square Park in New York
City. A seventy-three-year-old lady driving a large car lost
control and drove headlong into the square, killing five people
and wounding many others seated on the benches in the park
before her car was brought to a stop at the Garibaldi statue.
Helen Yglesias's son Rafe had just walked home through this
park on his way to his apartment, which looks down over it.

I thought of all the times in the late thirties I had sat on a
bench near the greened-over image of the Italian patriot
Giuseppe Garibaldi to study for final exams, of the elderly
actress I talked to once on that same bench who then,
twenty-five years later, turned up unexpectedly in a novel I was
writing, of the madam who sunned herself beside me on a bench
near the entrance at Washington Square South in 1939 and who
tried to persuade me that her profession was preferable in every
way to the career in scholarship for which I was preparing.

And I remembered my grandmother, a third-generation
New Yorker, who used to go every afternoon 'to the benches'
that lined the divider strips on Broadway. One day, feeling ill,
she stayed at home. On that afternoon a taxi driver, who was
drunk, drove up over the curb and killed three of her elderly
friends as they sat 'schmoozing,' as she said, with each other.

The benches, in Riverside Park where I played as a child
without my mother and in Central Park, all once seemed to be
oases of safety in the traffic-ridden city, until muggers, rapists,
and harassers occupied the parks, and yesterday, when their
protective nature was violated by a bloody accident. At best,
safety is a temporary and transient condition in cities, a mirage
even. My memories are a throwback to a time when most of
Manhattan, like a small island, could be traversed safely on foot.
Sargentville has no sidewalks, no parks, no benches. It resides on

a wooded peninsula surrounded by coves, bays, ponds, and the Reach. It needs no zones of security. As yet.

᧤

Yesterday I tried to dig up some of the common daylilies that threaten to smother our rock in June. Elizabeth warns me to stay away from the crocuses almost hidden among the lilies. She says they will wither at the slightest touch. All too true. My shovel slips. This morning two of the brave little purple advance scouts for spring are wilted.

᧤

While I uncover perennials and bushes, Los Angeles is in the grip of rioting, looting, burning, and murdering following the announcement of the Rodney King verdict. The police officers who beat the defenseless speeder mercilessly as he lay on his stomach on the road have been exonerated of wrongdoing.

Now the police, more than ready to take the offensive against a single black, are said to be helpless against the rioters. 'Public Sector is Overwhelmed' is the *Times* headline after the second night of turmoil. A whole district of the City of Angels is a giant bonfire, while I sit here in peace and safety, my tunnel vision limited to the silent sea, the burgeoning woods and fields.

Today the National Guard moves into the city. Patty Smith, my companion in Kailuum this winter, comes up from Camden to spend her fiftieth birthday here, bringing some wet suits that belonged to her good friend Myrna. They are intended for Sybil to use in the Cove and stem from a remark Sybil once made that if she possessed a fur-lined wet suit she would venture into the chilly waters of the Cove.

We take the wine Patty has brought, a bottle from Myrna's excellent cellar, to the beach and drink some of it in the enclosed serenity of the Cove, inspecting the great stones to see how they have wintered over. No one has come back as yet to open the houses I can see across from Byard's Point, no boats are in the water, the Davies and the Marsden houses, the only other places in sight, look uninhabited from here (although I am certain they are not), and the seabirds have not yet arrived from their winter in the southern sun.

We are alone in all this sane, pullulating splendor while across the country a city burns, and men and women lie dead in the streets. There is a striking inequity in the life I am permitted to live, and the one the blacks of East Los Angeles are forced to endure.

ᔅ

'But time runs on, runs on,' writes William Butler in 'I am of Ireland.' (I am reading his *The Tower*):

> What shall I do with this absurdity—
> . . .
> Decrepit age that has been tied to me
> As to a dog's tail.

ᔅ

I remember a riot in Harlem when I was quite young. My father's friend owned a men's clothing shop there on 125th Street. My father considered him a fool for staying in that location, but Mr. Silverman liked his customers and often gave them large discounts when he knew they were up against it. At three o'clock in the morning of the riot (I no longer remember what caused it but I think it might have been the way an anti-dispossession rally ended, the same one that Ralph Ellison wrote about in *The Invisible Man*), the police telephoned the Silvermans to tell them the store had been burned to the ground.

Mr. Silverman took the call, fell to the ground, and died of a heart attack. Mrs. Silverman (this begins to resemble a soap opera, but it is tragic fact) attended her husband's funeral, came home in a state of shock, served a supper to the other mourners, and, when they had all departed, jumped from a window of their eighth-story Riverside Drive apartment house, and died. There were no immediate survivors.

∽

The frowning child that I was: Martie Dickson told me during dinner last night that when she was a child she believed that all her thoughts were prominently displayed on her forehead for everyone to see. People always knew what she was thinking; she had no place to hide.

∽

Two foolish sentences, heard this week when I listened to two young women discuss their friends, and themselves: 'She needs to feel good about herself' and 'I need to find myself.'

∽

I read in the paper that newsreels of the years 1914–1950 are turning to dust because they were made on nitrate-based film. This is another way that history is wiped out: aging technology fails. The fragility of history becomes greater all the time, with every new invention for preserving it. We, of course, are part of the fragility. We forget, or ignore it, or rewrite it to suit our purposes. Every time I see the word 'revisionist' in the subtitle of a new book on history I shudder.

I have come to believe that the best history is fiction, the impressionistic, egocentric views of the past that have all the validity of acknowledged selection, formulation into 'good' style, and conscious omissions. Read *War and Peace, The Red*

Badge of Courage, The Naked and the Dead, and *Going After Cacciato* for the true histories of the Napoleonic invasion of Russia in 1812, the Civil War, World War II, and the Vietnam War.

✑

Last night we watched the film *Amadeus* on VCR. It is splendid, moving entertainment and the music is fine, but I am aware that its portrait of Mozart is dubious, as is its view of Antonio Salieri. Is it history? Well, I suppose, of a kind. Millions of viewers will accept it as 'the truth.' It will be all they will ever know of Mozart, which is too bad in a way, but better than complete ignorance. Absolute truth (if that is ever possible) is rarely the best entertainment.

✑

This morning an ax fell. My agent telephoned to tell me that our tenant-to-be had bounced six rent checks at her previous house and had failed to pay agreed-upon utility bills listed under the landlord's name. In our trusting innocence, we had not checked her references, had not even given it a thought, because, after all, she was one of us, part of the moral literary sorority.

I remember my youthful conviction that only good people wrote good books, and evil persons inevitably produced bad ones. I had to surrender that belief quickly, and now I know that good writers are not necessarily honest, and bad ones may well be the soul of probity. Sybil's disillusion and disappointment are sad to see, because she was so delighted to think she would be able to keep the apartment for another year.

My feelings are different. I have wanted to live full-time and permanently in Maine. I am fearful of cities and glad to think about having all my books and belongings in the one place I think of as home. I am tired of lugging my heavy computer from place to place, and of trips back and forth, thousands of miles each year in cars overloaded with new things for the house and old things for the apartment. But, knowing her frustration, I say nothing of this to Sybil.

Shall we try to find a new sublessee? There is very little time between now and the date Sybil is scheduled to leave Washington for Maine. You decide, I say to her, and hang up on the hour-long debate we have had on the subject. Next morning she says, 'I've made up my mind to bite the bullet. Let's give it up.' I agree to come down in a week to help her pack and prepare to relinquish the apartment.

ᔢ

My fantasy life has sometimes been aided by the help-wanted ads. I read them carefully and, completely forgetting my age and infirmities, seriously consider the possibility of employment. I read there is a search for a new director of the Peace Corps. Without a moment's hesitation, I think: That would be an interesting job. Or a manager of a pet store is sought: I think I would enjoy taking care of animals, fish, birds. That's a good job for me. In those fine, dreaming moments I am able to consider making a living as the night clerk in a Holiday Inn, the secretary to a dentist, an assistant librarian in a small town in Nebraska, a teacher of the blind ('We will train you'). I am especially taken with ads that contain the consoling sentence 'No experience necessary,' because I know how scant is my experience in almost everything. Then harsh reality steps in to remind me of my age, my condition, and the fact that being old is the single great limitation upon potentiality. There is not time to become anything else. There is barely enough time to finish being what it is you are.

ᔢ

It is still cool, usually foggy, always muddy, and quite often
raining up here in April. Sybil calls to boast that, in
Washington, 'it is beautiful, in the eighties, and everything is in
bloom.' Nothing is in bloom here but, I console myself,
everything will be, soon.

ᔐ

I spend an evening going into Ellsworth to the Grand Theater
to see a mediocre film. To do this I drive forty-four miles.
Coming home that night on dark, winding roads I have a
sudden flash of memory about the Loews theaters I used to
attend.

When I achieved the age of nine I was allowed to walk the
two blocks from our apartment on West End Avenue to the
Loews 83rd, as we called it, every Saturday noon. With me I
carried the precious little red book of passes my family was
given every year by virtue of our being 'related' to Marcus
Loew, my great uncle, the builder of all those grand palaces that
set off my childhood imagination.

Enterprising Max Loew started with peep machines installed
in a penny arcade. From this modest but profitable beginning
(I think it may have been from the cascading of pennies in that
first 14th Street arcade that my grandmother derived her saying
about taking care of small coins), Loew made his fortune, and
we got our annual book of passes.

I never knew in advance what 'the picture show,' as we
called it, would be. There were always two pictures, known as a
double feature. I did not care; I liked everything that was
shown. Before going in, I would always buy two cupcakes,
invariably a vanilla and an orange one, at the Horn & Hardart's
at the corner. Then I would present my pass to the man in the
box office and enter a side-aisle door. There a solid-looking

matron in a white dress would point me towards the section she oversaw.

I was never permitted to choose my seat, but this did not bother me. I rather liked the security of the children's section. In those happy days, this was the quietest place in the vast theater. Children like me were in tremendous awe of the whole experience and rarely moved from the moment when we groped our way down the dark aisle and into the black row, pushed the seat down behind us, and sat, never once having taken our eyes from the screen from the moment we entered. We were hypnotized, enchanted, captivated, obsessed by the miracle of the moving picture.

So I grew up, fed by at least 120 films a year, some of which I remember, most of which, in the early years, I did not fully understand. My view of the world I hoped to enter was Hollywood's, my only concept of the entrance to that world my Uncle Max's theater. My small triumph always came when classmates called the theaters *Lowees,* and I would correct their pronunciation.

'How do *you* know?'

'He's my uncle,' I would proudly announce.

It was inevitable that, leaving graduate school with a useless degree in medieval studies, I would look for a job in 'the family business,' as we always called Loews, Inc. I was hired in 1940 to work in an office on Broadway and 45th street, in the Loews State building, on the tenth floor. I wrote subtitles for films going abroad and stayed at this mechanical occupation for about a year, until I was fired for irreverence toward one of the pictures I had to subtitle.

The only virtue of the job was getting to know one of my fellow title writers, Felicia Lamport. She was a witty Vassar graduate, prosperous (I surmised), and a very clever practitioner of the craft I never mastered. I didn't know how talented she was until her books of light verse and short satiric essays began to appear in 1961. Even the titles of these volumes were witty: *Scrap Irony* and *Cultural Slag* and *Light Metres*.

I remember how delighted I was with the first sentence of a satire on Henry James in her first book: 'Author Winner sat serenely contemplating his novel.' Last week, going through my shelves of poetry to eliminate volumes I will never read again, I came upon three books of hers, and found a verse she wrote soon after Watergate, called 'Sprung Lamb':

> After a sudden religious conversion
> The shrewd politician can get off the hook
> By answering any who cast an aspersion
> 'The Lord is my shepherd and I am his crook.'

Reading Felicia's 'Southern Comfort' I recall Sybil's unspoken pleasure (or did I imagine it?) when she heard about Maine's terrible weather:

> No meter can measure
> The infinite pleasure
> Of people in tropic resorts
> Who squirm with delight
> Through the sweltering night
> At their home town weather reports.

Ogden Nash. Dorothy Parker. Phyllis McGinley. Felicia Lamport. Who in the eighties and nineties has been able to take a humorous poetic view of mankind and its corrupt and polluted world? It may be that no lyrical breasts contain light hearts, that it is not possible to laugh aloud at ourselves and at others, for fear we will be thought frivolous and uncaring, or unaware of the great tragedies of our times.

In a mood for more levity, I am pleased to receive from Bob
Emerson a clipping from *Newsday* published in New York City.
It contains some lovely Yogi Berra witticisms: 'You come to a
fork in the road,' Yogi once said, 'take it!' And 'You've got to
be careful if you don't know where you're going. Because you
might not get there.'

But no matter. This is no time for humor. I call the airline and
make a reservation to fly to Washington in a few days, to help
with the misery of yet another move, this one, we both swear,
to be our last. A vain threat: For everyone alive, the final move
is into Emily Dickinson's 'House that seemed / A Swelling of
the Ground' with its 'Cornice—in the Ground— .'

May

*When a man tries himself, the verdict
is in his favor.*
—*Thomas Williams,* The Hair of
Harold Roux

*W*ashington: Packing. Every day I come upon something I know I can live without. I place it in the 'Sell' or 'Give Away' or 'Throw Away' heap. Sybil returns in late afternoon from the Vassar Book Sale, inspects the piles while I am in the bathroom or at the computer, and removes two-thirds of my discards to the 'Save' or 'Pack' collections.

I remind her how much that object will cost to ship. She reminds me how much it will cost to replace. I think she errs in being too saving; she thinks I am wrong in being so profligate. So it goes. I suppose it is often true when two people live together: one is a hoarder, one a disposer, and each thinks the other is making terrible mistakes.

La Rochefoucauld: 'If we had no faults we should not find so much enjoyment in seeing faults in others.'

∽

To us, the Vassar Used Book Sale is a movable feast. Once a year, wherever we happen to be, sometime in the month of April or May, it is necessary for us to be in Washington for this

fabled event. In the old days, that is, the seventies, I remember
that it was held in some huge, vacant ground-floor store. Book
dealers, collectors, readers, and buyers would begin to line up
outside at midnight, settling down in sleeping bags or cushions
on the street near the building to await the opening of the doors
at ten in the morning.

The first year we went to the sale, the leaders in line were
Larry McMurtry, the co-owner of Booked Up, an excellent
used-book store in Georgetown, and his friend Calvin Trillin of
The New Yorker. Sybil and I were late: we arrived at five in the
morning, so we were quite far back in the line. Volunteers
would leave for coffee, their places being saved for them while
they performed breakfast errands of mercy. In later years an
enterprising dealer thought up the gimmick of handing out
numbers to early arrivals to enable them to go home for a few
hours of sleep. This worked for a while, until the stalwarts who
stayed in line objected to those who drove by, picked up a
number, and returned to get in their numbered places at a
quarter to ten.

So intense was the competition for early entrance into this
behemoth of Washington book sales that all sorts of trickery
came to be practiced. Close to the opening hour, late arrivals
would inch their way to the front, talking to friends along the
way, arranging to arrive at the head of line as the doors opened.
Others would exert extreme pressure at ten, so that the orderly
one-by-one progress would be swelled by persons from the
back, until pandemonium resulted—all in order to be the first at
the poetry table, or the cookbooks.

Collectors believed that the worst-behaved and most pushy
persons at the sale were dealers. Dealers thought that collectors
of military books were unbelievably aggressive, and old-timers
knew enough to stay away from Jacques Morgan, a local dealer
who had the strength of ten in his hands and arms. He could

insert himself into any small space near the book tables in order to sweep large numbers of books into his boxes.

All in all, the first twenty minutes of the sale were life-threatening. To the fleet-fingered, the rapid readers of book spines, and the effective elbowers belonged the spoils: valuable first editions, underpriced rare books, difficult-to-find volumes.

Two years ago (by this time I had stopped going to the opening day of the Vassar Sale for fear of losing life or limb in the initial melee) Sybil succumbed to torn carpeting and the pressure of the mob and was trampled, but not before a television camera had caught her fall and rise.

So her personal charge into the vast room containing thousands of used books is recorded for all time. Stories about her subsequent conduct are narrated, I am told, at the start of each year's sale. In falling, she sprained her right wrist very badly. Not a whit deterred, she went onto the sale floor carrying her canvas bags and collected hundreds of dollars' worth of 'stock,' as she calls it, to be shipped to the Sargentville store. She packed up cartons of the books she had bought, carried them to her van, then up to the apartment. Only then did she give in to the extreme pain and allow me to drive her to the emergency room of the Capitol Hill Hospital to have her severely sprained wrist treated.

It is of such stoic and ferocious stuff that used-book dealers are made.

⌒

The apartment has begun to look like a warehouse. It is piled and lined with packing cases marked for their destinations: 'bookstore' and 'house upstairs' and 'kitchen.' But we cannot figure out what will happen to them when they arrive. The Maine house is already overstocked with objects and furniture, the kitchen cabinets hardly close because plates, glasses, and cups

obtrude from the shelves. I try to practice the 'Good Riddance'
school of packing, but Sybil is faithful to her mode of saving,
collection, and preservation. I say, 'Let's throw it out.' She says,
as she wraps, 'You never know when we may need it.'

The rooms of the apartment grow smaller each day. We find
ourselves living in the middle spaces, surrounded by brown
carton walls. Still, there is a lot left, so we advertise in the
Washington Post that we are moving and selling. We nail hand-
printed signs to streetlight and telephone poles in the Seventh
Street–Eastern Market area. From noon to five on market day,
Saturday, people pour in. By the end of the day what we haven't
sold we give away, except for the larger pieces of furniture.
Word spreads about them; by Monday they too are gone.

The phenomenon of 'moving sales,' 'yard sales,' 'garage
sales,' and 'tag sales' did not exist, I believe, until the eighties.
Before that time I remember sedate 'estate sales,' handled by
professionals, and auctions. These were formal affairs, with no
haggling or 'offers' permitted. The buyer felt somewhat
intimidated by the process.

Flea markets date back to the early twenties and are probably
the forerunners of yard sales *et al.* I never went to flea markets
when I passed them 'in the country' (they were not city
phenomena), thinking that only junk would be offered there:
the name suggested small, cheap, insignificant objects to me. But
now! It is impossible to drive out on state and country roads on
weekends without encountering hand-lettered signs with
arrows, directing us to the nearest yard sale. And it is nearly
impossible for us to pass one in Maine without stopping.

In the past, in towns outside of Washington, Sybil would
lure me to one that advertised books among other things for sale
by saying: 'Who knows, there may be a first edition of *Huck*
there.' Years ago, in a good bookstore in Santa Barbara, I
bought a copy of Jean Toomer's *Cane* that had belonged to Paul

Robeson and had all the worn signs of having been carried everywhere for years by the great singer. We sold that unusual copy. But the promise of a first edition of that scarce-as-hen's-teeth novel would drag me into garage sales for many years. Of course, we never found another *Cane* or a *Huck,* but we did come upon interesting books selling for very little that we could add to the bookstore stock.

I have heard that these sales, large and small, are now an important part of contemporary American economy. People buy what they need, it is true, but as often they are persuaded by the price to buy what they think they need or do not need but take a fancy to at the moment. Comes the time when there is no more room for what they have acquired at sales, they solve the difficulty by holding a yard sale of their own.

So it comes about that objects of use, near-use, and no use circulate, from one yard to the other, from a garage in Stonington to a barn in East Blue Hill. I like to imagine that, eventually, the first seller of the little sailboat mounted on the face of a clock which stands on an abalone shell will change hands for the fifth or sixth time, and at the end, will be presented as a fiftieth anniversary present to the original seller.

In this manner, old purchases will move from house to barn to yard to other house. There is the pleasant sense of making a profit from what one no longer wants. But I suspect the profit is delusory, because persons caught in the yard-sale circuit will use their profits to acquire more 'things' in the next season of sales. The pleasures of acquisition are fleeting, profits only temporary. But the yard-sale economy seems active and vital.

Sybil is already packing objects to send to Maine 'for our yard sale up there.' She assures me: 'People in Maine will appreciate these things.'

∽

The saga of the bicycle named the *Queen Mary:*

Stored for three years on the balcony of the apartment is Sybil's old bike, vintage about 1939. When her older brother Joel came back from a student tour of England in that year he brought as a present to his ten-year-old sister a lovely three-speed Raleigh bike. For fifty years it has accompanied Sybil everywhere. But in her last years of city life she had rarely ridden it. This week, after much agonizing self-examination, she was able to entertain the thought that perhaps she might bring herself to sell it now.

At the apartment sale on Saturday a few people examined it with interest, but no one was willing to part with seventy-five dollars to buy it. On Monday Sybil and I walked it (one tire was flat) to a bicycle shop on Pennsylvania Avenue. We made a somber progress; she was desolate about offering it 'to the trade.' On the way we passed a panhandler who asked her if she was going to sell that fine bike. If so, he said, he would buy it 'when I get paid at the end of the week.'

No, the fellow at the shop said, he had no use for it. But the former owner of the store, a man now in his eighties who is the world's largest collector of bicycle *drums,* might be interested. Drums, or hubs, I learn from Isaac Wheeler, my grandson who works summers in a bicycle shop, are the axle-and-gear housings on old three-speed bikes. He was not able to tell me why anyone would collect them.

The shopkeeper tells us that so notable is Henry Mathis's collection that he has left it to the Smithsonian Institution. Sybil dwells lovingly on her bike's history as we all stand looking at the relic, pointing out that only the kickstand and the basket are not original. She explains that it is named the *Queen Mary* because one rides it sitting aloft in lordly fashion, high above everyone else on the road or street. 'None of this abject crouching that they do on bikes these days,' she says.

Next day she takes the *Queen Mary* to Maryland. The collector of drums (or hubs) admires the bike, and buys it. So upset is she by her callous abandonment of an old, trusted friend that she forgets to ask if he is going to polish up the original, now-dull black paint and sell it, permitting the new owner to mount the shiny black antique and ride away down Branch Avenue, aloft and regal, or dismantle it for its parts. She is somewhat consoled by the thought that if the old collector does disassemble it, the drum will serve to immortalize the whole bike when it is displayed in a national museum. She thinks it would be like an historic transplant—taking a healthy part from it and preserving it in another place.

Sybil comes home, saddened. But I notice she puts her helmet, the old bike bell, and two sets of cables and locks on the pile marked 'Pack.'

ᘐ

For some reason (perhaps the sight of the helmet), I remember Queen Elizabeth I's threat to an unruly courtier: 'I will make you shorter by a head.'

ᘐ

The time for John Kidner's moving men to arrive is approaching. Our living quarters have shrunk even further. We now have a couch, a chair, a demountable Ikea table, and about fifty cardboard cartons in the living room. The remains of a Mother's Day bouquet, three tulips and a few carnations, sit in a bottle on the table. We are stripped down to basic needs. After all the years of overdecoration, it feels rather good.

I break the rhythm of compulsive packing and go to noon Mass at St. James. Mother Barbara Henry, 'curate,' as she is listed

in the bulletin, is the celebrant, Iris Newsom, of the Library of
Congress, is the server, I am the congregation. It is a quiet,
decorous liturgy, during which the confusion and roil of the
streets outside die away, and only the peace 'that passeth all
understanding' seems to inhabit the beautiful church.

Afterwards we three meet in the nave, and realize we have
all been aware of the same thing: how extraordinary it is that it
is now possible for three women to come together to celebrate
Mass, legally, in an Episcopal church. The institution itself
proceeds into the modern world with the speed of a
hippopotamus, as T. S. Eliot observed, but as Galileo insisted, in
another context, *'I pur si muove.'* Nevertheless, it does move.

∽

We have dinner with a good friend who is HIV-positive and
has been living with the specter of AIDS for years. His
symptoms are not yet major, so few of his fellow workers, or
even his family, I believe, are aware of the cloud that hangs over
his life.

For some sufferers, this is the worst part of this plague: in
order to be treated humanely they must hide the truth from the
misinformed or pusillanimous persons around them. They must
approach the darkness alone instead of in the company of friends
and family. Only at the last, when it is too late, when extreme
illness turns one in upon oneself, creating a hermitage of one's
pain, do the disapproving and the frightened ones come,
carrying their fears for themselves in their faces, almost useless to
the one who is dying.

We say goodbye to our friend and urge him to visit us this
summer in Maine. He says he will come. But we doubt we will
see him there. We feel honored to be among those he took into
his confidence. We are his fellow travelers, even at a distance,

moving with him for part of the way, into the dark wood. He
has permitted us the journey with him toward the chasm.

⌒

The last three days of festivities before we leave. Each year the
PEN/Faulkner Foundation awards prizes for the best American
fiction of the year. This time I was one of the judges, so we are
included in the ceremonies in Washington that surround the
event. It is significant that we will leave the city, not from the
humdrum daily life of the apartment, but from the luxurious
hotel suite we have been assigned for the weekend.

On Friday evening, judges, winners, supporters, and literary
friends meet at Lael and Ron Stegall's house on East Capitol
Street. A few years ago Sybil and I went there to buy books.
Another time we acquired our prized library steps from their
house sale, so we know the place well. We walk from the
Capitol Hill Hotel, through the heavy-with-rain leaves of the
huge trees on that lovely avenue. My feet in their unaccustomed
party shoes hurt badly.

But I forget my discomfort in the presence of so many
people I know. Faith Sale has come down from New York,
fresh from the triumphs of two of her authors, Alice Hoffman
and Lee Smith, and Harvey Simmons, whom I knew when he
was an editor for the Eakins Press, and an old friend of the
Stegalls, is here. Leslie Katz, owner of the press, published
well-designed letterpress books, which Harvey always sent to
me, to my great pleasure. Then Harvey disappeared from the
publishing scene. Now he reappears (to me), having been for the
last twenty years a Cisterian brother in New York. He tells me
that the order's prime source of income is the sale of fruit cakes
at Christmas time. How large is the community? I ask. 'Down
to twenty brothers and five priests, from sixty,' he says. He is a

spry, bearded, almost elfin man with a cheerful mien, full of loving memories of 'Mr. B.' (Balanchine, of course) and his friendship with the great choreographer while he was working on books by and about him.

Elena Castedo, a South American novelist and now a board member of PEN/Faulkner, throws her arms around me and kisses me when we are introduced. I am startled, trying to decide why. She probably has heard I am a founding board member, but I am unused to such instant effusiveness.

Standing near by is this year's first-prize winner, Don DeLillo. He too looks startled. I move over to talk to him. He does not throw his arms around me. In fact, he is leaning against the wall and looks cornered when I approach. I congratulate him, he thanks me for my choice of *Mao II.* Then he points to a large abstract painting on the wall, full of colors that whirl, a mass of chaotic figures. 'There's the first chapter,' he says, unsmiling.

His novel is a searing account of the futility and irrelevance of writing fiction. Bill Grey, its hero, is a Thomas Pynchon–like writer who has published two books that have attained cult status. He becomes hermitic, wanting only to work without the intrusion of the world, while outside, having made of him a mythic figure as important as his work, the world waits eagerly for another book (in this he resembles Harold Brodkey). Years pass without its appearance (J. D. Salinger?). He has been writing and rewriting it in his cell, surrounded by walls of files of everything he has ever written.

The absurdity of mass culture ('The future belongs to crowds'), the fatuous world of the book and the writer, the media that feed on it, are DeLillo's subjects. When a photographer breaks into his seclusion she tells him she loves writers but is afraid she cannot speak their private language. Bill Grey says:

The only private language I know is self-exaggeration. I think I've grown a second self in this room. It's the self-important fool that keeps the writer going. I exaggerate the pain of writing, the pain of solitude, the failure, the rage, the confusion, the helplessness, the fear, the humiliation. The narrower the boundaries of my life, the more I exaggerate myself. If the pain is real, why do I inflate it? Maybe this is the only pleasure I'm allowed.

And later:

I'll tell you what I don't exaggerate. The doubt. Every minute of every day. It's what I smell in my bed. Loss of faith. That's what this is all about.

Yes.

Sybil has read the book, and liked it well enough. But she claims it is a writer's book, and that it is significant that the three judges are all novelists themselves. She is probably right. For it is a well-known maxim (Le Rochefoucauld? Montaigne? Twain?) that we most admire in others what we know to be true of ourselves.

Next morning Richard Wiley, fellow judge and novelist, Allan Gurganus, runner-up for the prize and my longtime friend, and Sybil and I have breakfast at Sherrill's, the Hill's oldest eatery, where the waitresses are all over fifty. One is so frail and old she has to hold on to the counter when she comes around to serve. They all have the surly dispositions of the waiters at the forties Broadway restaurant called Lindy's, another place where longevity bestowed upon the help all the privileges of incivility. The food at Sherrill's is plentiful, cheap, and rather poor. Hill

dwellers are so used to the historic place they prefer it to glitzy
newer restaurants with pretty young waitresses and good food.

We ate and talked for two hours, of the Iowa Writers
Workshop, where I taught after Richard and Allan were
classmates there, and of other PEN/Faulkner events we had all
attended. Allan told a story about the last gala, which took place
during the Senate Judiciary Committee hearings on the
nomination of Clarence Thomas to the Supreme Court. The
honored writers were asked to talk about their heroes. Two
famous black writers confined their remarks to black movie
actors who never got the fame they deserved, and jazz. Allan
decided to talk about the matter on everyone's mind. His hero
was Anita Hill.

The audience gasped. Afterwards, an official of the affair
asked him, reprovingly, if he knew that Senator John Danforth's
daughter was on the Gala Committee. Others, like Hodding
Carter and Susan Stamberg, congratulated him. Apprised of this,
the official informed Allan that his was 'the best talk.'

After breakfast, Richard and Allan go off to see a
demonstration on the Mall in support of aid to the cities. For
the last time, we go to the apartment to empty it of trash. We
strip it of everything, down to the penny that had dropped
behind the bed. We turn off the refrigerator, leave the keys on
the counter, and shut the door. We are gone, leaving for the last
time our home away from home, I with relief, Sybil with
reluctance.

⟳

Saturday's *Washington Post* has a sad story about Lowen's, a toy
store on Wisconsin Avenue that is closing after almost fifty
years in business. One employee has worked there for
thirty-seven years. In the shadow of Toys R Us, the world's
largest toy store, as it calls itself, the small, beloved Lowen's

could not survive the competition, the rent rises, the recession. Small, it would seem, is both beautiful—and fatal.

⌣

The central event of the PEN/Faulkner Award ceremonies. Again we 'dress up,' although I long to wear my comfortable L. L. Bean clothes, and walk to the Folger. The judges and the winners sit on the platform, I explain to the audience how we came to choose the five books. Then, with the example of Allan's story clearly in mind, I interrupt what I am saying to protest the censorship of grants to so-called sexually offensive art by the NEA's acting director. . . . We give the winners their prizes; I am openly very pleased to give Allan his. We hug a long time in full view of all the assembled notables.

⌣

At seven next morning we rescue our overladen van from the garage and leave the city. In the late afternoon we stop for coffee at a Dunkin' Donuts shop just inside the Maine border. Two old men, one black, are talking to each other about the work they do on their computers. I cannot resist joining the PC fraternity, asking about their instruments. As we leave, we hear one man tell the other: 'We'll be home all weekend. The grands are coming over.' Now we know we are close to home.

⌣

In Saco we stop for a late supper. There is a place to eat that Sybil remembers vaguely. We are fortunate to find it, since the entrance and parking are far off the road. There is an obscure sign that says 'Kerryman's PUB.' We enter through a dilapidated door into what resembles a back alley. Inside the pub is fine, a large room with booths, artificial flowers and plastic decorations, and food so plentiful that one portion would feed two heavy eaters. Most of the patrons are middle-aged Mainer locals dressed in the familiar L. L. Bean uniforms: jeans, heavy sweaters, sneakers. Add peaked caps for the men who have driven their wives here in their pickup trucks, and you will recognize the people we have dinner with.

We are even closer to home. We share a beer and talk about the contrast between this comfortable, poorly lit, unpretentious place and the lavish houses and expensive restaurants we have been frequenting in the past few days. I think of the elaborate, pretentious food catered for the PEN/Faulkner event, *expected* to be served by the people who pay a goodly sum to attend. Much of the money collected will go to pay for the awards and the judges, the hosteling and feeding of these persons, and the lady who arranges the affair they are attending, a kind of incestuous and circular round of finance and events.

I fantasize: What would happen if we called it all off one year, gathered in a publike place somewhere in an ordinary section of the city, wore our easy old clothes (especially the shoes!), had beers and the $5.95 blue plate special, and gave all the money collected for the affair to the homeless who live on the cold corners and grates of Capitol Hill.

∽

Aha! My feelings about the elaborate affairs accompanying fund-raising at Washington's PEN/Faulkner have been satisfyingly echoed by the Hospice of Hancock County, the county that encompasses Sargentville. A nicely offset invitation arrives this morning announcing that there will be no gathering this year. It requests the pleasure of my company at an Imaginary Candlelight Dinner to benefit Hospice patients and their families. 'The dinner will not be held anywhere at any time so you need not attend,' it reads. I am relieved of buying a 'new outfit for the dinner,' 'I don't have to eat another chicken dinner,' 'I won't need a sitter,' and 'I won't have to go to the hairdresser.' For each of these savings a contribution is suggested. 'I am pleased to accept your invitation to stay home.' With pleasure I check that box, and write a check.

⟍⟋

Early next morning we *are* home. This time it is permanent. We make a walkabout, inspecting everything we have left, and find nothing out of order. My unlocked car sits placidly in its place where it has been waiting for us for two weeks. I say nothing to Sybil, because her joy in being here is somewhat less than mine. But I think about what I heard at the gala on our last evening in Washington: The morning after Friday night's party at the Stegalls' on East Capitol Street, they left their house to do some errands. No car. It had been stolen.

⟍⟋

The quiet of the Cove swept over me this morning, the absence of people, the feeling that I was in sole possession of sky, water, meadow, and woods at our end of the peninsula. Two days ago, making our way north through the state, we thought we might stop for lunch at Barnacle Billy's in Perkins Cove to have a first taste of lobster. But it was not to be: Ogunquit has turned into a clone of Provincetown, Lake George, Taos, Carmel, the Hamptons, and other such overcrowded and overbuilt tourist places. We make a slow, ten-mile-an-hour trip through the main street, down the road, and into Perkins Cove. But stop? *Park?* Impossible.

Inexorably we make the loop because we cannot get out of it, catching a quick glimpse of the sea on our way. We are shocked by the number of people on the street and in the fancy, shoulder-to-shoulder shops. This is mid-May, and already the Cove and the town are fashionably crowded with tourists. I

remember what this town was like when we summered at
Moody Beach, the extemporaneous excursions to Barnacle
Billy's for a lobster. . . .

Standing on our sun-filled deck this morning, within sight
of no one, the silent, calm sea spread out before us, I wonder:

How long before creeping tourism moves up the coast and
reaches us? How long before we too become 'fashionable'?

⟋⟍

I am reading Julia Blackburn's account of the last years of
Napoleon's life on St. Helena. My ignorance of the subject is so
abysmal that I thought Napoleon died on Elba. Not at all. He
returned from his exile there, was defeated at Waterloo, and was
sent into a second exile by the British to its island, St. Helena, in
the South Atlantic Ocean.

The little general led a curious life there, isolated from
everything and everyone but a group of sycophantic French
aristocrats and army officers. Once, from France, a friend sent
him a crate of books. Blackburn writes: 'He is so eager that in
the middle of the night he cracks the lid off with a chisel and
reads without pause for several days until he is exhausted.'

⟋⟍

A letter from a man who has read *End Zone*. He made a list of
the books I talk about reading and having read, and intends to
pursue them systematically. It is strange, but I have noticed that
some people feel more secure about their reading if they do not
do the choosing themselves. The same preference characterizes
people who belong to book clubs that, figuratively, chew the
cud of book choice for their members.

⟋⟍

A large moose has been seen crossing a field near us by our neighbors Ken Grindle and the Parkers. I have never seen a moose and wish I had spent more time watching the edges of our woods and less at the too-often-unproductive clipboard. We *did* see a brown bear crossing the road into Blue Hill last year, drivers slowing down to watch his/her dignified progress. When Elizabeth was here she thought she saw a fox, although I thought it might have been a raccoon, and Grace and Martie are sure what they saw near the edge of their clearing was a mountain lion. Deer, leaving clear hoofmarks, regularly visit our rudimentary vegetable garden and nibble the lettuce, the cabbage, the beans. We have seen signs of beaver in the pond at the side of our woods.

Can it be that the recession and overpopulation have affected the wild creatures in our area, so that they are coming closer to cultivated places for free sustenance? Like the gulls feasting at McDonald's waste heap?

∽

Deer Isle folk are insular, if that is not tautological. Families have lived there since the eighteenth century, rarely leaving it until the bridge to the mainland was built fifty years ago. A story told to us in the bookstore recently: A teacher in the Deer Isle grade school assigned each member of her third-grade class a United States President on whom to write a report. This, *in toto,* was what the little boy who wrote on George Washington read to the class:

'George Washington was born off island.'

∽

The Davieses' Friendship sloop was put into the water yesterday while I was not looking. So the seascape has changed subtly. The handsome, handmade wooden boat, which took six years to build in John Davies's garage, has provided me with a new focus, a new place for my eyes to rest as they move toward the sea from shore to boat to the Point to Eggemoggin Reach to Deer Isle, a series of restful coulisses stretching toward the horizon. In such an arrangement there is the variety and interest that a view of the ocean's horizon lacks. Perhaps I am justifying to myself the absence here of surf and rolling sea, or, more likely, I am finding contentment where I am.

∽

I learn today that John Updike's first published poem, thirty-eight years ago in *The New Yorker,* was titled 'Duet, with Muffled Brake Drum.' *That's* what we should have done on that last, sad journey of the *Queen Mary* to the bike shop: muffled its brake drum.

∽

Living near us are two friends, who have been together for many years. Now they have decided to 'split up,' as it is now termed. They had bought a house together, worked in the same place, shared a car. So established were they as a couple in the community that they seem unable, together or singly, to tell anyone about what has happened. One will appear at a party to which both (as was always the custom) have been invited and, when asked about the other, will say, 'She is away for the weekend,' or 'She is traveling.'

   Although they are of the same sex, they were never timid about being regarded as having a permanent alliance. Once, one told me that theirs had been a case of 'true love' at first sight. The years had confirmed how right the initial glance had been. Now that they are no longer together, and so have achieved the respectable status of single persons in the world's eyes, ironically, each one appears shy, reserved, more closeted than they ever were together. Yesterday at the post office I met one of them and asked how the other was.

'I have no idea,' she said coolly.

I decided to be brave. 'Is it all . . . er, over?'

'Is what over?'

I thought it better not to define my terms or to inquire further. I had embarrassed her into denial. I should have buried their long history as she seemed to wish me to do. Driving home I thought how alike all human relationships are, of whatever origin, duration, or sex. I have grown suspicious of the reality of 'true love,' believing it is a state of mind that exists only in adolescence, fiction, and romantic poetry.

'True love is like a ghost,' La Rochefoucauld said. 'Everyone talks of it, but few have met it face to face.'

∽

Miscellany: I read back over what I have been thinking and writing this month and see that, slowly, I seem to to be sinking back into the slough of despond. Why? I wonder. Is it the insidious approach of another birthday in two months, another signpost on the last mile? I do absurdly despairing things like pick up in the bookstore to read something called *The Raft Book,* sixty-four pages of instructions for using seabirds, fish, insects, winds, and waves as directional aids when you are lost at sea. The first sentence in this essential guide: 'Upon abandoning ship you may have to be your own navigator.' Abandoning ship: a good metaphoric title for a novel? For a memoir? For the end of life?

∽

I put out money for Don Hale who comes by on Monday to collect our trash. He fails to arrive. It rains. I forget to take it in until Friday, when he does come. I mention to him that the bill is probably sodden. He says, "That's okay. I will think of it as laundered money."

∽

> *The Lord is my shepherd.*
> *Hallowed be thy name.*
> *Behold the lamb of God.*

Are these truly beautiful sentences, or do they seem so because they have worn a groove on my tongue, so comfortably familiar that they have been elevated into poetry?

∽

I hear of a new used-book store that has opened on Deer Isle. The proprietor is an elderly man with a long beard who has refused to reenter our store since the time Sybil denied him the discount he thought he deserved. (At the time he was not an active dealer.) It is a clean, well-lighted place with moderately interesting books. We buy a few. He gives us a small discount. We thank him.

He tells me that the area around Stonington, the town at the end of Deer Isle, has a very high ozone level. I question how that can be on this seemingly pure peninsula.

'Oh yes, it's true. If you had known that, would you have called your book *Coming into the Ozone?*'

∽

Agnes de Mille, still actively at work every day at the age of eighty-six, talked to a *New York Times* reporter this week about the mystery of creativity:

The best things I've done come from way below thought. You
have to wait and wait, like teasing a wild animal, get yourself
ready. You do bad work, you throw it away. And suddenly it's
there. It's a surprise, always. I don't have it happen often.

She has been choreographing for sixty years. I wonder if 'it'
happens more often in her old age or less frequently. She doesn't
say. My suspicion is that the richer the compost heap that is the
mind of the old person, the greater the hoard of examined
experiences, tag-ends of ideas, conversations, stories heard and
overheard, dreams, memories, places seen and lived in, persons
known, loved and unloved, the more chance there is for
something useful to be there when it is needed.

In the bookstore, we sell what are called 'remainders,' books
consigned at wholesale rates to dealers by publishers who have
given up on the effort to sell them as new books. This is a
last-ditch effort to make a little profit out of a now profitless
enterprise. That mental compost heap I have been talking about
is full of remainders. When one writes, or composes or
choreographs, or whatever small creative things one happens to
do late in life, it is out of these absorbed, roiling remainders that
ideas come, from 'way below thought,' in de Mille's words.

∽

The first poem in Brad Leithauser's book *The Mail from
Anywhere* contains a useful epigraph by Paul Gauguin: 'Could
you ever have as much light as nature, as much heat as the sun?
And you speak of exaggeration, but how could you exaggerate
when you always fall short of nature?'

I think of the Holocaust, of the terrible twentieth-century
wars, of the plague years of AIDS, of mass starvation in Africa,
mass slaughter in Central and South America, of genocide in

South Africa and on the streets of North American cities, of millions of homeless persons and refugees on this earth, and I think: What can one write about in fiction that could possibly seem exaggerated?

Summer

*Driving a carload of baseball players
to their next game, he said:
'We may be lost, but we're making
good time.'*

—*Yogi Berra*

A little after two in the afternoon: The sun clouds over. It has been visible for an hour so, a brief visit by a very shy guest, typical of the manner in which the sun comes and goes up here. The water is still; the mast of the Davieses' sloop stands perpendicular to it. A sea breeze arrives at the deck, the little wind I always expect about this time. It dries the sweat on my neck and forehead (I've been weeding in the rock garden). Tiny brown tree sparrows leave the ugly dying-brush pile in the meadow to sample the seed in the feeder. We are waiting to burn the brush, but Don Hale, who gives out the permits, says it is too dry to have a fire.

For the first time all day, the leaves on the horse chestnut, somnolent and heavy in the warm air, move quietly, unlike those of the scrubby poplars and maples, which are stirred to noisy chatter by the least wind. An abbreviated family of eider ducks make its daily advance across the Cove. In late spring there is an extended family of them, but now only three or four, a nuclear group. Black butterflies leave one fireweed spire for another some distance away. Two minuscule white sails are on

the Reach, from this distance looking like toy boats on the pond
in Central Park.

The end of the day is signaled by this activity: the breeze
from the sea, the retirement of the sun, and the finches, young
jays, the doves, recovered from their siestas, at the feeder having
their early supper.

～

A woman dying of cancer (not of the lungs, strangely, although
she is a chain smoker) calls Sybil to say she has books to sell. She
lives in a low-cost housing project on Deer Isle. I read in the van
while Sybil goes in. When she returns, half an hour later, she
tells me I am lucky: the apartment is so full of smoke that it is
hard to breathe in it. The books she carries out smell of smoke;
she wonders if sun and air will ever remove the odor. With the
bags of books loaded in the back, the van now reeks.

But the books are interesting, mostly art history, because the
seller was a teacher of the subject at Harvard. She is ridding
herself of her books, for she is not well enough to read. She is
now alone; her daughter is in Boston, hard at work on her law
degree. A visiting nurse comes by once a week and her
neighbors are good about bringing food, but her appetite is gone
and she does not think about eating. She smokes ('What
difference can it make now?') and sits in her small apartment and
waits.

The end of life is too often like this, mean, without the grace
in which a woman like this must have lived. A woman of
learning and sensitivity, who has been a wife, a mother, a
teacher, is letting her possessions go, lessening her hold on life in
a colorless and lonely small space. Without family nearby,
without close friends, without hope of recovery.

In the van we talk about going to visit her but realize we

would be repelled by the air in the apartment. Her solitude is ensured by her smoking. Perhaps it is her wish, to be left in peace behind a smoke screen. But I doubt it. There is no justice in such a coda, only a sense of tragic waste, a good and useful life come to so little, the disappearance forever of what Schopenhauer observed about persons who die: 'There is in every individual something which is inexpressible, peculiar to him alone, and is, therefore, absolutely and irretrievably lost.'

Summer neighbors, David and Loni Hayman, are back in their newly built house on Deer Isle, having spent part of June in Ireland. He is a Joyce scholar who teaches in Wisconsin. It is only to be expected that he would go abroad to celebrate Bloomsday, but he reports that he found the occasion less interesting than usual. . . . The fine thing about living in this area is that sooner or later, and especially in good weather, my far-flung acquaintances who are writers, scholars, artists, bookmakers, editors, and even one college president come by to enrich my rural life with good 'away' talk.

Short of sailing myself I take pleasure in watching the Davieses' sloop go out to sea. The mainsail is raised. On my deck I can hear its rings clatter against the mast. The sailor is alone. With the mainsail up he starts for the Reach. As he tacks into the Petersons' water I see the jib go up, and now he is truly off, leaving behind small white marks of wake on the water. He settles into the stern, takes the tiller, and heads out. I am with him as his boat becomes a chalked spot on the horizon. Almost.

A letter from a lady in Geneva, New York, who says she disliked the unjustified-type right-hand margins on the pages of *End Zone.* 'Was this your idea?' she asks, suggesting that if it wasn't, my publisher has wronged me. I answer: Yes, it was my idea. I thought irregular margins looked more like a handwritten journal than the strict, regular ones, just as I liked italic rather than roman faces for headings because the slope of italic suggests handwriting. I apologize for displeasing her, but still, I think . . .

~

Seasons in this corner of Maine are a matter of the color of blueberry fields. In early April, every other year, they are black, having been burned off to increase the crop. In the summer, now, they are green and low to the ground. Then the first wave of migrant workers, *bees,* arrives. They are rented and brought to the fields to carry out the need for fertilization of the bushes. Three thousand colonies of them arrive from Florida. The report this year is that they have been performing well, 'flying hard despite the weather.'

Why don't they use local bees? Because, I read, they have had a high mortality rate this year, the result of tracheal mites. But a good winter in Florida contributed to the health of the hives there. Those bees are granted a health certificate (literally) and come north to do their salubrious work, pollenizing the blueberry barrens. In August the fields turn blue with the happy results of their activity.

And then in October, to accompany the glory of reddened and yellowed leaves, the denuded expanses will celebrate their victory over burning, tracheal mites, and picking by turning scarlet, a color so deep and pure that my breath is short in their presence.

∽

A terrible day of resistance and rebellion: My computer has refused to obey my instructions. I press F6 to delete a line. Instead, two prints of the line I wish to take out appear. I want to move up a line. It refuses to obey. I press ^G to delete a letter. *Two* of that letter appear on the screen.

At first I believe that my little IBM clone is rebelling against what the manual calls my 'commands.' It seems afflicted by what the Germans say is *Schadenfreude,* satisfaction and pleasure the clone feels at my misfortune. It gloats at my frustration, adding unwillingness to its resistance. It will not move a block of type I have it in mind to put in another place in this memoir.

Suddenly, everything becomes clear. The clone is tired of being ordered around like a common servant. I have underrated its intelligence, its talent, and its judgment. It has stopped being my amanuensis, my gofer, and decided that, for six years, my instructions have been foolish, ineffective, poorly chosen, lacking precision and wit, indeed, dictatorial. It will now do what it thinks best. It has become *a critic.*

∽

An old friend, Woodie Crohn, comes by from Buffalo. He is retired from medical practice. We talk about his famous father, for whom Crohn's disease is named. I hear, for the first time, that Burrill B. Crohn was one of twelve children of an impoverished immigrant family. Then I remember Burrill telling me years ago that he had no carfare to get to City College of New York, so he would walk the hundred blocks early in the day and home again after dark. He earned his expenses for medical school. He became one of New York City's most eminent internists, practicing still when he was in his nineties. After the celebration of his ninety-ninth birthday with his family and many friends, he was hospitalized for two months, and died.

I recall a funny (and terrible) story he once told me. He had treated a patient in her home on Park Avenue and taken away with him a urine specimen. He wrapped the bottle in a brown paper bag and placed it on the front seat of his car when he went on to the next patient. He was returning to his parked car from that call when he saw a hobo (what a homeless man was called in the thirties) reach into the car and grab the paper bag. Horrified at what he realized was the hobo's intention, he shouted after him. The hobo heard him and ran. Burrill began to chase him, and only gave up when he realized he was outdistanced.

He said he spent some time imagining the man's first mouthful. He wondered if it might not have been the beginning of the poor chap's rehabilitation.

Burrill and I became friends when I was a college freshman. In the days of house calls, he came to treat me for infectious hepatitis. I stayed in bed for months, feeling so sick that dying seemed an attractive alternative. Dr. Crohn's visits were the only virtue of that awful winter. After he examined me, he would stay to talk about books he had read recently, and often, when I showed some valetudinarian interest, would bring them on his next visit for me to read. I remember that in this way I became acquainted with George Santayana's only novel, *The Last Puritan, The Letters of William James,* and the novels of his brother.

I often find it hard to believe in the death of someone at whose demise I was not present. The past, for me, is increasingly present. So Burrill is still over there on Park Avenue, packing his black bag full of syringes, brown urine-specimen bottles, and maybe a novel by Edith Wharton, whom he admired, on his way to our apartment on West End Avenue to medicate me, tell me a funny story, and ask what I thought about *The Wings of the Dove.*

Conversation overheard in the bookstore:

A grown daughter and her middle-aged mother are looking at books. The mother shows the daughter (or it may be the other way around) a volume by Eudora Welty.

'She's a good writer.'

The other replies: 'I never heard of her.'

'She's won prizes—that Swedish prize, you know, what's it called?'

'The Pulitzer Prize?'

'That's it. She's won that.'

They both inspect *The Optimist's Daughter,* and then return it to the shelf.

Sedgwick, the town of which the village of Sargentville, population two hundred or so, is a part, held a town meeting last night. A plan has been drawn up by an appointed committee to control growth in the area. Based on responses from the citizenry, it provides for very little commercial growth, and very tightly controlled residential growth. 'Development' (that despised word) would seem to have been circumvented by the required size of acreage on which it is possible to build, and by the amount of waterfront required for a single dwelling.

But still, there is ground for dissension. The village has one lovely, elevated site, Caterpillar Hill, from which, on a clear day, it is possible to obtain a panoramic view of Walker Pond (actually a large lake), Penobscot Bay, the Reach, and far out, the sea. It is a wondrous sight, and many tourists, as well as

residents, stop their cars there and climb out to take pictures or
to enjoy the view. We often go up to watch the sun set over the
Castine Hills.

The plan calls for the preservation of the outlook from that
place at the top of the hill to guarantee that 'our children and
grandchildren will be able to enjoy it.' But protection of
personal property is to be the theme of the rest of the meeting.
A longtime resident, who owns almost one hundred acres of
blueberry fields on the hill and whose property encompasses the
view area, demands to know if someone is going to tell her
what to do with her land.

'Oh no, not at all,' says the selectman. 'We're just suggesting
what might be done to preserve . . .'

'That's what I mean,' says the redoubtable lady.

So it goes, back and forth, nothing won or lost or settled,
only the occasional Maine expression of fierce, outspoken
opposition to any intrusion upon property rights, any hint of
communal use or preservation for the future.

ᗡ

I read in yesterday's *Times* that the newly refurbished
Guggenheim Museum will open today in New York City. The
new café area is not quite finished. So the hot dog wagon just
around the corner is doing a very good business, its owner says.
But then, he and his father before him have sold hot dogs on this
spot for many years. What is more, the frankfurter entrepreneur
has contributed one thousand dollars to the renewal work on the
building.

ᗡ

My two-year-old grandchild, Maya, and her newborn sister,
Hannah, will not come here to visit this summer. Maya dislikes
flying, because her ears plug up upon descent; this is very

painful. But she may go to see her New York aunt because she can be taken there by train.

Telephone conversation between her and her Aunt Barbie, reported to me this morning:

'Will you come to New York to see us? Sam and I will take you to the movies.' (She is devoted to *Beauty and the Beast*.)

Maya: 'Oh yes, I'll come.'

Her aunt: 'You can bring your mother and father.'

'Yes.'

'And Hannah can come too.'

Maya, very quickly: 'Oh no, Hannah doesn't like movies.'

∽

After talking about the possibility for four years, we have finally plowed, fertilized, and dug a trench for an asparagus bed. What is more, after a few weeks, some wispy spears have appeared, so thin that Sybil says they have only one side. . . . Next year, *Deo volente*, they will be somewhat thicker, but still not edible. An asparagus bed is an act of faith in the future. With luck we will be able to eat the vegetable in 1994.

∽

Last evening Harold Casey brought my new hard disk, transferring everything I need from the ailing, moribund one (now named for the eminent critic Edmund Wilson) to the Duracom Desksaver in about fifteen minutes, whole books, everything that took me years to enter into it. The new computer is two-thirds the size of the old one, but its capacity is the same. It works so fast that it embarrasses me, like the electric typewriter when first I took it up. That machine put me to shame with its impatient humming while I sat frozen and mute, unable to think of anything to write.

A new addition is an expensive gadget called a Tripplite,

which will provide me with fifteen minutes of additional power
in case of an outage or brownout, more than enough time to
turn off all the gadgetry and save the doubtless immortal prose I
have been endowing it with. In this part of Maine there are
frequent failures of this kind; I am now protected against them.
But not, I fear, against the failure of ideas or imagination.

∽

This morning I put the new PC to work. I write, enter, print
out, and then rewrite and correct. I change and rearrange. I take
out and bring back. Insert and omit. The new draft (the third)
bears very little resemblance to the first. Later, I talk by
telephone to Helen Yglesias, who listens to my bragging about
my technical skills. I ask her: 'Do I do all this maneuvering out
of love for the versatility of the program and the machinery, or
because I believe it improves my prose?'

She reminds me that things are sometimes better before one
rewrites them.

∽

For the summer, at St. Francis-by-the-Sea Church (a name no
longer pertinent, since the old Methodist church has been moved
to a meadow in Blue Hill at least three miles from the water and
rechristened Episcopal), there is a substitute priest who lives near
here in the summer and is professor of music at Wheaton
College during the academic year. Carlton Russell gives good
sermons, full of learned references, and he is sensitive to
questions of language. Last Sunday he bemoaned the fact that
the new translation of the Bible had made 'earthen vessel' into
'clay pot,' a simplification William Strunk would have
approved of, but which has singularly little poetry to it.

On the other hand, we listened to the news last evening,
hearing about Republicans who 'utilize' dirty tricks in their

political campaign. Sybil asked: 'What happened to "use"?' And
then we witnessed the funeral of a policeman in Washington,
D.C., whose 'casket' was borne by his fellow officers. And once
again she wondered, whatever happened to 'coffin'?

∽

This year the winter lasted well into early June, so there was
almost no spring. The cold went on until yesterday, Bastille
Day. Today feels very much like fall. Sybil builds a fire in the
bookstore's woodstove, and I put on a wool sweater. There are
two blankets on the bed. By the end of June we had not yet put
our dinghy in the water, and I, the inveterate swimmer, have
not tried the Cove.

Summer comes to central coastal Maine at noon about once a
week in August. It is the view of some that summer here is a
minority opinion, or a kindly judgment, or a tenet of faith, or a
debatable figment of the local imagination.

Last evening we heard a weatherman describing the rain,
fog, and cold we are to expect this week. He ended his report by
saying:

'There's a lot of weather out there.'

∽

Senator Everett Dirksen, quoted on the radio this morning: 'A
billion here, a billion there. Pretty soon it adds up to real
money.' My grandmother and her pennies. . . .

∽

Tourists seem not to be deterred by weather. They come to
Maine in *their* season of summer. They come for strange reasons,
I learned on the plane to Washington last week. I sat next to an
attractive young woman, a college student from Texas, who
told me she had been visiting her roommate's parents in Boston.

When she asked, I told her I was from Maine, words that come slowly to me because I am so recently a Maine resident.

'Oh, my roommate and I went to Maine for a week,' she said.

'Where in Maine?' I asked, expecting to hear of the camping places, Baxter State Park, Acadia, a whale-watching excursion off Northeast Harbor perhaps.

'Kittery,' she said. 'Shopping in the discount stores in the mall.'

〜

Abigail McCarthy came to lunch today. She is visiting her friends the Dudmans, and Helen drives her down from Cranberry Island, where they summer. I ask Abigail why we did not see Eugene on TV at the Democratic National Convention in New York. The new 'young Turks' of the party offered him two tickets to the affair in an obscure section of the hall, she said, and he thought there should have been five, as he was a candidate, no matter how unrecognized by the party. So he did not attend. The much-revered (in my time) Senator Edward Muskie was offered two tickets; he went instead to Moscow.

These are McCarthy's spiritual children who are now in the spotlight. Bill Clinton did not wish to go to Vietnam; 'Clean Gene' was the leader of the objectors to that insane war. Now it is probably not politic to recognize him in his old age, in their flourishing youth.

After we have exhausted politics, Helen Dudman tells me she has a friend who hates Maine. She claims it is 'east of the United States.'

〜

Reluctantly, I go to Washington, D.C., for a committee meeting, an ad hoc offshoot of my senatorial duties in the Phi

Beta Kappa Society. The weather there is terrible, the capital's usual hot and humid summer days, known as humiture, the discomfort one feels in such conditions. (Did I wonder in Maine where summer was? Ah, it is here.)

The two days of meetings are worse. I cannot remember how I allowed myself to be put on this committee (PBK has so many committees that it maintains a Committee on Committees), or why I ever agreed to take this step back into the time-and-energy-consuming activities of the academic world by becoming a member of the Senate. Ego. I am paying for it now.

(Footnote on Committee on Committees: It reminds me of another foolishness that took place during a faculty meeting at the College of Saint Rose. After four fruitless hours of debate on some subject I can no longer remember, we took a vote on whether to take a vote. On *that* vote, one member of the faculty, famous for his timidity in the presence of the nuns, voted to abstain.)

All the things I most disliked about academic meetings in the old days were present at this one: the fraudulent surface of civility, the undercurrent of prearranged and determined agendas, the rude disregard of a woman chairman by male members of the executive committee accustomed to dominating every occasion of their privileged lives, their loud (or contrivedly too-soft) and always obtrusive voices carrying every question and insisting on every answer. My humiture was intense. I came away feeling sick, tired, discouraged, and angry at myself for spending four days of my diminishing supply of time in this absurd way.

On the plane I decided to resign.

But there was one saving grace to the trip. I learned that Alice Walker would be at a midtown store signing books. I left the offices of PBK, heated almost to exploding, and calmed

down, cooled down, when she and I had a short, warm reunion.
She is an old acquaintance from MacDowell days. I have always
admired her talent and her person. A long line of admirers
buying her new book and waiting for her to sign it stretched
out the door of Vertigo, a bookstore devoted in large part to
black writers.

The queue was composed of black and white readers, a good
sign that the best black writers have a mixed following, as it
should be. Soon there will be no need for separate courses in
black fiction. I noticed, last Sunday, that three black women are
on the *Times* best-seller list: Terry McMillan, Toni Morrison,
and Alice Walker.

ᔎ

May Sarton comes for a short, overnight visit, with her friend
Susan Sherman. Susan is young (by our standards), energetic,
and devoted to May. May tells me she has been feeling better
since the Westbrook College gathering to which more than
three hundred persons came to read papers about her work and
hear her read her own new poems written for her eightieth
birthday.

But the days she was here she was not well. She was
constantly in bad pain (she told me later in a letter), and yet her
determined spirit made her hide it from us. She talked of her
delight in the recognition ('at last,' she said) by the academic
community, and of her new journal, which had to be spoken
into a dictaphone because she was not up to long spells of
writing by hand or typewriter. It is to be called *Encore,* and will
appear for her eighty-first birthday, another achievement by a
gallant writer whose job, she has always believed, is to write,
quand même.

I thought of Henry James. In the midst of writing *What
Maisie Knew* he developed a rheumatic right wrist. He

abandoned writing his novels and letters by hand and began to dictate them to a typist. When he saw his typed letters he said they suffered from 'a fierce legibility.' He grew fond of the sound of the typewriter, and said his prose came to the page 'through an embroidered veil of sound.' The odd thing was, the longer he dictated the more complex grew his writing.

I would have thought that the opposite would be true, that speaking one's prose would make it simpler, less prolix, more unadorned. The highly wrought result of his dictation came to be known to critics as James's 'later style.' His biographer, Leon Edel, describes James's 'indirections and qualifications, the rhythms and ultimate perfection of his verbal music . . . his use of colloquialisms and in a more extravagant play of fancy, a greater indulgence in elaborate and figured metaphors, and in great proliferating similes' brought about by dictation.

All that, from the almost public act of speaking to a typist rather than the customary elaborations that result from the privacy of the pen to paper.

∽

The mail brings a copy of the May Sarton *Festschrift,* a well printed volume of tributes to her octogenarian year from her professional friends and acquaintances. Most of them are genuinely admiring paragraphs common to such tributary books. But Maggie Kuhn, founder of the Grey Panthers and now eighty-six years old, defies the genre by contributing an amusing line. One of the things she likes about being old, she writes:

'We have outlived our opposition.'

The observation reminds me of George Burns's remark that he liked living into his nineties because 'I don't have to worry about peer pressure.'

∽

By mere chance I pull from a shelf a collection of Diane
Trilling's book reviews, written for *The Nation* in the forties. I
had been thinking of gathering together some of my short
reviews from the 'Fine Print' column of *The New Republic* and
Saturday Review (twenty years ago) and combining them with
comments written today. Do I still think highly of this book?
Did I overpraise it? Did I neglect other good books of that time
to give it space? But after reading Diana Trilling's trenchant
short reviews of fiction, I have serious second thoughts about
my own. No one since her time has been able to make an art of
this difficult form.

Her talent was to recognize so well the paucity of ideas, the
failures of thought, the pretentiousness of books that others were
taken in by, and to encapsulate her comments in a few effective
words. Here is what she wrote about Ayn Rand's *The
Fountainhead:*

> [It] is a 754-page orgy of glorification of that sternest of arts,
> architecture. What Ruth McKenney's Jake Home [in a novel by
> the same name] is to the proletarian movement, Ayn Rand's
> Howard Roark is to public and domestic buildings—a giant
> among men, ten feet tall and with flaming hair, Genius on a scale
> that makes the good old Broadway version of art-in-a-beret look
> like Fra Angelico. And surrounding Howard Roark there is a
> whole galaxy of lesser monsters—Gail Wynand who is Power,
> and Peter Keating who is Success, and Dominique who is
> Woman. When Genius meets Woman, it isn't the earth that rocks
> but steel girders. Surely *The Fountainhead* is the curiosity of the
> year, and anyone who is taken in by it deserves a stern lecture on
> paper-rationing.

This is the entire review. In four sentences she has summarized
the plot, accurately suggested the tone, stated the theme, and
made a judgment so sharp, so intelligent, and, as it turns out, so

prescient that it deserves to last as a piece of inspired criticism long after that now-cultic, empty volume has gone back to well-deserved dust. Some months later she referred, in a phrase, to the 'operatic excesses' of Ayn Rand's novel.

On the other hand, her praise for the three short, elegant novels of Isabel Bolton (Mary Britten Miller), who wrote her fiction after she was sixty years old, should have raised that now entirely forgotten novelist to serious and permanent notice. She said Bolton was 'the best woman writer of fiction in this country today,' and her novel, *Do I Wake or Sleep*, 'quite the best novel that has come my way in the four years I have been reviewing new fiction for this magazine.'

If Diana Trilling convinced no one else with this extraordinary praise she moved me to find Isabel Bolton's books, to read them, and then, in the 1982 *Writer's Choice*, to recommend them, along with Edmund Wilson and Babette Deutsch, once again, to readers. Now, ten years later, no one, so far as I know, has made a move to reprint the novels. It is hard to see how it is possible for such distinguished work to fall into total oblivion.

∽

Rarely does the *New York Times* manage to print two stories that, running consecutively, make an interesting point about society's contrasts. This morning, in its 'Chronicle' column, I read first about the star Madonna, who arrived in a tinted-window limousine in front of a restaurant and boutique, Serendipity, on East 60th Street in New York City. The window of the store was full of baseball paraphernalia. Madonna's companion got out and told the owner that 'someone in the car wanted everything in the window.' Everything was duly removed and gift-wrapped: T-shirts, sequined baseball caps, bats.

Then the lady wanted food to be served in her car. After some protest by the owner that he did not provide curb- or carry-out service, Madonna rolled down the window. Overwhelmed by the identity of his customer, the owner promptly brought out what she wanted: foot-long hot dogs with chili and frozen hot chocolate (surely this must be the ultimate food oxymoron).

The second story in the column: Clara McBride Hale, known as Mother Hale and founder of Hale House, the group home for babies born addicted to drugs and alcohol and recently those born HIV-positive, is eighty-seven years old. She has had a series of strokes, and recently fell and broke her collarbone. Still, she visits her beloved little patients every day and is sad because she cannot pick them up 'for fear of dropping one.' But her daughter, who runs Hale House, brings her a seven-week-old baby to hold. He nestles in bed with her and she talks to him: 'I tell him about my past—he is the only one who will listen to me anymore—and about his future.'

Blond Madonna has gift-wrapped baseball bats and frozen hot chocolate brought to her parked limousine. Black Mother Hale has a sick baby brought to her bed to comfort, not gift-wrapped. Two small but significant portraits of the closing years of this century.

ᔆ

At the height of the summer some of the bookstore's customers are tourists who have visited it before. I am in the store one day when a lady asks me:

'What are you doing now?'

'I'm working on a book.'

'Oh, really. I thought you were doing that *last* year.'

ᔆ

This is said to be one of the coldest summer seasons on record. No humid days, and the average temperature, taking the cold nights into account, is about sixty. Only our guests have used our boats: we have not been on or in the water. In August there are still yellow flowers on the vestigial tomato plants and a few tiny green tomatoes. The blackberry bushes seem to have frozen before the fruit matured. We wear sweaters in the early afternoon. We hear rumors of a possible August frost. Sybil wants to know what has become of global warming.

Yesterday we saw, at a distance, what we think were geese flying south. To date there have been three hot days. They may constitute the summer.

❧

A student writer asks me to tell him 'how I write.' I take it this means 'With a pen? a pencil? a computer?' I answer him. But I would like to have found the courage to tell him the story of the would-be composer who asked Mozart how to compose a symphony. Mozart told him that a symphony was a complex and demanding musical form and that he had better start with something simpler.

The young man: 'But you wrote symphonies when you were younger than I am now.'

Mozart: 'I didn't have to ask how.'

❧

Sybil is reading Terry McMillan's new novel, *Disappearing Acts,* and I am finishing Alice Walker's *Possessing the Secret of Joy.* We talk about this and decide we chose to read these books because we miss the sight of black faces around us. We live among an unvaryingly white homogeneity. The two novels give us pleasure because, for the time being, we can move into the worlds of persons of color.

At the same time I am reviewing a novel by Susan Straight, *I Been in Sorrow's Kitchen and Licked Out All the Pots*. Written by a young white woman, it is a remarkable and welcome immersion in the life of a black community, and has a memorable South Carolina Gullah-speaking heroine.

჻

A MEDITATION ON HOME
SEPTEMBER 15, 1992

Now, as this year of a book (the one I am writing, the one I have written) is ending, I have been thinking about what it means to be home, to have learned that the place where I am *is* home. Finding it is pure good fortune. Being lucky enough to procure it, settle into it, and the prospect of remaining there for what one hopes may be the rest of one's life: that is a consummation devoutly to be wished.

This spring Marlene Dietrich died in France, where she had lived for many years. According to her wishes, she was buried in Germany, her native country, where she felt she could not return to live after the Nazi regime. But still, it was to be her final home, to which her aged body and extraordinary reputation was returned, at the end.

For some writers—William Faulkner, Flannery O'Connor, John Edgar Wideman, William Kennedy, Eudora Welty, Wendell Berry, others—home, the place of their birth, becomes their invariable subject matter. They leave it rarely in their fiction, traveling widely in their native places. Their characters are born there. There, those parochial inventions live out their lives. For such writers, home fires their imaginations and moves their pens.

In Sanskrit, *ksemas* means safe dwelling and is the word for
home. The verb *ksi* means to dwell secure. Home and safety
are part of the same concept. For some childhoods, I suppose,
this is true. Some of us have felt safe at home, and unsure,
threatened, when we were removed from that secure place.
It has been said: Home is where you hang your childhood
and later, your hat. For some this will always be true. For
others, the home of childhood is a place to escape from, to
put behind them, to remove from their memory, even to
deny the existence of. For some writers, like Katherine Anne
Porter, home is a place so unsatisfactory you have to
reinvent it.

The word is the subject of numerous aphorisms. T. S. Eliot's
home is where one starts from. The best country is at home.
Thomas Wolfe's title, you can't go home again. Huck's no
home like a raft. Robert Frost's home is the place where,
when you have to go there, they have to take you in. Oliver
Wendell Holmes thought that where we love is home. The
question we have framed and written in calligraphy in the
entry to our house is: If I follow you home, will you keep
me?

Homelessness is the great social disaster of our time. The
homeless are the politically exiled. Those who leave for a
better place, only to find they are unwelcome there. Those
sent to gulags or concentration camps. The exiled, dwellers
on street corners and grates, park benches and in doorways.
People dispossessed by earthquakes, tornadoes, floods,
volcanos, avalanches, wars. Refugees. Immigrants. Boat
people.

For me: At long last, I have overcome my sense of displacement
and homelessness, my need to find the one place to which I
feel I belong. To which I come with a sense of inevitable

return. The place I leave, even for a few hours, with regret. I
take pleasure at every vista from these windows:
'Everywhere you look there is something to see,' as Ted
Nowick once observed. I feel a foolish nostalgia for the sight
of the Cove when I go as far away as the post office or the
local store. Homesick? Looking out of every window
toward the sea, I know where home is.

I remember the Sisters at Saint Rose had a clear idea of its
location. One early morning one of them stopped me in the
breakfast line to tell me of the death of an elderly nun that
night. She smiled as she said: 'Sister Rosaleen has gone home
to God.'

I am now prepared to see my life as a journey to arrive here. It
has been a somewhat narrow, constrained, unadventuresome
trip to this place where I am, for the time being, home free,
for good. Finally, of course, there will be the last expedition
when I am 'called back,' in Emily Dickinson's phrase.
Shakespeare's metaphor for death: 'The latest home.' Mary
Oliver's image for death: 'that cottage of darkness.'
English sermons of the fourteenth century speak of death as 'the
long home.'

An elderly acquaintance whose permanent home in her late years
has been Brooklin, Maine, said at tea the other day, while
reviewing her life: 'We lived temporarily in Chicago for
twenty-five years.'

In games nomenclature, the fourth, final, and scoring base in
baseball is home plate; crossing it is a home run. . . . In
hide-and-seek, the place safe from discovery is home. The
object of backgammon is to bring the counters round to
your own home.

Home for me might have been an apartment, a condominium
in a high-rise building, a brownstone looking beyond
parked cars and streams of traffic to another brownstone.

A ranch house in the suburbs with a manicured lawn
indistinguishable from the ones on either side. A room in a
boardinghouse, a shelter: in one of these places I might have
spent the seventh segment of my life.

But Fortune has provided me with a rocky Cove off a Reach, a
meadow, two shallow woods, one great oak and a towering
horse chestnut tree, a huge, immovable rock that sits, in
Maine fashion, in the middle of a scrabby lawn, a deck
(substitute for a ship's side) that is attached to the house and
stretches toward the water.

Together with this parochial gift, it gave me more: an interior
landscape made of serenity, isolation, solitude. the flowering
desert of the heart, the mountains (and valleys) of mind, the
pools of imagination. Perhaps I am truly at home when I am
at peace with myself, surrounded by the serenity that comes
from the Cove, a quiet so deep I am able to hear the roar of
the sea in my inner ear, to see in my mind's eye absent
friends as well as the dead I have loved, to taste on the buds
of fantasy the great meals I am no longer able to digest, to
restore the scraps of a quiescent past long buried in my
memory by an overactive present.

I live in these landscapes. Here I dwell secure, looking inward to
learn the ancient, neglected truths about myself, and outward
to find God in this small piece of the beautiful world I have
been granted, and in my fellow human beings nearby. I
celebrate what I have, but sometimes mourn what has been
lost in the world. For I take to heart what Robert Finch
wrote: A celebrant of nature is now forced to become a
'writer of epitaphs for moribund places . . . one who speaks
well of the dead or dying . . . [I] celebrate things that no
longer are. . . .'

I have been lucky. I did not find this place too soon, too early.
(For if I had, I might face the danger of losing it and not

being able to come home again. I might have been expelled,
or transported, or exiled from it.)
Ecclesiastes contains a good metaphor. Worthless, vain ambition
is said to be 'chasing the wind.' In another translation it is
rendered as 'a striving after wind.' To be home is to stop
chasing the wind. To know thy place.
And knowing it, to learn to sit still. Here. For the time being.

Sargentville, Maine